FOREIGNERS IN THEIR OWN LAND

PENNSYLVANIA GERMAN HISTORY AND CULTURE SERIES,
Number 2

Publications of The Pennsylvania German Society,
Volume 35 (2001)

FOREIGNERS
in Their Own Land

PENNSYLVANIA

GERMANS

IN THE

EARLY

REPUBLIC

STEVEN M. NOLT

THE PENNSYLVANIA STATE UNIVERSITY PRESS

UNIVERSITY PARK, PENNSYLVANIA

Library of Congress Cataloging-in-Publication Data

Nolt, Steven M., 1968–
Foreigners in their own land : Pennsylvania Germans in the early
republic / Steven M. Nolt.
p.   cm.
(Publications of the Pennsylvania German Society ; v. 35.
Pennsylvania German history and culture series ; no. 2)
Includes bibliographical references (p.   ) and index.
ISBN 0-271-02199-3 (alk. paper)
1. Pennsylvania Dutch—Ethnic identity. 2. Pennsylvania Dutch—Cultural assimilation.
3. Pennsylvania Dutch—Religion—History—19th century.
4. Lutherans—Pennsylvania—Social conditions—19th century.
5. German Reformed Church (U.S.)—History—19th century.
6. Pennsylvania—History—1775–1865.
7. Pennsylvania—Ethnic relations.
8. Pennsylvania—Religious life and customs—19th century. I. Title.
II. Publications of the Pennsylvania German Society (2001) ; v. 35.
III. Publications of the Pennsylvania German Society (2001).
Pennsylvania German history and culture series ; no. 2.
F160.G3 N65 2002
305.6′410748′09034—dc21
2002003803

It is the policy of The Pennsylvania State University Press to use
acid-free paper for the first printing of all clothbound books.
Publications on uncoated stock satisfy the minimum requirements
of American National Standard for Information Sciences—
Permanence of Paper for Printed Library Materials,
ANSI Z39.48–1992.

CONTENTS

ILLUSTRATIONS

Figures

Maps

For Rachel

ACKNOWLEDGMENTS

In the course of research, writing, and seeing this manuscript to publication, I have incurred many debts. During the research phase, library and archive staff members provided valuable assistance. I would especially like to thank Diane Rimert and Dianne Russell of the Evangelical and Reformed Historical Society, Lancaster, Pa.; Sarah Mummert of the A. R. Wentz Library and Archives, Lutheran Theological Seminary at Gettysburg, Gettysburg, Pa.; John Peterson of the Krauth Memorial Library and Lutheran Archives Center, Lutheran Theological Seminary at Philadelphia, Philadelphia, Pa.; the staffs of the Historical Society of Berks County, Reading, Pa.; the Lancaster County Historical Society, Lancaster, Pa.; the York Heritage Trust, York, Pa.; the Krauth Library, Concordia Theological Seminary, Fort Wayne, Ind.; the Shadek-Fackenthal Library, Franklin and Marshall College, Lancaster, Pa.; the Hesburgh Library, University of Notre Dame, Notre Dame, Ind.; and the Harold and Wilma Good Library and Mennonite Historical Library, Goshen College, Goshen, Ind.

Helpful comment, counsel, and direction came from faculty and graduate students at the University of Notre Dame—particularly George M. Marsden, Jay P. Dolan, Nathan O. Hatch, and R. Scott Appleby. L. Allen Viehmeyer, Youngstown State University, suggested bibliographic additions and sources, and made other comments as well. André Gingerich Stoner assisted in checking several of my translations from German.

I owe a special debt to the Connelley Foundation Program of Elizabethtown College, Elizabethtown, Pa., which funded my spring 1997 tenure as Connelley Fellow at the Galen S. and Jessie M. Young Center for the Study of Anabaptist and Pietist Groups. Young Center interim director Theron F. Schlabach and Connelley Program director Conrad L. Kanagy offered a base from which to consult many Pennsylvania sources and depositories.

During the spring of 1997, as well as on other trips to Pennsylvania, my parents, Wilmer G. and Doris L. Nolt, provided lodging and otherwise underwrote the miscellaneous expenses of itinerant research.

More recently, my colleagues in the History and Political Science Department at Goshen College have provided an uncommonly pleasant and supportive environment in which to work, and the Goshen Dean's Office supplied a Summer Research Grant to help cover related expenses.

For publication itself, special thanks must go to the Pennsylvania German Society and its support of the Pennsylvania German History and Culture Series, and to Series Editor Simon J. Bronner. Penn State University Press Editor-in-Chief Peter J. Potter and Editorial Assistant Timothy L. Holsopple were most helpful and gracious throughout the publication process. John B. Frantz, Mark Häberlein, and an anonymous reviewer provided thoughtful comment on the current manuscript. To all of them I am most grateful.

Some of the material in this book has appeared in other forms. A variation of the material in Chapter 4 appeared as "Liberty, Tyranny, and Ethnicity: The German Reformed 'Free-Synod' Schism (1819–1823) and the Americanization of an Ethnic Church," *Pennsylvania Magazine of History and Biography* 125 (January/April 2001): 35–60. A shorter version of Chapter 5 appeared as "Becoming Ethnic Americans in the Early Republic: Pennsylvania German Reaction to Evangelical Protestant Reformism," *Journal of the Early Republic* 20 (Fall 2000): 423–46. A variation of the material in Chapter 6 appeared as "The Quest for American Kinship: Liberty, Ethnicity, and Ecumenism Among Pennsylvania German Lutherans, 1817–1842," *Journal of American Ethnic History* 19 (Winter 2000): 64–91. I thank these journals and their editors for permission to use this material. The nine anonymous reviewers for these articles provided helpful comments that were incorporated into the present volume.

Closer to home, two people played roles of a different, but more important, sort. Since the fall of 2000, Lydia has given me innumerable opportunities to catch the wonder, mystery, and joy of life. Meanwhile, Rachel has provided more encouragement, support, patience, and love than can be recounted here. The dedication to her is too modest a token.

INTRODUCTION

In the middle of the nineteenth century, a German visitor to North America made his way through the valleys of eastern and central Pennsylvania. There he encountered a population that intrigued him: in manners, dress, speech, and custom, they appeared to him to be Germans who had transported Old World ways of life to another continent. Yet when Johann G. Kohl (1808–78) introduced himself as a fellow countryman, the Pennsylvania Germans he met returned quizzical looks. Two pipe-smoking Pennsylvania German women, for example, quickly corrected Kohl and informed him—in German dialect—that they were "Americans." Kohl discovered this attitude throughout the region. "They might, it seems to me," he noted, "at least pay the Fatherland the compliment of saying 'German-American,' but on the contrary, it seems to me that if they spoke of the Yankees, the New Englanders, the Irish, and so on, that they wanted to reserve the name 'American' for themselves and wanted to be taken as definitive Americans."[1]

Kohl had stumbled upon one of the most significant stories of the early nineteenth century: the creation and formation of American identity. He found, however, that the tale had a complicated plot. The Pennsylvania Germans he met were surely not Crèvecoeur's new humanity, engaging in exogamy, easy anglicization, and reflexive cultural melding. On the contrary, as Kohl and many other European and North American travelers testified, the Pennsylvania German population was easily identifiable and remarkably stable and cohesive. Historical demographers have detailed their homogenous settlement patterns and unusually high rates of in-group marriage. Even as late as the 1930s, a German ethnographer marveled at their cultural persistence.[2] Yet by the 1850s the mass of Pennsylvania Germans had come to think of themselves as quintessential Americans and showed scant interest in the life and activities of the millions of German immigrants arriving during the middle and later nineteenth century. Pennsylvania Germans were, even by the eve of the Civil War, the most "inside" of "outsiders."[3]

The story told here explores how this transformation happened. This is a cultural history of Pennsylvania German Lutheran and Reformed adherents, with special attention to the thought and action of ordinary lay members as well as clergy.[4] It is the tale of people who began with Continental notions about liberty, religion, and community, but coupled them with Anglo-American[5] ideas and rhetoric to fashion identities simultaneously rooted in and resistant to their New World home.

The Pennsylvania German experience of the early nineteenth century certainly confounded observers such as Johann Kohl, but it also illustrates the paradox of Americanization. And given the pioneering role played by Pennsylvania Germans in that development, their experience illuminates a path that others traveled in the following decades. A nation of immigrants, the United States has perennially faced the question of national identity without recourse to claims of exclusive bloodlines, ancient territorial homeland, or a universal folk culture. Becoming American has been a process, one that has challenged generations of newcomers and their descendants. Even today, debates continue over the meaning and pace of assimilation and the value and desirability of multiculturalism. In some settings, the appropriateness of identifying a dominant or mainstream national culture is no longer assumed, and the role and future of minority groups remains a closely argued topic.

In the early nineteenth century (no less than in the twenty-first), the discrete groups of people claiming American identities formed complex relationships and intricate ways of interacting. Becoming American has not frequently been an experience that simply pitted the power of assimilation against the forces of cultural resistance; rather, it has involved an adaptive process in which majority demands and minority wishes mixed and even furthered ironically complementary ends. Typically, ethnic groups have engaged an American mainstream that in turn has marked and changed them. Yet despite—and often even because of—that process, they have reforged their identities to reflect the reality of a new cultural context as much as a heritage from another era or continent. Thus, creating an ethnic identity and becoming American are integrally related processes. This sometimes counterintuitive connection has surprised many observers since the time of Johann Kohl. Yet Kohl's Pennsylvania Germans—adherents of Lutheran and German Reformed churches and descendants of colonial-era German-speaking immigrants who settled in Pennsylvania, Maryland, and the Appalachian backcountry—were the first major group to experience this sort of ethnicization-as-Americanization.[6] Their story represents the complex way in which minorities have managed assimilation to their own ethnic advantage.

Historians of immigration generally define ethnicity as, most basically, a sense of peoplehood.[7] While anthropology suggests a more objective definition tied to bloodlines and discrete, ideal membership,[8] American historical scholarship has tended to stress ethnicity's subjective nature in a context where those outside the group assign (or ascribe) meaning to the identities asserted by insiders. Historian Dale T. Knobel has described ethnicity as "a social classification. It is neither strictly biological nor precisely cultural, [but rather] a category of ascription and self-identification with boundaries defined by custom."[9] In the United States, such self-identification has often risen from a heritage of similar national origin, language, folkways, and beliefs, as well as from dynamic interaction with surrounding, contrasting traditions.[10] Indeed, literal common ancestry—a *sine qua non* of ethnic identity in traditional societies—has not always been an exclusive principle in the creation of ethnic groups, because self-identification always exists (sometimes uneasily) alongside ascriptive definitions created by others. Immigrants may have arrived as Palatinates, Hanoverians, or Hessians only to receive the common appellation "Pennsylvania German" from their neighbors and thereby take a first step down the path of "ethnicization."[11]

If ethnicity is partly defined by those outside a particular group, it is cultivated within a group through the formation and perpetuation of *culture*— the learned patterns of behavior, intellectual assumptions, and reflexive social responses with which people make sense of their world and through which they integrate new experiences and encounters. Culture provides the outer boundaries and the guiding core principles of ethnicity, because cultural values set the terms of negotiation with the surrounding society. In the resulting interaction, minority cultures change, selectively adapt, and modify their traditions and practices in conversation with a larger host society. In the period of the Early Republic (roughly 1790–1848), a British-stock majority created a dominant culture with which Pennsylvania German traditions interacted. The fact that Anglo-Americans were still unsure how best to construe their own national and cultural identity after the Revolution only added yeast to the mix.

For Pennsylvania Germans, as for many other minority groups without direct access to other structures of social power, religion and religious institutions were often the chief means of mediating and propagating culture.[12] Religious affiliation is often a central building block of group identity and a regulator of cultural change, but this is not the only reason that religion is a primary factor in the process of ethnicization and Americanization. Rather, religion is primary because, from the founding of the republic, religion has been an arena in which the state—in theory, and very often in fact—cannot intrude. The federal Constitution barred religious tests, and the federal First Amendment and the Pennsylvania Constitution of 1790 guaranteed freedom from religious coercion. Both meant that religion was a different category among the elements that contributed to both national and ethnic self-understanding.[13] In rallying to religious particularity or bolstering arguments with religious rhetoric, ethnic Americans could resist the claims of the larger society in the name of common American principles. Ultimately, they might even claim that their approach to religion made them better Americans.

Conceiving ethnicity as a created, dynamic category in the American context assumes that ethnicization may also be a form of Americanization, because the process of constructing ethnicity is derived from and stated in terms of the American experience.[14] The process of choice, the surprise of contingency, and the interaction between groups and the dominant American culture are at the heart of the construction of ethnicity in America, and together they constitute an underlying motif in this study.[15]

As the largest group of white, non–British-stock people in the new nation, Pennsylvania Germans pioneered the process of ethnicization-as-Americanization, and religion functioned in a critical way to frame and legitimate the resulting arguments and outcomes. The Pennsylvania German experience is particularly fascinating, because the negotiation of ethnic and national identity took place in the context of a fragile young republic whose cultural majority was itself struggling to define and secure the practical legacy of the Revolution. Moreover, the role and function of Pennsylvania Germans' most important community institutions and culturally influential structures—their Lutheran and Reformed churches—faced uncertain futures in the face of the religious competition, popular revivalism, and evangelical reformism that imbued the period.

If the Pennsylvania German experience illustrates a critical opening chapter in the unfolding tale of Americanization and demonstrates the connections between national identity, religion, and ethnicity, it has perhaps gone largely unnoticed because scholars charting these histories often missed connecting themes. American religious history and American ethnic history emerged as major fields of scholarly inquiry at about the same time, yet historians of Protestantism have yet to engage ethnic history to the degree that scholars of Catholicism and Judaism have.[16] More recently, historical attention to the American Early Republic has blossomed, but while the interaction of Early Republic historiography and religious history has been notable, connections between ethnic historiography and scholarship on the Early Republic have been almost nonexistent. Thus, ethnic Protestants in the Early Republic have remained a shrouded group, despite the prolific activity of academics working in three fields in which such people are potential subjects.

Inattention to ethnicity in the Early Republic stems mostly from the fact that immigration was slight during most of the period. In fact, the percentage of foreign-born residents in the United States declined steadily from the 1760s to the mid-1840s; the Early Republic thus stands as one of the least immigrant-stocked epochs in American history.[17] Moreover, many of the standard topics of ethnic history, such as nativism, anti-Catholicism, urban ghetto life, and the Western frontier emerged only after the upturn in arrivals following the 1830s. Thus, it seemed that historians of ethnicity had little important work to perform on the years between the writing of the Constitution and the flight of famine-stricken Irish.[18]

This study begins to fill that gap by examining the Americanization of the Pennsylvania Germans in the Early Republic.[19] Although Pennsylvania Germans have long been the subject of ethnographers, folklorists, and linguists, they have attracted few historians.[20] Recent scholarship has produced several excellent studies detailing aspects of Pennsylvania German life and thought in the colonial and revolutionary eras,[21] but their experience in the republic's first five decades remains largely unexplored.[22] Moreover, the written histories that cover Lutheran and Reformed church life during this period have generally dealt with narrower denominational issues or focused on Pennsylvania Germans only during the Mercersburg debates or the Lutheran "Americanist" controversies that occupied leaders in the 1850s.[23] For their part, historians of religion in the Early Republic have created a significant body of work, but even they have largely ignored Continentally rooted churches, thereby obscuring some of their subject's complexity and leaving readers with an incomplete sense of Protestant evangelicalism.

But Pennsylvania German religion, like other aspects of its adherents' culture, was never isolated from the surrounding currents of mainstream American society. True, relatively few of the Early Republic's Pennsylvania Germans lived in cosmopolitan Philadelphia (in 1793, there were three Lutheran and three Reformed churches in the city). Most resided in smaller towns, such as Reading, Pennsylvania, or Frederick, Maryland, or in tiny hamlets and rural farm communities in the counties of Berks, Northampton, Lancaster, York, Dauphin, Adams, and Schuylkill. And even in the second quarter of the nineteenth century, future German Reformed pastor William Helffrich (1827–94) passed through a childhood he later characterized as "very limited and my vision of life narrow." When his family temporarily boarded the son of a leading English-stock American family, young Helffrich realized that the boarder "understood the world and the people of America as I didn't."[24] But interaction with larger American political and religious ideas continued to expand after 1800. During the colonial era, Pennsylvania Germans had begun to understand Anglo-American legal tradition and religious culture, and in the decades that followed, they started to transform and defend their particular notions of faith and freedom—notions that often set them apart from the social and cultural mainstream—with the rhetoric used by other patriotic Americans.[25]

This book explores the Pennsylvania German encounter with American political and religious culture—two areas of lively concern in the Early Republic, and two themes central to ethnicization and the development of a broader American national identity. It is hardly remarkable that Pennsylvania Germans would pick up themes of American exceptionalism, given the prevalence of such notions in early national life and the fact that the Pennsylvania Germans' forebears had, in many cases, immigrated to North America in hopes of bettering themselves.[26] What is significant, though, is what Pennsylvania Germans *did* with the common notions of American political and religious identity, and how they employed such notions (in ways often very different from those of their neighbors) in order to construct and defend alternate, ethnic visions of the United States.

The first three chapters of this work illustrate Pennsylvania Germans' "outsider" status in the young nation by looking at the story of their initial interaction with American approaches to faith and civic life. In the political realm, their understandings of freedom and community often separated them from their anglophone compatriots, even if they joined in expedient alliances. In the realm of popular religion, Pennsylvania Germans debated and often resisted the overtures of the powerful evangelical Protestant vanguard that set the prevailing terms for public conversation and new religious trends. Yet these encounters with mainstream American political and religious cultures did more than foster a Pennsylvania German sense of separation and sectarianism. They actually provided resources for building and maintaining identity in terms suited to the American scene; they permitted ethnicization to be a side door to Americanization.

The second half of the book explores this latter process through ecclesiastical debates in Lutheran and German Reformed religious bodies, or communions. These debates involved ordinary laity as well as religious leaders, and they offer a window onto the participants' intellectual worlds, revealing Pennsylvania German discussions of liberty, democracy, American identity, and community and church boundaries. Pennsylvania Germans successfully combined elements of their Old World tradition with several emerging versions of national identity. Many took up democratic populist rhetoric

7

to defend local cultural particularity and ethnic separatism. Others wedded rather Whiggish notions of reform and national purpose to their traditions of clerical authority and idealized German virtues. Religion played a central role in the process because it provided intellectual resources, structural identity, and an arena sanctified by republican principles of disestablishment and noninterference. It was a realm within and about which particularity could be construed as properly American.

By 1850, Pennsylvania Germans were ethnic Americans at home in their own land, sure that their religious ideals and related cultural commitments best represented core civic and political values of the United States. As essays in the Pennsylvania German youth periodical *The Guardian* would insist, readers' ethnic distinctiveness and dissent from the mainstream only made them better, more representative Americans.

The Pennsylvania German Lutheran and Reformed experience of ethnicization and Americanization in the Early Republic foreshadowed many of the themes, debates, and concerns that would surface repeatedly among subsequent generations of other immigrants who sought to negotiate an American identity in cultural terms they could understand and embrace. Nevertheless, the experience discussed here also differed significantly in certain ways from that of other German-speaking Americans. As a predominantly rural, yeoman population, Pennsylvania Germans did not wrestle with issues of class in the same way that German-American Protestants in New York City did. There, as Stanley Nadel has shown, the second half of the nineteenth century saw economic interests overwhelm traditional group identity markers such as geography, endogamy, and religion, leaving class as the major channel for engaging (or resisting) the larger society.[27] Nor was the Pennsylvania German experience like that of German-speaking Catholics who—after a brief public battle with English hierarchs—took up a more internal ethnic agenda, addressing questions of how to be German in an Irish church, or how to be Catholic in a Protestant society.[28] Pennsylvania German Protestants could seek to become Americans without having to justify their faiths' compatibility with republican principles. Yet given their colonial-era status as tolerated aliens, their transition to American citizenship did position them as political outsiders—unlike the German speakers in frontier Milwaukee, who, as Kathleen Neils Conzen notes, founded and defined a political culture into which *others* integrated themselves.[29]

For their part, Pennsylvania Germans appropriated the universalizing propositions on which American identity was predicated, but they used those principles to defend ethnic particularity. In the process, they fashioned themselves as representative Americans. By the middle of the nineteenth century, they had found a rather comfortable niche in American society; their interaction with its culture and their understanding of their place within it had made them Americans without assimilating them.

Map 1   Selected place-names mentioned in this study. Political boundaries, 2002.

IN THE BOSOM
OF THE STATE

In June 1787, as delegates labored in oppressive Philadelphia heat to draft a new frame of government for the
young American republic, a group of Philadelphia's leading civil and religious figures traveled sixty miles west to
the borough of Lancaster to witness the dedication of a
new academy of higher education. Unlike the state's two
other such schools—the University of Pennsylvania and
Dickinson College—this institution was to serve a German-
speaking population. Dubbed "Franklin College" in honor
of its most prominent benefactor and Pennsylvania's leading political figure, the school was a joint endeavor of the
Lutheran and German Reformed communions.

Philadelphia physician, evangelical activist, and social
commentator Benjamin Rush (1745–1813) was among
those who attended and spoke at the dedication. An ardent
federalist, Rush used the forum to speak optimistically

about an emerging nation and nationality in America. Franklin College, he announced, would break down "the partition wall which has long separated the English and German inhabitants of the State" so that "in the course of a few years ... the names of German, Irishman, and Englishman will be lost in the general name of Pennsylvanian." Sectarian differences and ignorance of the English language would fade together as educated, ecumenical, anglicized "sons of the Germans" would "be qualified to shine in our legislature, and to fill with reputation the professions of law, physic, and divinity."[1]

In private, Rush was far less sanguine about the success of his assimilationist goals. Writing several days later to relatives, he noted that the German-speakers he met "exhibit[ed] the most melancholy proofs of ignorance," and otherwise seemed poor prospects for becoming the sort of new American he hoped would populate the republic.[2] His dream of creating a new society united by common republican political principles and his commitment to evangelical religious reformism were balanced by his recognition that the Pennsylvania German community might easily resist any attempts at managing its future. They had, after all, remained decidedly separate and distinct despite almost a century of life in America. Indeed, Rush's subsequent *Account of the Manners of the German Inhabitants of Pennsylvania,* which referred to the German population as "an inexhaustible treasure in the bosom of the state," was prompted as much by his apprehension as by his admiration of the group.[3]

Rush sensed that Pennsylvania Germans resisted the homogenizing forces of assimilation that he had extolled in his Franklin College address, that they stood apart from his vision of America. That Germans remained distinctly "in the bosom of the state" was cause for both nervous calm and gnawing concern. The embryonic metaphor suggested that their place in society was underdeveloped. That so large a population was maintaining such a sharply identifiable position posed a problem for the nationalist Rush. Could these people find a place in American culture and society? What was their relationship to the republican vision and evangelical religious causes that Rush saw as the unifying foundation of the rising new nation?[4]

Germans in a New World

The Pennsylvania German population Rush lauded and feared had grown from some seventy thousand German-speaking immigrants who had arrived through the port of Philadelphia before the American Revolution. As Aaron Fogleman has summarized, eighteenth-century German immigration to North America was a "calculated risk, one of many choices [European Germans] could have made to try to improve their steadily deteriorating [economic] situation at home."[5] Yet during the second and third quarters of the eighteenth century, the number of German immigrants to the New World was substantial. Scholarly estimates suggest that between 1717 and 1775, speakers of German constituted more than 27 percent of all white arrivals to the thirteen colonies, and more than 80 percent of these Germans came by way of Philadelphia.[6] While German-speaking newcomers hailed from Hesse, Baden, Württemberg, Alsace, Switzerland, and elsewhere, many were from the Palatinate, and that geographic designation frequently served as a label for all of them.[7]

German immigrants tended to leave Europe in groups as extended or nuclear families, or associations of village neighbors. According to Fogleman, this strategy of communal migration enabled them to succeed in the expensive and arduous process of transatlantic migration.[8] Their success and the networks they replicated in North America encouraged others to join them in a process of chain migration, the results of which startled English observers. In 1742, the Pennsylvania government acknowledged "that some look with jealous eyes upon the yearly concourse of Germans to this Province," but tried to calm critics by reminding them that "every industrious laborer from Europe is a real addition to the [colony's] wealth."[9]

German immigrants settled in southeastern Pennsylvania and backcountry regions linked to Pennsylvania by trade and culture. Known to colonial historians as "Greater Pennsylvania," this area included southern and eastern Pennsylvania, western Maryland, and the backcountry of Virginia and North Carolina.[10] Indeed, the thousands of German-speaking settlers living throughout Greater Pennsylvania soon acquired the appellation "Pennsylvania Dutch," or "Pennsylvania German," regardless of their actual province of residence.[11]

Examining the social and economic motives for emigration to Pennsylvania, Fogleman has argued that the ability to acquire and secure title to land was the Germans' most important New World goal. During the late seventeenth and early eighteenth centuries, Rhine Valley villagers had participated in a vigorous reassertion of their traditional communal rights in the face of efforts by lesser nobles to break community bonds. The German-speaking immigrants who populated Greater Pennsylvania possessed a strong corporate spirit that they put to use in establishing communal land claims for themselves and their kin.[12] Historical geographer James Lemon has demonstrated the way in which immigrants of differing national origin segregated themselves in the process of taking up land in colonial Pennsylvania, rather than mixing with one another.[13] Further, demographers have shown that German residents in particular were even more ensconced in ethnic enclaves than Irish, Scots, Welsh, or English residents.[14] Rather than automatically settling along an ever-extending westward frontier, Germans tended to take up lands among fellow ethnics, and historians have uncovered relatively low rates of geographic mobility among Pennsylvania Germans.[15]

These communities also shared a common set of Pennsylvania-evolved folkways and material culture.[16] For example, customs of dress set Pennsylvania Germans apart from the practices of British neighbors in Greater Pennsylvania. In 1797, Polish nobleman Julian U. Niemcewicz (1758–1841) arrived in Frederick, Maryland, and observed that while even the oldest German inhabitant he met "was born in America, nevertheless by dress and way of life it is easy to recognize them as Germans and even to place them as Germans of the 16th century." For example, instead of British-style bonnets, women wore "large white hats without crowns like huge flat plates," while men sported "long, wide linen trousers."[17]

In addition to folk culture, emergent ethnicity had institutional structure, and the establishment of regular patterns of religious life was a significant factor in the formation of stable German-speaking communities in Pennsylvania. Nearly all Pennsylvania Germans were Protestants of one sort or another.[18] Early German immigrants represented a wide array of confessions and creeds—a variety that caused some colonial commentators, such as Lutheran schoolmaster Gottlieb Mittelberger, to complain about the "blind zeal of the many sects" he encountered in the province.[19] Yet while sectarian plurality was sure to strike European observers as the most remarkable aspect of the middle colonies' religious life, it was, in the end, the so-called church folk—members of Lutheran and German Reformed communions—who dominated the German American landscape in Greater Pennsylvania and created what amounted to a practical ecclesiastical establishment.[20] (Fig. 1.) With more than sixteen thousand actively communing members (and many more baptized members) in Greater Pennsylvania by 1740, these church bodies were already well established, and they

Fig. 1   Falkner Swamp Church, Montgomery County, Pennsylvania, was in 1725 the
first German Reformed congregation in Pennsylvania. This building, erected in 1790,
was photographed sometime between 1869 and 1925. It has undergone several
renovations and modifications, but it is still being used today by the Falkner Swamp
Reformed Church of the United Church of Christ. Courtesy of Falkner Swamp
Reformed Church of the United Church of Christ.

continued to grow in the years that followed as the total number of German arrivals swelled and the proportion of sectarian immigrants shrank.[21]

Though representing historically distinct Reformation traditions, Lutheran and Reformed churches in Greater Pennsylvania developed close relations, often shared church buildings, and lived within a common cultural context that often meant more than their dogmatic differences. In fact, early American Lutheranism was not as confessionally conscious as some of its nineteenth-century descendants would later become, and a number of early Reformed pastors had been trained at the Reformed school in the German city of Herborn—a school known for its irenic approach and rather open stance toward Lutheranism.[22] In short, the experiences of these two confessions in Greater Pennsylvania would be cordial and closely intertwined.

In either case, for those in the Lutheran and Reformed Pennsylvania German mainstream, religion was a critical part of their cultural identity. Throughout Greater Pennsylvania, the number of congregations expanded quickly and acted as ethnic magnets. Later-arriving Germans tended to settle in Pennsylvania townships that had established German churches rather than in those with commercial markets or county seats.[23] Although settled clergy were often in short supply, the laity acted to organize congregations even without clerical help, and then they appealed for ministerial service. (Maps 2 and 3.) The dearth of German clergy in North Carolina, for example, did not dissuade lay members from organizing eighteen congregations by 1760—and six more in the decade that followed.[24]

Indeed, ecclesiastical identities became more important as the eighteenth century wore on, in large part because of the course of the Great Awakening in the middle colonies.[25] While the revival of interest in religion in the mid-1700s was destabilizing and even revolutionary in parts of New England and the South, where it gave birth to dissenter movements, divided the local standing order, or upset old elites, the Awakening in Pennsylvania was a consolidating, denomination-building event that strengthened member loyalty and structural authority. During the 1740s, under the active direction of Lutheran pastor Heinrich Melchior Muhlenberg (1711–87) and Reformed cleric Michael Schlatter (1718–90), both communions organized further.[26] "Paradoxically," historian John B. Frantz has noted, "this revival of religion that transcended nationality ... accentuated their group consciousness to such a degree that their religion became an ethnic as well as spiritual refuge."[27] Theologically, Lutheranism was an "outsider" tradition in a British Protestant religious context, and German Reformed clergy were always quick to contrast their traditions' lone adherence to the German-language Heidelberg Catechism with the allegiances of Reformed believers from the British Isles or Holland, who ascribed dogmatic significance to a longer list of English and Dutch confessional documents.[28]

If ethnic religious loyalties, endogamy, and geographic community stability marked Pennsylvania Germans, these factors did not cut them off from the surrounding society.[29] Ethnic sensibilities mediated and regulated, rather than precluded, such encounters. Pennsylvania Germans' relationships to provincial law illustrate this pattern. Because the vast majority of German-speaking immigrants had come to the New World to obtain clear land titles, securing property rights became a priority for Pennsylvania Germans and prompted their initial forays into political activity.[30] Yet such involvement was far from straightforward, because Anglo-American notions of liberty and law were rarely self-evident to German-speakers schooled in Continental traditions of local privilege and hereditary rights. As A. G. Roeber has explained, German American Lutherans had to learn the language of this new political culture, and they did so in the context of church life: they secured ecclesiastical property and drew up valid personal wills and bequests.[31] Such training might lead its participants into the wider world of public service, and several Pennsylvania German church folk did become deeply involved in colonial and postrevolutionary government. The first speaker of the U.S. House of Representatives, Frederick A. C. Muhlenberg (1750–1801), was the most visible of these figures.[32]

Nonetheless, by the 1780s, Pennsylvania Germans had actually taken only initial, cautious steps toward any significant involvement in mainstream public and political life, and the Revolution itself would so transform anglophone American society that in the war's wake, Pennsylvania Germans would find their surroundings even less familiar.[33] Thus, nationalist observers like Benjamin Rush could be concerned that Pennsylvania Germans' civic isolation was becoming more salient at the very time that their neighbors were participating in the defining, nationalizing events of constitutional creation and debate.[34]

Such was the situation in the spring of 1787, when Pennsylvania political figures such as Rush and financial supporters such as Benjamin Franklin backed the idea of a German college in Lancaster. They were eager to draw the German population—a population that by 1790 would comprise

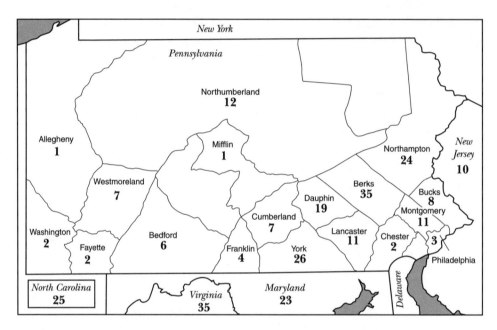

New York

Pennsylvania

Northumberland
12

Allegheny
1

Mifflin
1

Northampton
24

New
Jersey
10

Westmoreland
7

Berks
35

Bucks
8

Dauphin
19

Montgomery
11

Cumberland
7

Washington
2

Bedford
6

Lancaster
11

Chester
2

3

Fayette
2

Franklin
4

York
26

Philadelphia

North Carolina
25

Virginia
35

Maryland
23

Delaware

Map 2   Pennsylvania German Lutheran churches, 1793. Numbers indicate
congregations in each county. Political boundaries are those of 1793.
SOURCES: Charles H. Glatfelter, *Pastors and People: German Lutheran and Reformed
Churches in the Pennsylvania Field, 1717–1793*, 2 vols. (Breinigsville, Pa.: Pennsylvania
German Society, 1980–81), and Jacob L. Morgan et al., eds., *History of the Lutheran
Church in North Carolina, 1803–1953* (n.p.: United Evangelical Lutheran Synod of
North Carolina, 1953).

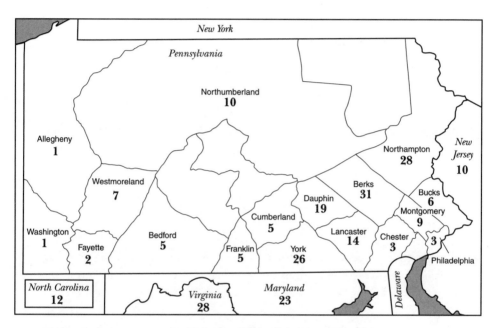

Map 3 Pennsylvania German Reformed churches, 1793. Numbers indicate congregations in each county. Political boundaries are those of 1793.
SOURCES: Charles H. Glatfelter, *Pastors and People: German Lutheran and Reformed Churches in the Pennsylvania Field, 1717–1793,* 2 vols. (Breinigsville, Pa.: Pennsylvania German Society, 1980–81), and *Historic Sketch of the Reformed Church in North Carolina by a Board of Editors Under the Classis of North Carolina* (Philadelphia: Publication Board of the Reformed Church in the United States, 1908).

almost a tenth of the country's white population, and one third of Pennsylvania's—into the task of nation building. The new college would be part of a network of regional institutions all aimed at producing freshly minted Americans schooled in the logic and language of the infant republic.[35]

But what Benjamin Rush and other non-German Franklin College boosters did not know was that the Pennsylvania Germans they eyed so warily would eventually learn their republican lessons quite well, indeed. Over the course of the next fifty years, many would turn those lessons and their accompanying language and logic against their Anglo-American tutors, defending ethnic particularism with the rhetoric of liberty, equality, and natural rights. Instead of nurturing new Americans who would transcend ethnicity and drown cultural differences in the "new order of the ages," as Rush and others had hoped, revolutionary ideology would in fact supply the very tools with which many Pennsylvania Germans would defend their refusal to assimilate. Becoming American would be more complicated than Benjamin Rush had imagined.

American Identity in the Early Republic

But what did it mean to be—or to become—American? During the half-century that followed the adoption of the federal Constitution, Pennsylvania German Lutheran and Reformed adherents encountered with greater frequency the political and religious movements, issues, and debates of larger American society. What made those encounters particularly challenging was the fact that the concept of American identity—with all its attendant political and religious assumptions—was still unsettled. Pennsylvania Germans found themselves not reacting against a given definition of what America meant or demanded, but participating in the very construction of those formulations. After the Revolution, American society underwent a marked transformation, wrestling with the new nation's purpose and the role of citizens in securing and furthering its meaning.

In one sense the notion of American identity was as young as the republic itself, and on the surface, it promised its potential subjects no immediate formulation. The expansive geography, diverse population, and various local histories contained in the states that constituted the nation seemed to mitigate against any single definition of what America was or might become. In fact, the central design for the "Great Seal for the confederated states" that the Continental Congress had considered adopting in 1776 was merely a composite of the coats of arms of six European countries whose people had arrived on the colonies' shores.[36] Although that design was ultimately not approved, it suggested the early leaders' derivative thinking about their new nation.

The largest number of Americans shared a heritage that included British notions of law, the English language, and religious outlooks shaped by and descended from the experience of the English and Scottish Reformations.[37] British-stock Americans were not a uniform lot, and distinct patterns of particular folkways from England and its borderlands took root in specific regions within North America.[38] Yet for all of these people, in an important sense, America's very existence as an independent nation represented a repudiation of Britain, a sudden and decisive break with the country that stood as cultural parent to so many Americans. Language and national origin could not adequately serve as explicit marks of identity for a people struggling to separate themselves from their ethnic ancestor across the sea. After all, Americans had shed blood to force the separation—and in the end, that War for Independence was the one thing they could hold in common.[39]

The Revolution provided those Americans not only with the practical foundation of their republican experiment, but also with the rhetoric and the ideology for its precarious existence. Almost immediately—and of necessity—the words and actions of the Founders took on mythic proportions. Fourth of July festivals quickly became public rites of dedication to the cause, one so novel that many citizens feared for its collapse as much as they gloried in its success.[40] The anxious and the triumphant, the radical and the cautious: all found the meaning of America in the struggle for liberty and the charge to carry its republican banner into the future. One historian has noted that within the widely held religious worldview of the day and in "an atmosphere of Christian responsibility . . . Americans thought about their nationality as a Trust and themselves as Stewards."[41]

Debates over American national identity thus drew more on the interpretation of recent events and abstract ideology than on a demonstrable definition of peoplehood circumscribed by geographic origin or religious persuasion. Combining classical republican ideals of self-government and Enlightenment visions of the universality of humanity, leading American thinkers in the wake of the Revolution saw America as a great social experiment in which a people championing self-reliance, virtue, and simplicity broke with the past and invited humankind to join them in realizing a republican future. So strong were these sentiments that the 1790 congressional debate of the nation's first immigration and naturalization statutes was wrapped in discussions of ideology, not national origins. On the surface, anyone committed to revolutionary liberty and interested in its promulgation could claim the name "American."[42]

One of the reasons an ideologically based and seemingly culturally blind conversation about American identity flourished during the Early Republic was that the nation's ethnic diversity waned throughout the period.[43] With few immigrants and a high birthrate, the United States increasingly became a land demographically dominated by British-stock residents—the very people who had produced the Revolution and then debated its legacy.[44] The federal government only began counting newcomers in 1819, and historians' estimates for the period before that date vary, yet all agree that the number of immigrants was small. One of the most comprehensive studies places the total number between 1800 and 1816 at less than 122,000. Though immigration picked up somewhat after the end of the Napoleonic Wars and the reestablishment of normal transatlantic trade, the number of new arrivals remained relatively low through the 1830s. Indeed, natural population increase dwarfed the impact of immigration, and immigrants accounted for less than 10 percent of all population increase (and thus a much smaller amount of the population as a whole).[45]

Yet the reality of American culture and identity during the course of the Early Republic was not as straightforward as its ideological foundations might suggest.[46] Commitment to the ideals of the Revolution and to the promotion of the republic may have been common features, but their meaning and future were unclear. John Murrin's apt description of the Constitution—the centerpiece of the republican experiment—as a "roof without walls" suggests the sort of cultural void that surrounded Americans' commitment to their political creation. Without the aid of tradition or external authority, Americans were left to glory in their ideals with the hope that given enough loyal devotion their nation-state would not collapse upon them.[47] They believed that Joseph Hopkinson's poem, "Hail, Columbia," was correct in praising the revolutionary generation as a "heaven-born band," but that belief only added to their burden of seeing that liberty and equality would remain marks of the republic. The responsibility of sustaining the Founders' work was a heavy one and produced ambivalent feelings and varied interpretations of the nation itself. The wild optimism associated with the establishment of this "new order of the ages," for example, was only a short step from a deep anxiety that the sacred trust would be lost through corruption or failure of nerve.[48] Carrying forward the Founders' legacy produced sharply contrasting visions of America and the role of its citizens.

Many of the Founders had subscribed to a classical republicanism that linked civic humanism and traditional Christian morality. They championed virtue, fraternity, and selflessness as characteristics that would lead to a near sublimation of the self into a pursuit of the public good.[49] Yet that sort of ideal would not—in fact, could not—support the American cause in the years that followed. In an atmosphere charged with aggressive optimism and nagging anxiety, safeguarding the legacy of the Revolution would require more than a virtuous posture of proper public disinterestedness. In place of their classical vision, Americans constructed several versions of national purpose and public responsibility. What bound them together was a common appeal to the Revolution and an interest in the legacy of the republic; what set them apart was how they construed that legacy.[50]

The Revolution had provided general propositions that many Americans embraced, including the idea of liberty unfettered by tradition and the idea of restitutionism—the notion that people could transcend history and re-create human society afresh. As a "new order of the ages," America stood as a repudiation of the "Old World"; the United States was a new vineyard in a new Eden. The desire to remake (if not forsake) the past was a favorite American theme and would mark the country's culture in innumerable ways. Similarly, appeals to liberty would play a part in each of the competing visions of America. Fierce debate over the purpose of that liberty would not dampen anyone's interest in claiming the language of the Revolution as holy text.

The American republic was not born free, liberal, and competitive. It had to become so, but the process of transformation did not take long.[51] Those changes, coupled with a steady appeal to the defense of the Revolution, conspired to create two leading visions of American identity during the Early Republic—visions that also shaped the process of Americanization for cultural outsiders such as the Pennsylvania Germans. From one side of the Revolution's legacy came a liberal, populist, and even democratic vision of America. In place of the vertically organized society predicated on monarchy and client-patron economic relationships, the Revolution ushered in an age of radical leveling that overturned conventional social structures. Gordon Wood has argued persuasively that the logic and language of the Revolution directly bequeathed such a vision of the new nation, and he adds that it was present among war veterans and the rising generation long before the so-called democratic Age of Jackson.[52]

The experience of Boston shoemaker George Robert Twelves Hewes (1742–1840) illustrated this shift.[53] Before the Revolution, Hewes had trembled in the presence of his "betters"—such as John Hancock. But Hewes's side-by-side participation with Hancock in the Boston Tea Party and his subsequent service in the Continental Army left him feeling that he was Hancock's equal, that he need not doff his hat to anyone. The republic, Americans like Hewes came to believe, was secure when citizens were unrestrained in their pursuit of happiness and acknowledged no superiors. Indeed, many politicians who tried to maintain the prerevolutionary patriarchal posture of public "fathers" failed to hold their offices, while those who adapted to seeing themselves as "friends of the people" were able to continue public service.[54] Even a war hero such as Henry Knox (1750–1806) ended his civil career ignominiously when he failed to see that the Revolution had produced a society that took its cues from market forces and the popular will. In the Revolution's wake, veterans on the frontier even formed guerrilla bands of Liberty Men and continued the struggle for freedom against the vestiges of power held by landed proprietors.[55]

The rapid rise of the market economy was a further validation of this vision of America. It incorporated horizontal notions of society into the very commercial fabric of the country and linked the concepts of liberty and license. Democratic republicanism eventually coupled geographic expansion, capitalism, and political self-determination. Market logic seemed to suggest that republican principles could simply imbue the nation and animate its life with little external guidance. The great danger to the republic's future lay in the limitation of individual liberty.[56]

Another vision of the nation simultaneously claimed descent from the Revolution, though its appeal to the country's founding events presented a contrasting version of American identity and the means to attain it. In an effort to secure the nation's destiny and legacy, some Americans sought to consolidate that legacy and manage it so as to avoid the pitfalls of anarchy and excess. Fear of disunion and apprehension over the rampant desire for material gain prompted these voices to call for a more disciplined commitment to republican principles, shielding them from mob tyranny, acquisitiveness, or the paralyzing grip of political and cultural factions.[57]

Promoters of this vision did not simply call for a return to the disinterested ideals of Enlightenment-era civic humanism. Like their liberal counterparts, they dreamed of an expansive land of enterprise, continental greatness, and boundless opportunity.[58] Yet they also argued the necessity of stability, honor, and discipline in the pursuit of those goals. Moreover, they believed that republican ideals would not simply permeate society: these ideals were fragile constructions that had to be inculcated and passed on through careful education. Patriot leader Benjamin Rush epitomized this understanding of America in his writings, which coupled references to the legendary exploits of the Founders with appeals to shun excess and luxury, promote common schooling, and encourage philanthropy and self-conscious reflection upon the common good.[59] This vision of America also accepted and embraced the emerging market economy, but sought to channel and direct its energy into public improvements and along lines that would secure the nation against hostile mercantile forces from abroad. Eventually this understanding of America became associated with a political culture dubbed "Whiggish."[60]

Although both sides differed in their appraisals and prescriptions, there was broad agreement that the republic's definition was ideological and that in appealing to the legacy of the Revolution, all parties shared something in common. Both liberal populists and Whiggish communalists could be optimistic or anxious. Populists could decry the rapid restructuring of American society that seemed to undo personal freedom as much as they could glory in unfettered liberty. Communalists could champion wild post-millennial hope as much as they could warn of the evils of unrestrained passions.

In any case, dominant American cultural assumptions and practices emerged out of debates among British-stock citizens struggling over how best to reconstitute their society on grounds that would actualize the Revolution's legacy and realize its promise. These ideas and definitions of national identity had a powerful, shaping effect on many aspects of American society, including the republic's religious culture. American

Christianity became associated, on the one hand, with restitutionism and anti-authoritarian populism; on the other hand, it became linked to arguments for the United States to take on a messianic role, one that would require religious leaders to identify and safeguard national public morals.[61]

But could ideology transcend culture? If in the midst of their debates over the ideological content and purpose of American identity, America's British-stock majority had actually been transforming their cultural heritage into something fundamentally new, something that would differentiate them from their counterparts in the Old World, then what role could such ideologies have among Continental cultural outsiders—those who had played a marginal role in revolutionary politics and who did not share all the political and religious assumptions of the majority? Could cultural particularism and a universalizing political ideology coincide? On the surface, at least, ethnicity was a problem for American nationalism. Thinkers such as Benjamin Rush believed that republican ideology, propagated through education, would eventually render existing cultural differences meaningless. For their part, liberal democrats (who worked only in terms of individual liberty) did not even consider collective claims—except as impediments to their own version of nationalism.

If they wished to find a cultural home in the United States *and* retain their ethnic sensibilities, Pennsylvania Germans would have to find their own way.

2

PEASANT REPUBLICANS
AND PENNSYLVANIA CULTURE

On Tuesday, 15 December 1808, the Pennsylvania House of Representatives set aside its normal routine of business and engaged in what one newspaper characterized as "a rather heated debate" on the public place of Christmas. Though a staple of twenty-first-century social life and commercial plans, Christmas had not yet become an accepted holiday among many early-nineteenth-century British-stock residents of Greater Pennsylvania: their Quaker- or Presbyterian-shaped cultures were decidedly Sabbatarian, but otherwise shorn of holy days.[1] Christmas's low public profile, however, posed a problem for those Pennsylvania Germans who had found their way into state government and who demanded a recess for the season, unwilling simply to adopt prevailing Anglo-American ritual rhythms. They objected to the Commonwealth's public calendar, challenging the ethnic assumptions that lay behind its ordering.[2]

Drawing on Continental Protestant tradition, Pennsylvania Germans held Christmas as an important religious and family festival—not only on 25 December, but also on the day that followed, the so-called Second Christmas. Now, however, they lived in an environment defined by neighbors who only grudgingly were becoming accustomed to one such holiday in late December, not to mention setting aside an additional Second Christmas. Since legislators gathered only a limited number of days each year and received per diem compensation, prudence dictated suspending work only for widely recognized and accepted holidays. In the midst of debate, however, House member George Spangler of York announced "that among the Germans Second Christmas is observed as a holiday just like Sunday. So on that day no business could be carried out in the chamber in any case since the Germans would not be present." In the face of such cultural conflict, the resolution to recess for both holidays eventually passed.[3]

The encounter illustrated the way in which Pennsylvania German forays into American public life did not necessarily signal or promote assimilation; they could also trigger a heightened sense of ethnic consciousness as members came face-to-face with the cultural differences that separated them from their neighbors. Moreover, engagement could provide minority members with the political tools to fight for recognition of their distinctiveness. Debating Christmas in legislative chambers was one small example of the paradoxical process of Americanization that Pennsylvania Germans experienced—a process made more interesting by the fact that these ethnic Americans were shifting their political posture from subject to citizen while trying to frame their understandings of liberty in terms recognized in an American environment.

On the Cultural Margins

Peoplehood, for Pennsylvania German church folk, was an evolving, created reality produced in a mixed North American environment, neither transported intact from Europe nor easily reducible to a single element. Stephanie Grauman Wolf has wisely warned historians that "modern models of ethnicity are ... firmly built on nineteenth-century notions of nationalism"; it is difficult to "reconstruct them" for use in the American colonial era and the Early Republic.[4] For Rhine Valley heirs, especially, political allegiance was a weak basis for group identity, given the patchwork political nature of German-speaking Europe.[5]

Instead, ethnicity rested on a conscious acceptance and perpetuation of culture—the interrelated collection of symbols, folkways, institutions, and ideals that defined and gave meaning to the good life and the accepted way of living it. For example, among British-stock Americans who demographically dominated the new United States, at least four major cultural traditions developed and flourished in identifiable geographic regions. Culturally significant in their own right, these systems produced a heightened sense of peoplehood when they existed in conscious competition with others. Pennsylvania Germans lived among two of these, one largely defined by Delaware Valley Quakers and the other by backcountry Irish and British borderland settlers.[6] While individual cultural components were rarely exclusive—Pennsylvania Germans and Delaware Valley Quakers shared a general commitment to non-ostentation, for example—other elements, such as language or the folkways of marking time, combined to provide a recognized set of ethnic borders.

One factor that marked Pennsylvania German peoplehood was language, especially since ethnicity in the eighteenth century was more often thought of in linguistic rather than political terms. Swedish church records in Pennsylvania for the years 1683 to 1784, for instance, suggest that "[a] Swede was a person, of no matter what ethnic background, able to speak the Swedish language."[7] For Lutherans and Reformed in Pennsylvania, the German language of printed texts and its American-evolved "Pennsylvania Dutch" spoken dialect were central marks of identity as well as means of communication. Even those who mastered English signaled their linguistic heritage with obvious accents—despite the best attempts by English newspaper editors to instruct them on proper speech.[8] The Pennsylvania Dutch spoken by descendants of eighteenth-century immigrants would also separate them from later-arriving Germans, who were appalled by the apparent corruption of the traditional tongue.[9]

The dialect thrived throughout Greater Pennsylvania wherever its speakers settled in large numbers.[10] As Lutheran pastor Gotthardt Bernheim (1827–1916) remembered it, Pennsylvania travelers visiting even portions of backcountry North Carolina in the 1830s would have certainly believed themselves "to have unexpectedly come upon some part of the old Keystone State," given the prevalence of Pennsylvania Dutch. In some places

English was actually uncommon, and Bernheim reported that "many of the negro slaves of these Germans spoke no other language" than the German dialect.[11]

Patterns of marking time also revealed Pennsylvania Germans' distance from the folkways of neighboring British Americans. While one of the English Reformation's legacies was a ritual calendar devoid of most religious holidays, Lutheran and Reformed people continued to set aside not only Christmas and Second Christmas, but also Easter Monday, Ascension Day, and especially Pentecost (Whitsun) Monday as both religious and social days of special note. Philadelphia patriot leader Christopher Marshall (1709–97), who was living in Lancaster, Pennsylvania, in 1780, discovered that Pentecost Monday was "a very high holiday in this place," given its Pennsylvania German population.[12] By the early nineteenth century, Pentecost Monday had become an ethnic festival commonly known as the Pennsylvania German equivalent of the Fourth of July. Storekeeper James L. Morris (1810–49) of Morgantown, Pennsylvania, reported that "Whitsun Monday" was a holiday among the "Germans of our neighborhood, but altogether disregarded by the English part of the community."[13] Even on the Ohio frontier, members of the German Reformed Church considered "due regard ... for the leading Church Festivals, such as Christmas, Good Friday, Easter, and Pentecost" important.[14]

Peasant Republicanism

But ethnicity (and the culture within which it rests) was always more than attachment to a particular language or a collection of distinctive folkways. At its heart were values and ideals that gave meaning to ordinary activities and relationships. As David Hackett Fischer has shown in his study of early British Americans, understandings and expressions of liberty and social order were among the most important of cultural elements.[15] They remained especially so in the Early Republic, as discussions of American identity centered on the terms of securing and perpetuating liberty and the American republican experiment.

While backcountry Irish settlers championed a version of libertarian freedom and eastern Pennsylvania Quaker culture nurtured a notion of reciprocal liberty, they shared a common Anglo-American sense of freedom as rooted fundamentally in property rights and the tools of individual economic advancement.[16] For their part, Pennsylvania Germans carried a different set of assumptions with which they initially began to negotiate their place in the American civic arena. Rhine Valley emigrants had left a political culture in which they related to governing powers as subjects who requested privileges and performed traditional duties; the notions of individual, isolated rights and responsibilities associated with a British, Lockean idea of citizenship were not a part of their cultural baggage.[17]

Instead, they carried convictions associated with and supported by southwestern German Pietism, sentiments that paradoxically accented both the importance of personal freedom and the authority of local custom and church structure to provide order and an effective measure of social control.[18] Transferred to the political sphere, such attitudes and assumptions amounted to what might be termed "peasant republicanism." Peasant republicanism regarded true liberty in negative terms—that is, as freedom from intrusive agents of change. Its proponents resisted the efforts of distant power brokers to meddle in their local and traditional affairs, yet ancient privileges and the authority structures that guarded them received honor and deferential respect, and peasant subjects dutifully filled their roles in a vertically organized society. The system of reciprocal relationships and localized mutual obligations that organized civic life thus supported a delicate balance of obedience and vigilance. Peasant republicanism endorsed a collective self-interest derived from a strong local base. It could produce seemingly passive subjects who compliantly yielded to hierarchies of merit, but its advocates actually based their actions on political principles that could also evoke stiff opposition and vigorous protest.

In many ways, the assumptions that surrounded peasant republicanism had only been confirmed during German immigrants' early years in America. For example, unlike colonial arrivals from Britain or even elsewhere on the Continent, the German-speaking newcomers who poured into the port of Philadelphia after 1727 and spread across Pennsylvania and into other colonies confirmed their relationally defined status through oaths of allegiance to the British crown and the colonial proprietary family. Household heads promised to "be faithful and bear true allegiance to His present majesty King George the Second and his successors ... [and] to the proprietor of this Province ... and strictly observe and conform to the laws of England," and many Pennsylvania Germans were slow to publicly abjure their promise when in 1777 a revolutionary state assembly mandated a new loyalty oath.[19]

But events in the colonial period also challenged Pennsylvania Germans' notions of liberty, prompting reactions that pointed to the strength of peasant republican commitments. For example, attempts by English Pennsylvanians to establish a system of "charity schools" for German-speakers met with frank hostility. Conceived and managed by distant authorities who were not accountable to local communities and who seemed to disregard local concerns, the charity schools promised liberty through individual advancement, but ran counter to Pennsylvania Germans' sensibility of proper freedom and order.[20]

For their part, Lutheran and Reformed church structures exemplified and reinforced their members' ideas of a locally ordered political culture. Although many Lutheran pastors had imbibed a Halle-derived version of Pietism that emphasized a more reflexive ideal of obedience, ordinary congregational life was in many ways still governed by peasant republican ideals.[21] Local Lutheran congregations elected their own trustees and pastors, yet those chosen exercised considerable traditionally assigned authority. Reformed polity allowed for lay member participation and voting at the synodic level, but tradition dictated deference to the leading of senior clergy. (Fig. 2.) Participation in church functions did train some lay members for wider political service, and almost all of the Germans who served in colonial government were also prominent congregational lay leaders. Yet, in the end, Lutheran and German Reformed members held disproportionately few public offices beyond their local communities.[22]

Order, Liberty, and Political Cultures

The Revolution was something of a turning point in the relationship of Pennsylvania Germans to the surrounding political order.[23] The war fundamentally altered American political culture and dissolved in an official sense any place for peasant republicans as semifeudal subjects. Unleashing a wave of sentiment that championed individual liberty and democratization as the corollaries of national independence, the Revolution undercut any lingering plausibility of a deferential, vertically structured society.[24]

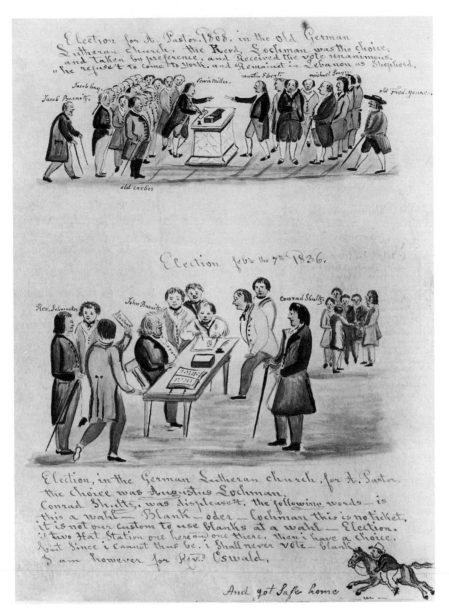

Fig. 2 Choosing a minister at the Lutheran church in York, Pennsylvania. This watercolor and the commentary by Lewis Miller illustrate the role of lay members in choosing church leaders—and the laity's jealous guarding of voting rights. In 1808, the members elected a pastor who then refused to accept their call. At the 1836 election, Conrad Schultz protested that a ballot with only one name was "no ticket" and that "it is not our custom to use blanks at a *wahl*—Election." "I shall never vote," Schultz insisted, unless "I have a choice." Courtesy of York County Heritage Trust, York, Pa.

The resulting and sudden societal shift caused members of the 1786 German Reformed Coetus—the church's governing body—to lament that "the blessing of peace has rather been attended with the sad consequences of display in dress, debauchery, and luxury," since "now there are few, very few, who do not live above their stations, so that a stranger on Sundays, or festival days, cannot possibly tell whom he meets."[25] Pennsylvania German folkways surrounding dress—drawing on a Rhine Valley intellectual orientation and the lingering effect of traditional German sumptuary laws—signified ascribed, stratified social rank and reflected the importance of a properly ordered society, monitored by local custom and authority, and given more to the household economy than to wider networks of trade. In short, it fit a peasant republican outlook. Such visual markers had disappeared in Britain long before they had on the Continent, but it was the leveling of society in the Early Republic that most clearly washed away such standards for most Americans.[26]

In a legal sense, Pennsylvania Germans were now citizens, and whatever their earlier disinterest in naturalization and in regular political participation, they stood on equal legal footing with their British-descended neighbors as common members of a new republican experiment.[27] Yet ironically, Pennsylvania Germans actually maintained a lower political profile in the years following Yorktown than in the period that had preceded the Revolution. Fewer Pennsylvania Germans held elected office in the 1780s, and that decade seemed to usher in "an era of stagnating German engagement in politics." Some analysts have credited this apparent withdrawal from the public sphere to a reassertion of "ethnic pride and distinction" marked by calls to preserve the German language.[28] However, successful political adaptation and the development and assertion of "ethnic pride" are hardly mutually exclusive developments.[29] Pennsylvania Germans' ambivalence in the wake of the Revolution stemmed not so much from qualms about cultural purity as it did from a more fundamental problem of needing to refashion traditional political purposes and habits of thought so as to connect them to the rapidly changing American political world in a meaningful way. That transformation would take time.

Two different approaches eventually emerged among Lutheran and Reformed Pennsylvania Germans trying to situate old ideals in a new political landscape, and each could rightly claim a portion of the heritage of peasant republicanism. On the one hand, there were those who cherished custom and tradition, deference to authority, and respect for predictable order above all else. They believed that Lutheran patriarch Heinrich Muhlenberg's counsel that "God is a God of order, and in His congregations everything must be done orderly," applied equally to the civic sphere.[30] The Revolution triggered a process that separated this older notion of order from its earlier context, which had also included tradition-guided local privilege and checks on the power of distant authority. But some Pennsylvania Germans were willing to give up those elements in the process of adapting to a changing American society; indeed, the speed of social change may have fueled their quest for stability.[31] Meanwhile, other Lutheran and Reformed faithful continued to think of government in rather minimalist terms and feared distant, oppressive state power, regarding it as a threat to their traditional ideas of local liberty. For them the path from peasant subjects to democratic citizens led toward even greater wariness of centralized authority and of the optimistic claims of reform-minded nationalist republicans—even if such conclusions required discarding traditional habits of deferential respect for social betters and honor for divinely sanctioned leadership.

Both approaches were visible already in the closing years of the eighteenth century. Philadelphia Lutheran pastor J. H. C. Helmuth (1745–1825), for example, clearly identified with the first. Helmuth championed the creation of a highly organized benevolent-paternalist social order that combined an activist Halle-inspired version of Pietism with a deep respect for and trust in the ability of public authorities to manage and direct society as a whole. As the American rhetoric of liberty increasingly took on an individualist flavor, Helmuth became more strident in his criticism of unrestrained liberty in politics and religion.[32] In 1795 Helmuth and his associate, Christian L. F. Endress (1775–1827), introduced Lutheran parishioners to constitutional theory and American government through a series of lectures insisting that the worthy replacement of monarchy was not popular democracy, but an updated version of ancient patriarchy in which virtuous republican public servants formed a governing hierarchy of talent and looked after the good of their charges.[33]

Nor were Lutheran divines alone in trying to communicate such sentiments. German Reformed pastor Samuel A. Helfenstein (1775–1866) was among the most influential figures in his denomination and prepared many candidates for the ministry, including Daniel Hertz (1796–1868), who compiled manuscript books of theological and practical notes given at Helfenstein's dictation. Rejecting the increasingly popular idea that "preference [in church government] is altogether a matter of human prudence and not of divine right," Helfenstein taught that "God has instituted a form of Gov. which is binding and necessary." That form, it turned out, while not "Monarchical," was certainly not "Democratical" either. Instead, it was "the form generally styled Aristocratical." Refuting the growing American notion that vested ever more power in "the body of the faithful," teacher Helfenstein told students that "the best objection" to such democratic notions was that "in all its consequences [it] tends to licentiousness & the destruction of civil government." Moreover, Helfenstein emphasized that the church, "its rules, its members, its laws, [and] its ordinances ... are all visible," not merely "spiritual," so the application of ecclesiological ideas to broader social settings was a short and easy step.[34]

While the sentiments of Helmuth and Helfenstein were doubtless influential, they were not the only way in which Pennsylvania Germans were beginning to reconfigure their ideas of what it meant to live as republican citizens. If some thoughtful members of the community were able to find a political home among the "Friends of Order and Good Government"—as the members of the Federalist political faction liked to call themselves—others found in the democratic rhetoric of the day a closer connection to their idea of local community privilege free from outside interference.[35] In 1805, for example, dissenting Philadelphia Lutherans simply left pastor Helmuth's St. Michael's–Zion congregation and formed St. John's Lutheran Church.[36] For his part, pastor John Peter Mahnenschmidt (1783–1857) discovered a similar spirit among German Reformed believers in northeast Ohio who resisted his attempt to implement a new church constitution and connect congregational life to the larger synod. "The argument against it," he noted about 1813, "was, 'We live in a free country, where no one should suffer himself to be bound.'"[37]

Yet the difference in spirit did not simply reflect a split between clergy and laity. Ministers could hold populist democratic views as well. For example, while Lutheran pastor John Casper Dill (1758–1824) complained bitterly about the egalitarian sensibilities of Pennsylvania German churchgoers in Northampton County, a neighboring Lutheran clergyman, Johann C. Jaeger (1768–1832), replied that Dill was living in America and should realize that here the minister raises his hat to his parishioners. Although

Dill retorted that "he would never do" such a thing, Jaeger remained a clerical defender of the more democratic-localist understanding of liberty.[38] Similarly, the esteemed German Reformed pastor Thomas Pomp (1773–1852) joined lay members in criticizing the Federalist-inspired "house tax" that in 1799 ignited the so-called John Fries Tax Rebellion in eastern Pennsylvania. (Fig. 3.)[39] Pomp's published attack in the *Easton Messenger and Intelligencer* on the Federalists and on a Moravian tax assessor bordered on libel.[40] Nearby, the Reformed pastor Jacob Eyerman also supported the tax resistance, denouncing Congress as a gang of *"spitz bube"* (bandits). If the federal government responded with force, he announced, he "would rather lay his black coat on a nail, and fight the whole week, and preach for them Sundays" than see his people lose their traditional privileges "as in the old country."[41]

In fact, responses to the Fries Rebellion marked an early and public divide among Pennsylvania Germans. The larger political context included international tensions with France and President John Adams's desire to levy a direct assessment to support what many saw as the nucleus of a standing federal army.[42] But Pennsylvania German opponents resented the tax assessors as much as the tax itself, because the Federalist-appointed agents were often drawn from the ranks of gentry elites or German sectarians aligned with distant, powerful officials in the state capital. In short, according to historian Kenneth Keller, Pennsylvania German supporters of John Fries and his tax resisters believed "that the taxes [meant] further oppression by persons who had unjustly dominated county politics."[43] In late 1798, using a tactic they would employ again in the following decades, Lutheran and German Reformed laity gathered in several heavily German townships and signed commitments to resist the tax assessors. Some claimed that they were willing to pay a property tax "if it was laid as they were used to," but they refused to concede the justice of a novel "house tax" collected by assessors who had—in the view of Lutheran and Reformed adherents—betrayed their community to foreign agents of meddlesome innovation.[44] While lay members and clergy such as Pomp and Eyerman had supported the rebellion, pastor Helmuth was horrified by such resistance to legally constituted authority. In March 1799 he composed a circular in which he asserted that "most of the Germans" still held a reputation as "industrious and religious inhabitants" of the state, and he denounced rebellion against governmental authority.[45]

REV? THOMAS POMP.

Fig. 3　Thomas Pomp served as German Reformed pastor in Easton, Pennsylvania, from 1796 to 1852. He was sympathetic toward Northampton County's John Fries tax revolt. Courtesy of Evangelical and Reformed Historical Society, Lancaster, Pa.

As the Fries Rebellion cooled, the autumn 1799 election for Pennsylvania governor—a contest that "exhibited more acrimony, malice, and indecency than was ever known on any former occasion"—became another theater of political struggle that enticed some Pennsylvania Germans into the realm of active citizenship.[46] The election pitted the democratically inclined Republican supporters of candidate Thomas McKean (1734–1817) against Federalist James Ross (1762–1847). Both were Irish Protestants, so neither national origin nor religion were partisan issues. Instead, the contest turned on debates over political philosophy: the Federalist supported the traditional power of rural gentry and hereditary elites in the cities, while the Republican forces, in contrast, championed constitutional and judicial reform that would decentralize government and give more power to local justices of the peace. Not only would such innovations have allowed legal hearings to be held in German (judicial proceedings above the level of justice of the peace were in English), but it would have brought power closer to the informal system of community control that guarded local custom and tradition.[47]

In the end, despite pleas from the likes of pastor Helmuth, most German churchpeople voted for McKean and against the Federalist party. Wealth and geographic sectionalism played little role in the democratic triumph, a triumph that "was not so much a victory of ideology or class as it was of local interest" that proved attractive to onetime peasant republicans.[48] Yet Pennsylvania German politics were not completely settled in 1800, and if the Federalist Party was finished, a version of Helmuth's and Helfenstein's benevolent-authoritarian ideal would continue to fuel one side of the Pennsylvania German political debate for decades to come.

In large part this ongoing debate was necessary because the collapse of the Federalist Party did not leave simply a single political option. Instead, the new Republican majority—in Pennsylvania and throughout the United States—faced a dilemma born of its own victory, its commitments to egalitarian republicanism, and their implications. For if democrats opposed the power wielded by distant Federalist elites, then they implicitly supported a system of equality that knew no geographic bounds and theoretically recognized no variation among citizens. Yet such political homogenization, in turn, threatened some of those same democratically inclined citizens' cherished claims of localism. Here the democratic coalition would founder: some argued that securing equality and democracy would require common schooling, universal militia service, and cultural uniformity, while others claimed that democracy really "meant a system by which local ethnic and religious subcultures claimed power and defended themselves against real or imagined threats that in the name of majorities sometimes attempted to homogenize the pluralistic commonwealth."[49]

The peasant republican heritage of many Pennsylvania Germans mitigated against their warming to a custodial role for government, and even the Calvinists among them were often skeptical of state-managed morality.[50] If most Pennsylvania Germans had opposed the Federalist elites, many now began to harbor fears of a tyranny of the democratic majority. Indeed, Pennsylvania German minorities in several regions successfully campaigned for the creation of new ethnically dominated counties—Lehigh (1812) and Lebanon (1813)—carved out of older jurisdictions.[51]

In terms of political alignments, Pennsylvania Germans tended toward Pennsylvania's "Amalgamation Party," which would later become the Jacksonian Democratic coalition,[52] promoting "a conception of minimal government" and cultivating a sense of outsiderhood turned to popular advantage.[53] John P. Helfenstein, a member of a leading German Reformed family, chaired the 1816 Amalgamation organizing meeting that advocated greater latitude for the exercise of local authority.[54]

The Republic Reborn

Just before the organization of the Amalgamation Party, however, the War of 1812—brief and militarily bungled though it was—provided a measure of evolving national identity. Through the struggle and anxiety of war, the republic was reborn in the popular mind, freed from the shadow of Europe and the threat of counterrevolution. Political orators and the popular press gloried in the strength of the republic. Many used the war and the changes it wrought on American society to promote democratization and economic leveling.[55]

In the midst of the conflict, German Reformed pastor Yost Heinrich Fries (1777–1839) found himself before a group of war volunteers from Northumberland County, Pennsylvania, and he felt obliged to preach "a patriotic sermon."[56] (Fig. 4.) Although such militia sermons had a long history in America,[57] Fries confessed that he "had never before in my life considered such a topic in proper seriousness." Indeed, as far as he could recall, during his entire ministry among his people in York, Pennsylvania, and now on the frontier, he had "never read anything of this sort."[58]

His sermon illustrated the degree to which Pennsylvania Germans had absorbed popular political rhetoric and ideas and yet remained out of step with national sentiments. Fries began by painting a picture of the biblical Joshua as a true patriot who loved God and his people, desiring nothing more than that the ancient Hebrews would "maintain noble peace in their own republic." Surveying biblical and secular history, Fries argued that virtually no other leader in human history compared with Joshua: "None was free of monarchy, aristocracy, or despotism, and most of them were, in the strictest sense of the word, arch-tyrants." Then acknowledging that among his German listeners, his next comments would surely provoke "a displeased face here and there," he drew a favorable comparison between Joshua and George Washington. Both men, Fries contended, were "genuine, pure, and truly republican patriots."[59]

Yet Fries also revealed Pennsylvania German skepticism about the self-confident and progressive claims of the United States.[60] He ventured that support for the war was weak among his people, who tended to believe "that selfish, even incompetent people serve in our government." Fries argued that if his people had a proper civic role, it was one of quiet, moral example. "What Germany is in Europe, that is what Pennsylvania is in America," Fries declared, carving out a special place for his listeners and implying that valuable contributions existed in spite of limited political power. Pious Pennsylvania German soldiers who avoided dishonesty and vice could model reserved self-control in the Yankee army marching to Canada.[61]

Although Fries could speak about citizenship in general terms and even suggested that it was "an honor to be a Pennsylvania citizen [*Bürger*]," when he came to speak specifically about his listeners' relationship to their Pennsylvania German governor, Simon Snyder (1759–1819), he suddenly shifted to more authoritarian language, publicly wishing that the governor "might rule over his subjects [*Unterthanen*] with wisdom and understanding."[62] Even in a patriotic sermon explicitly drawing on widely shared American political rhetoric, Pennsylvania German churchgoers in Northampton County heard a message that fell back on traditional notions of relating to the state as peasant subjects.

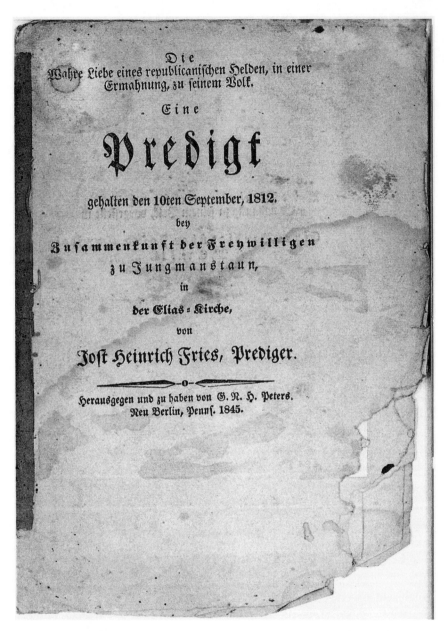

Die
Wahre Liebe eines republicanischen Helden, in einer
Ermahnung, zu seinem Volk.

Eine

Predigt

gehalten den 10ten September, 1812,

bey

Zusammenkunft der Freywilligen

zu Jungmanstaun,

in

der Elias = Kirche,

von

Jost Heinrich Fries, Prediger.

Herausgegen und zu haben von G. N. H. Peters,
Neu Berlin, Penns. 1845.

Fig. 4 Title page of Yost Fries's 1812 militia sermon. Courtesy of Evangelical and
Reformed Historical Society, Lancaster, Pa.

To some observers, Pennsylvania German Lutheran and Reformed adherents might well have appeared still to be acting as subjects rather than as politically engaged citizens. In the early nineteenth century, they were less likely to hold political party leadership positions, and although they occasionally represented their coethnics in legislative bodies, districts with non-German majorities almost never chose them for such posts. They were also noticeably absent from both major and minor judicial offices and militia leadership.[63] Moreover, a comprehensive study of the German book trade during the Early Republic found that "[t]angible evidence of interest in political and philosophical thought" was "largely absent from book-sellers' lists."[64]

Yet by the time of the battle of New Orleans, Pennsylvania Germans had begun refashioning aspects of their subject-oriented peasant republicanism to fit the American scene. Many apparently found the localist orientation of Pennsylvania's emerging conservative Democratic party attractive. Nevertheless, they were not simply refighting the old colonial battles that they had waged over charity schools and the like. While the debates that would erupt in the 1820s through the 1840s over the meaning of liberty echoed some of these eighteenth-century discussions, the nineteenth-century development of Pennsylvania German ethnicity and American identity were not merely the triumph of an old, negatively defined liberty. What would be new was Pennsylvania Germans' casting arguments in patriotic American rhetoric that joined ethnic parochialism and national intention—claims that assumed both an identification with the United States and a commitment to define what that identification meant. Pennsylvania German separatism would be increasingly and perhaps somewhat paradoxically linked to larger visions of American purpose. In that process of negotiating their place in national political culture, Pennsylvania Germans were not maintaining a distant heritage so much as formulating new means of defining their distinction.

A brief look at Pennsylvania German responses to public school legislation illustrates this dynamic. As in the 1808 debate over the public place of Christmas, such interaction hinged on cultural particularity but moved Pennsylvania Germans into the currents of mainstream American public discourse. After 1834, debate in Pennsylvania over the role of public and parochial schools highlighted questions of local autonomy and particularity and their intersection with ongoing discussions of American national purpose. That year, legislation provided for local taxation and the establishment of common township schools free from specific ecclesiastical control. The idea was one dear to those Americans who promoted a guarded, Whiggish vision of their nation. Many citizens who saw America as a land of unrestrained personal liberty also viewed the schools positively, sure that they were engines of social and economic leveling, though some did question whether the plan might create a new class system.[65]

In either case, Pennsylvania Germans saw the introduction of public schools as a threat to their understanding of liberty. They were eager to save their locally controlled parochial primary schools—the most extensive in the state, with some 250 classrooms operated by Lutherans and 160 by German Reformed. While there was some opposition to the public school plan from Scots-Irish Old School Presbyterians, a careful study has concluded that their resistance was quite limited compared with that of the German churchpeople.[66] Of 987 potential public school districts in the state, 264 refused the common school plan, with the vast majority of these in the Pennsylvania German pale of Adams, Berks, Bucks, Lancaster, Lebanon, Lehigh, Northampton, Schuylkill, Union, and York counties.[67] Pennsylvania German townships' resistance continued in many cases through the 1850s, and some did not replace parochial schools with public ones until after the Civil War.[68]

Yet despite the ethnoreligious origins of Pennsylvania Germans' opposition to the public schools, their resistance assumed the language and logic of secular democratic argument. Pennsylvania Germans insisted that the new institutions were *zwing Schulen* (forced schools), not free schools, and that they infringed on their liberty as free Americans to maintain local particularity.[69] The common school struggle pulled Pennsylvania Germans into the public political arena and brought them face-to-face with the debate over American purpose waged by Whiggish communalists and democratic populists. Pennsylvania Germans had significant ethnic stakes in the outcome of this mainstream political contest.

Throughout the period, Pennsylvania Germans had remained culturally distinct, prompting British travelers to marvel over their retention of so "many of the customs and prejudices of their countrymen"—and cosmopolitan writer Anne Royall to note how they differed "from all other nations that have settled in America."[70] Yet such differences could easily be exaggerated and stereotyped. (Perhaps travelogue writers simply fixed on the exotic?) What was fundamentally important was the connection between symbol and worldview in these folkways and ideological orientations, and the relationship of Pennsylvania German identity to the larger discourse of American identity and values. Ideas and convictions that, on one level, Pennsylvania Germans shared with their anglophone neighbors could also define, defend, and bolster ethnicity. And the Lutheran and Reformed churches—still the most important Pennsylvania German institutions of the period—provided the issues, personalities, and arenas in which the formidable task of ethnic negotiations took place.

But Pennsylvania German church folk were not the only people to find connections between their religious orientation and political sensibilities. Many English-speaking Americans who began to champion universalizing, reformist ideas as a means of securing the nation also drew upon new and popular religious currents coursing through the Early Republic. Those religious impulses, however, were not unchallenged in Lutheran and Reformed communities.

3

FIGHTING FOR THE
PENNSYLVANIA GERMAN SOUL

Toward the end of 1828, well-known evangelist Charles
G. Finney (1792–1875) concluded a series of revival meetings in Philadelphia and headed northwest to the Pennsylvania manufacturing borough of Reading. There, amid
the rolling Berks County hills, Finney found himself in the
heart of the nation's Pennsylvania German population.
But the evangelist who had turned towns of similar size
in western New York on their heads found the situation
in Reading something of a shock. Although it had taken
much of the country by storm, Finney's brand of evangelical religion registered little effect among the so-called
Pennsylvania Dutch, who "had no conception of revivals
of religion," he lamented. Calls to conversion fell on deaf
ears, he noted, since "the German population supposed
themselves to have been made Christians by baptism, and
especially by receiving the communion. Nearly all of them,

if asked when they became Christians, would reply that they took their communion at such a time of Dr. [Muhlenberg], or some other German divine. And when I asked them if they thought that was religion, they would say, yes, they supposed it was."[1]

Locals told Finney that for Pennsylvania Germans to adopt even the most modest of his "new measures"—his revival techniques—was tantamount to "saying that their ancestors had all gone to hell; for they had done no such thing." Finney complained that German pastors spoke "severely of those that forsook the way of their fathers," and he bemoaned "the influence of the daily press," which shaped the opinions of "the German population particularly." During the winter that Finney remained in Reading, he settled for reviving local Old School Presbyterians. While his autobiography characterized the Reading experience as a success, it was surprisingly candid about the Pennsylvania German opposition he encountered.[2]

By the time Finney had arrived, that opposition had been building for several decades. If Pennsylvania Germans were somewhat hesitant to engage the Early Republic's political culture, they were often even less keen to embrace the new forms of American evangelical religion[3] that also flourished in the wake of the Revolution. Unlike their encounter with a political process that beckoned but did not necessarily demand involvement, the confrontation with American popular Christianity was marked by a combative spirit of competition and proselytizing that actively challenged Pennsylvania German notions of how they should order their natural and supernatural worlds.[4] Given the growing discussions that linked national identity with a popular religious rhetoric and social vision, however, participation in the wider evangelical movement also offered Continental outsiders a means of merging with the cultural mainstream. But Pennsylvania German Lutheran and Reformed encounters with American evangelicalism—even in the form of direct appeals in the German language—ultimately did not result in mass defections nor in the easy adoption of an Anglo-American evangelical orientation.

Christianity in a New Nation

Charles Finney represented the development of a particularly American style of religion that had already begun to emerge in the late 1700s. In the decades that followed the Revolution, American Christianity entered a tumultuous and tension-filled period that witnessed the radical reconfiguration of the ecclesiastical landscape.[5] Methodists, Baptists, and other upstart sects and populist religious movements challenged and displaced the once-dominant colonial-era denominational establishments. In an atmosphere charged with the ideas of self-evident truth, inherent human equality, sovereignty of the people, and restitutionist calls to create "the new order of the ages," the old religious order gave way to an energetic evangelicalism that tended to disparage tradition and clerical authority, often claiming no creed but the Bible. The common touch of Methodism and the democratic structure of Baptist churches fitted them for the prevailing mood of the country, as did the restitutionism of groups such as the Christian Connection and the egalitarian tenets of the Universalists.

In some situations, the new religious orientation expressed itself through boisterous, enthusiastic revival meetings in which participants claimed simply to yield bodies and minds to the work of the divine Spirit. In other cases—including those involving figures such as Charles Finney—revivalists sought to create tactically an atmosphere in which this new brand of faith would be most effective. These strategies included Finney's innovative "new measures," such as calling on the unrepentant by name or asking them to sit on an "anxious bench," where they could publicly claim salvation before the service concluded.[6] Either way, the result was a faith that prized individual, experiential validation over inherited authority and discontinuity over tradition. This revivalism was a means to and hallmark of true faith insofar as it represented a populist appropriation of belief on the parishioners' own terms.

Not surprisingly, practitioners of a type of Christianity so closely connected to a democratic and optimistic American mentality quickly understood its political implications for public life. Revivalism linked hands with community reform—either through the promised regeneration of citizens or combined with programs of religiously informed social management—to suggest connections between national destiny and the success of evangelical Protestantism. Soon, appropriating the message of evangelical Protestantism and its methods of revivalism also meant subscribing to a host of related commitments and assumptions about American society and an identity tied to the redemption of the nation. Even apart from its spiritual draw, then, this new faith became a powerful force in shaping American identity in the first half of the nineteenth century.[7]

Yet even as Charles Finney—the most skillful evangelical revivalist of the period—discovered, some Pennsylvania Germans could resist participating in the nation's religious revolution. Nor was theirs a rejection born of isolation or ignorance. The Pennsylvania German population spawned several popular evangelical movements that carried class meetings, camp meetings, circuit riders, and an enthusiastic, egalitarian message into the heart of ethnic enclaves. In addition, some Lutheran and Reformed clergymen themselves worked to introduce similar innovations into their own churches. But in the end, the popular evangelical appeal and the new German-speaking denominations connected with only a limited portion of their potential audience. Certainly they achieved nothing compared with the Methodists, Baptists, and similar groups that overtook and nearly eclipsed the older, traditionally dominant, English-language denominations during the same period.[8] The struggle for the Pennsylvania German soul highlighted the cultural gap between many Lutheran and Reformed adherents and the Protestant religious mainstream, a distance that would often contribute to ethnic conflicts and skepticism about schemes that linked religious and civic renewal on a national scale.

Ethnic Revivalists

As an army of evangelical enthusiasts spread their message across the country, they came upon communities that tested the limits of their English-language message. In 1810, for example, Methodist preacher William Colbert (1764–1833) was assigned a preaching circuit that included that "infamously wicked place, *Hamburg* [Pennsylvania]"; he decided that he "might almost as well be in the heart of *Germany*." Unable to communicate effectively, he complained bitterly to Methodist bishop Francis Asbury (1745–1816) about "the influence of wicked Dutch Priests" who warned parishioners to shun Colbert's class meetings.[9]

Although Colbert apparently had little success in presenting his message, Pennsylvania Germans had not had to wait for the opportunity to hear, in their own tongue, America's popular new religious idiom.[10] German-language equivalents of the burgeoning Methodist movement had already appeared in the form of the United Brethren and the Evangelical Association.[11] The United Brethren organized around the revivalist preaching and earnest enthusiasm of German Reformed pastor Philip William Otterbein (1726–1813), who had built a small network of like-minded, revivalist German clerics.[12] In the religious tumult of the postrevolutionary years, the Otterbein circle organized under the name United Brethren, and in 1800, it elected Otterbein and onetime Mennonite minister Martin Boehm (1725–1812) co-superintendents and bishops. Otterbein's United Brethren approach included not only new methods of achieving religious revival, but also populist theological innovation. When a Reformed pastor complained that Otterbein had fallen under the influence of American-style theological self-determination and had jettisoned predestination, Otterbein confessed, "I cannot side with Calvin in this case.... I believe in election, but cannot persuade myself that God has absolutely and without condition predestined some men to perdition."[13]

Another German evangelical group of the period, the Evangelical Association, sprang from the ministry of Jacob Albright (1759–1808), a third-generation Pennsylvania German and Lutheran layman. When the deaths of three of Albright's children left him in a state of spiritual crisis, conversations with a Methodist neighbor and a United Brethren exhorter led to Albright's joining a local Methodist class in 1791. Granted a Methodist license five years later, he became frustrated with that denomination's refusal to aim its message specifically at non-English-speakers.[14] In response, Albright launched an independent German-language ministry; local class meetings, a general conference, and his role as bishop all followed.[15]

German evangelicals patterned their approach on the wildly popular Anglo-American evangelical movements rising to public prominence around them—particularly on the Methodists. The United Brethren adopted a Methodist-style confession and discipline, and they eventually organized four regional conferences that in 1815 formed a combined general conference.[16] Their itinerants, such as Christian Newcomer (1749–1830) and Andrew Zeller (1755–1839), adopted the Methodist mode of circuit riding. Nor did they always ride alone; in 1805, for example, Newcomer traveled with the noted Methodist Lorenzo Dow (1777–1834).[17] Albright's Evangelical Association patterned its polity and discipline even more closely on the Methodist model.[18] Members of all three groups worshiped together and attended one another's conferences.[19] Popular revivalist-style camp meetings and singing were also part of the German evangelical repertoire. A native of Lebanon County, Pennsylvania, who observed German evangelical camp meetings as a boy, later recalled "scenes of vociferous and extravagant enthusiasm."[20] Like their anglophone compatriots, they made much of dreams, visions, and ecstatic utterances.[21] Indeed, one United Brethren chronicler noted that "the worldly-minded" endowed his forebears with "the nickname, *Dutch Methodists,* which in those days was considered rather slanderous."[22]

After 1830, in addition to these groups, a small Pennsylvania German restorationist group known as the Church of God also competed for ethnic souls. Organized by a onetime Reformed pastor in Harrisburg, Pennsylvania, John Winebrenner (1797–1860), the church spread a primitivist message similar to that of Alexander Campbell's "Christian movement," playing on the American desire to forgo all inherited ecclesiastical tradition.[23]

Appealing to the democratic commoner, German revivalists belittled formal theological training. In the leveling, democratic spirit of the time, their sermons criticized fancy dress and upper-class imitation. The Evangelical Association, for example, "resolved [in 1818] that none of our ministers be allowed to wear gloves during the Summer, nor to use silver-plated bridle bits or stirrups, or loaded whips, and in no case to adorn their person with large watch keys."[24] In most ways, in fact, the German evangelicals' experience ran at close parallel with that of their numerically more successful and effective English-speaking counterparts—even following in the process of gradual gentrification.[25] The new groups adopted the style and substance of a populist American Christianity that drew on the ideals and social reality of the new nation, but they had targeted a different audience.

That targeting produced religious conflicts in dozens of Pennsylvania German communities as Pennsylvania German church leaders and laity debated their response. In a few cases, the battles took place on traditional ecclesiastical turf, such as the Lutheran Ministerium's 1783 warning to Heinrich Möller (1749–1829) "to be careful in his dealings with the Methodists," or in the 1804 German Reformed Synod's dismissal of pastor George A. Geeting (1741–1812), one of Otterbein's associates, who was increasingly given to novel American revivalist tactics.[26]

More often, however, the conflicts involved public denouncement, published argument, and open competition. In 1810, German Reformed minister Yost H. Fries (then in York, Pennsylvania) complained that he "was much annoyed by Methodistic fanaticism and [the] proselytism" of the United Brethren.[27] German Reformed pastor Joel L. Reber (1816–56) of frontier Centre County, Pennsylvania's Brush Valley, lamented in his journal: "Sect-people persecuted us much—mocked at our assemblies, because we did not, like them, permit all kinds of disorder."[28] On the other side, the Evangelical Association's legendary bishop, Johannes Seybert (1791–1860), faced churchly hecklers at some of his preaching appointments. "I believed that I had come to a Christian Lutheran community," Seybert called to noisy disrupters on one occasion. "Now it seems, however, that I have come to Sodom and Gomorrah."[29] One Evangelical Association preacher was said to have attributed lightning that struck Lutherans' barns to God's judgment on that church.[30] And as late as the 1840s, the Association distributed a handbill containing the supposed confession of Reformed minister William Hendel Jr. (1768–1846), in which he feared that he had the form of religion without true faith.[31]

In a particularly dramatic move in 1802, North Carolina Lutheran pastor Paul Henkel (1754–1825) took the battle to his opponents' turf by attending a camp meeting. Deciding that the spiritually deceived needed to hear his message and that they were most apt to be at such a gathering, Henkel arrived at the revival and began preaching against the subjective and individualist message of the other orators assembled there; he offered a counter-sermon in the midst of the camp meeting.[32] Several years later, in western Pennsylvania, a Lutheran pastor stumbled upon an Evangelical Association gathering where he found "an awful scene." Some participants were "singing with the 'holy swing' and rocking to and fro, clapping their hands and stamping their feet," while others "were shouting at the top of their voices" or were "stretched out on the floor." The horrified minister grabbed a "hymn book and commanded order with his rough, harsh voice. 'I want you to be still; this is not the way to worship God; bodily exercise will not save your souls,'" he thundered. A sympathetic observer reported that "all became silent as the grave," and the pastor "preached them a good, faithful gospel sermon ... which no doubt did the people ten times more good in the end than their noisy and turbulent meeting."[33]

Stories of those who moved into the evangelical fold and later returned to their old loyalties also circulated in Lutheran and Reformed communities, aiming to show the wisdom of the desire to "live and die" in the church of one's ancestors and the need to rethink initial attraction to the Pennsylvania German evangelicals. John Dietrich Aurandt (1760–1831) of northeastern Pennsylvania's Buffalo Valley, for example, had been catechized in the Reformed Church as a child, but fell out of regular ecclesiastical connections after his mother's death. Coming under the influence of a United Brethren itinerant, Aurandt even began preaching under Brethren license around 1800. His own pastoral work, however, led to an inner struggle—not over the experience of salvation, but over the theological foundations of such an experience. In response, he began attending the Reformed Synod, "regularized" his ministry with theological study and ordination in 1809, and took his own Buffalo Valley audience into the churchly fold.[34]

The contest for loyalty seemed particularly heated on the frontier, where "democratized Christianity" was often especially active and traditional ecclesiastical structures were relatively weak. Calls for Lutheran and Reformed pastors to fill charges in the west and south were staples of East Coast ministerium and synodic gatherings. John George Butler (1754–1816), a Lutheran pastor traveling in 1805 and 1806 among scattered faithful in Virginia, Kentucky, and Tennessee, found that "for lack of a German preacher," some Lutherans had even "connected with an English church." Yet he believed that "they would all, without doubt, come back again if German preachers would visit them."[35] Lutheran leaders even took to licensing migrating schoolteachers in theology to make sure that parishioners moving into Kentucky or Ohio received doctrinal as well as rudimentary knowledge.[36] Some Pennsylvania German clergymen, such as James Ross Reily (1788–1844), combined charismatic personalities with denominational authority and became frontier folk heroes. Reily's travels among Reformed adherents in North Carolina included run-ins with local toughs and armed standoffs with bandits.[37]

Yet confessional allegiance among Lutheran and Reformed believers was not an eastern phenomenon that melted as they moved west and joined in the supposed assimilating experience of the frontier. North Carolinian Paul Henkel led in the formation of two regional Lutheran synods, Ohio (1818) and Tennessee (1820), which were composed of westward-moving Pennsylvania Germans and stressed traditional confessionalism as a mark of true Lutheranism.[38] Although a friend of Pietist-style emotive spirituality, Henkel did not subordinate tradition to experience. His catechisms and writings on the sacraments stressed loyalty to received confessional authority that was not based on individual sensibilities.[39]

After 1799, Lutheran and Reformed adherents in North Carolina migrated to what would become Cape Girardeau and Bollinger Counties, Missouri, where pastor Samuel Weyberg (1773–1833) became the first

American Protestant clergyman to undertake a settled ministry in the 1803 Louisiana Purchase.[40] When wandering New England preacher and school-teacher Timothy Flint (1780–1840) passed through the area about 1820, he found that the members of the Pennsylvania German community had "preserved their peculiarities in an uncommon degree." Flint suggested that the Pennsylvania Germans had not imbibed the American popular evangelical sentiments of their neighbors.[41] In any case, the frontier setting and distance from major Pennsylvania German population centers had not led to the community's demise.

Wherever they were located, Pennsylvania Germans tended to maintain their Lutheran and Reformed connections, despite aggressive evangelical proselytism.[42] Although the United Brethren and Evangelical Association gained converts, they did not approximate the proportional success of their English-language counterparts. By 1820, the United Brethren claimed approximately 9,000 baptized members throughout the country, yet that year the German Reformed Church accounted for at least twice that many actively communing members in its Eastern Synod.[43] And in 1830, Albright's Association had a nationwide membership of only 3,245, while Lutherans had more than four times that many communing members in the Ohio Synod alone—a body covering a western region supposedly difficult for established churches to hold in the face of upstart evangelical proselytizing.[44] In fact, the United Brethren and Evangelical Association became sizable denominations only after they abandoned their focus on Pennsylvania Germans and began appealing generally to English-speaking Americans. As one United Brethren chronicler remarked, the "tendency in holding to [the German language] ... worked against the numerical growth" of his group. "But when once the speech of America had obtained the mastery in the United Brethren pulpits," the church grew significantly, "this increase coming largely from the non-German elements of the American people."[45]

The direct challenge of upstart German "bush preachers," however, was not the only source of revivalist influence. During the later 1820s and 1830s, several Pennsylvania German Reformed and Lutheran church leaders themselves introduced popular evangelical techniques and tendencies into their own congregations. Though they did not take up itinerancy and tried to limit excessive emotionalism, they did employ successive weeknight "protracted meetings" in an effort to build interest, along with spirited calls to conversion that were not necessarily tied to orderly catechetical instruction.[46]

A notable promoter of this effort was German Reformed pastor John C. Guldin (1799–1863), who served several churches in Montgomery and Chester Counties, Pennsylvania. Earning the nickname "the weeping prophet" because of his impassioned pleas to parishioners, Guldin used evening meetings and other novel approaches to press the call for conversion, and he organized a temperance society for the faithful. Guldin also invited neighboring Presbyterian revivalists to share his pulpit in an expression of their united message that bridged denominational divides.[47]

Then, too, such revivalism—whether in Chester County, York, or Philadelphia—received prominent print attention in Lutheran and Reformed circles. The editors of the new *Magazine of the German Reformed Church* and the *Lutheran Observer,* begun in 1827 and 1831, looked favorably on the efforts of evangelical revivalists and endorsed greater participation in American evangelical activities. Indeed, these fledgling English-language periodicals were themselves innovative instruments. Modeled on similar magazines produced by anglophone Protestant groups, the papers highlighted reports of Reformed or Lutheran revivals and reprinted similar accounts from other evangelical magazines.[48]

Although opponents did not have the same tools to broadcast their opinions, dissent at the local level could be sharp and adamant. Even when established ministers introduced revivalism into their local congregations, lay members did not always welcome it. The popular but innovative Guldin lost the support of his people and saw his East Vincent Church split in 1837. His opponents locked Guldin out of the church building and brandished clubs to keep his supporters away. Soon after, Guldin's enemies seceded, hired a tradition-minded pastor, and formed their own congregation—St. Vincent German Reformed Church. Quickly receiving recognition from the denomination's East Pennsylvania Classis, the new St. Vincent charter pointedly insisted that it should never be served by a clergyman who "has or will deviate from the long established forms and usages of the German Reformed Church."[49]

Solidifying Tradition in America

"Why was the German reformation, in the middle states, that sprang up with Boehm, Otterbein, and their helpers, not more perfect?" asked *The*

Methodist Magazine in 1823. English-speaking evangelicals had noticed the Pennsylvania German reluctance to embrace popular modes of religion otherwise sweeping the country, and they struggled to explain the discrepancy. It was not for lack of effort, the Methodist publication decided. Perhaps the blame lay with denominational loyalty and cultural attachments, it suggested; even the United Brethren, who had popular evangelical sympathies, "brought along with them the formalities, superstitions and peculiar opinions of religious education."[50]

The disappointed Methodist editors identified cultural factors that were both theological and social in the Pennsylvania German resistance to the populist religious style of the Early Republic. Lutheran and Reformed resistance to evangelical revivalism relied on a heritage of Continental Pietism, confessional catechesis, and the authority of tradition. Such Pennsylvania German religious convictions and social habits had provided both individual spiritual experience and a corporate identity that met the demands of faith in a way that rendered the popular religious message less appealing. Yet religious conflicts now accentuated these characteristics and helped define what being Pennsylvania German meant in the context of a new nation.

Continental Pietism was one such characteristic common among the Reformed and Lutheran Rhine Valley immigrants who populated Greater Pennsylvania in the eighteenth century. Although occasionally overused as a category of historical inquiry, Pietism was an identifiable religious orientation marked by an experiential, practical, and somewhat separatist approach to Christianity, though its experiential inclination did not form the basis of religious allegiance (as it had in the more populist orientation of the Early Republic's revivalists).[51] The Pietist impulse placed a premium on confessional dogma combined with a religion of the heart.[52]

The 1783 gathering of the Lutheran Pennsylvania Ministerium, for example, discussed "[h]ow the necessity of conversion is to be declared to those who are merely respectable and externally Christians."[53] The most widely used catechism among American Lutherans during this period included (in its section on the "orders of salvation") the idea that Christians "feel [*verspürt*] the power of reconciliation with God" in addition to having a knowledge of divine forgiveness and justification.[54] The charge of dead formalism that evangelicals brought against the young republic's Anglican and Puritan heirs, then, rang somewhat hollow when directed toward German churchly establishments. German Reformed pastor Casper Wack

(1752–1839) was apparently not alone in being remembered as one whose "sermons, like his conversation, were always práctical and experiential. He believed religion to be a matter of the heart, mainly."[55] Growing up in an atmosphere infused with Reformed Pietism, future theology professor Lewis Mayer (1783–1849) found that "[h]is convictions of sin were unusually deep and pungent. He clearly saw his lost and helpless condition as a sinner, and felt himself exposed to the awful wrath of God."[56] (Fig. 5.)

Significantly, the Pietist cast of German spirituality also differentiated Pennsylvania German faithful from British-rooted denominations that were similarly cool to revivalism but did not share the Pietistic sentiments of Lutheran and Reformed adherents. In 1839, a young German Reformed traveler who had been raised in the Pietist environment of Easton, Pennsylvania, had the opportunity to hear an Old School Presbyterian sermon; he found the conservative doctrinal teaching familiar, yet somehow incomplete. "The discourse contained many excellent thoughts, well expressed," he concluded, "but it was directed almost exclusively to the intellect, and it was, therefore, one-sided."[57]

Although many Pennsylvania German church folk rejected the rhetoric and methods of new measures revivalism, their Pietism did encourage them to expect special "seasons" of spiritual renewal—though they believed that these events would generally accompany orderly catechetical exposition by an ordained religious authority. Members who insisted that they were made Christians through baptism, and not at a camp meeting, also saw their baptisms as one step in a process of sanctification—a caveat their evangelical competitors may not always have appreciated.[58]

The experience of the Loysville Lutheran congregation in what would become Perry County, Pennsylvania, was typical. During the pastorate of Frederick Sanno, from 1802 to 1809, the group "enjoyed a glorious revival of religion," while Sanno "lectured on the Catechism diligently and with great unction." Even years later, those "who were then catechumens ... [could] scarcely find language to describe the ... deep feeling on days of confirmation when all the catechumens were publicly examined on the doctrines of our holy Christianity as set forth in our Catechism." Confirmation combined teaching, hymns, and prayers, "so that the interest of the occasion was sustained for hours."[59] Throughout the process, however, the source of authority and manner of proceeding were established by tradition and external to the participants.

ENGRAVED BY JOHN SARTAIN — THE ORIGINAL BY EICHHOLTZ.

REV. L. MAYER. D.D.

Lewis Mayer

Fig. 5 Lewis Mayer, who was born in Lancaster, Pennsylvania, served Reformed congregations in Maryland, Virginia, and Pennsylvania before becoming the first professor at the German Reformed Seminary in 1825. Courtesy of Evangelical and Reformed Historical Society, Lancaster, Pa.

Here, Pietism yielded its role as an ecumenical middle ground as parishioners absorbed specific theological convictions regarding their approaches to faith. Training in a historic confession—in conscious opposition to others—blunted the often restitutionist call of popular Christianity to abandon tradition and appropriate an existentially based faith. Among Lutherans, Luther's *Small Catechism* was ubiquitous—even in areas where pastoral care was intermittent. "Deface and alter anything we have," cried the editor of the *Evangelical Lutheran Intelligencer*, "take everything from us but leave us our Bible and Catechism . . . just as our Fathers had them."[60] Lutherans published no fewer than 246 editions of 29 German and 30 English Lutheran catechisms by or for American faithful between 1749 and 1850. By far the most influential was the 1785–86 Pennsylvania Ministerium Catechism, which included Luther's text and appeared in no fewer than 73 editions. That work alone contributed significantly to "keeping a degree of confessional consciousness alive among both clergy and laity" in the face of American populist revivalism.[61]

Among Reformed Germans, the Heidelberg Catechism—which served as the denomination's only officially recognized statement of doctrine—presented an order of salvation that balanced experiential sanctification with an objective faith.[62] In an autobiographical essay from 1810, venerable Reformed pastor "Father" Nicholas Pomp (1734–1819) recalled that by the age of fourteen, he could "recite the Heidelberg Catechism by memory. The instruction in the catechism by the preachers was, through God's grace, so powerful in me, that I became a new man, and I loved the Triune God with all my heart. I would have nothing at all to do with other children of the world."[63] Even Philadelphia pastor Joseph F. Berg (1812–71), a convert from Moravianism who continued to hold populist evangelical sympathies, could announce that "[a]s a denomination we have our land-marks, and there is one old standard, which is pre-eminently '*the* ancient land-mark, which our fathers have set.' I mean the compend of Christian doctrine known familiarly as the Heidelberg Catechism. *Remove not that ancient land-mark*."[64]

The catechism determined the churchly preaching year, and during the course of a lifetime parishioners heard extended commentary on doctrine from pastors such as Bernhard F. Willy (1751–1810), who served in Tennessee and Virginia. His "Lectures on the Heidelberg Catechism" ran to 351 manuscript pages. In Lebanon County, Pennsylvania, pastor Thomas H. Leinbach (1802–64) integrated worship and catechesis by "fixing the truths taught permanently upon the heart and mind" by correlating appropriate hymn verses with each clause of text.[65]

The very process of catechesis challenged the American notion of the "sovereign audience" upon which many American preachers relied to build popular support. Handing down received truth placed listeners in the debt of their elders. Such a debt was enough to carry Joel Reber back to his ancestors' tradition after experimenting with American revivalism. "*In me* something called 'Woe is me if I preach not the gospel,'" he recorded in his journal. "But [the] Methodist[s] said, 'You must not study—not have recourse to flesh and blood,' etc. A severe trial for me." Reber came to see the popular prejudice against inherited tradition as an error and an evil temptation, and he concluded, "'I must study, and preach in the German Reformed Church'"—a conclusion for which he often "thanked God."[66] Even the editor of the *Evangelical Lutheran Intelligencer,* a Maryland and Virginia Synod publication given more to expressions of emotive piety than to the details of doctrinal teaching, took pains to emphasize that "ministers are under the most binding obligations to expound the whole Catechism," because "wherever this course is duly pursued we know vital religion is gradually produced and our people speak and answer not mechanically, not merely as committed to memory, but as they feel and have experienced."[67]

Pietism and catechesis fit into a system of community life marked by peasant republican sensibilities and structured around traditional notions of clerical authority. These notions were balanced, however, by local congregational vigilance (and a corollary distrust of distant agents of innovation). Congregational meetinghouse charters often contained clauses prohibiting their use by outsiders for teaching novel doctrine.[68] British evangelicals visiting Union County, Pennsylvania, in the 1830s sensed that a localist and conservative spirit guided Pennsylvania German religiosity. "In this respect they resemble the Roman Catholics more than Protestant denominations," the travelers remarked. Perhaps not fully understanding their subjects' religious principles, the visitors continued: "One of the natural effects is that they are cold and formal in their religious observances; and they seem to regard modern improvements in science with equal apathy."[69]

Personal piety could certainly appeal to the affections, but clergy and laity believed that it should lead people down time-honored paths, not produce novelty or disorder. Lutheran pastor John William Heim (1782–1849), an advocate of plain dress and opponent of English preaching, represented such an understanding of personal piety. Heim "never opposed genuine revivals of religion ... where properly conducted," but "he set his face ... against those bastard excitement[s] *gotten up* by foreign elements ... that despised knowledge and gloried in deriding the Catechism and catechetical instruction," so that "fanaticism said sometimes hard things of him."[70] The desire to maintain congregational order and properly balanced roles for clergy and laity became more important in the face of German evangelical appeals. Even somewhat sympathetic observers, such as Reformed pastor John William Runkel (1749–1832), expressed reservations. Runkel had appreciated much of Otterbein's United Brethren preaching, but he noted in his journal in 1818 that while he could stomach much of the conversion theology in Methodist sermons, he found the "crying, shouting, clapping their hands, and stamping, to cause a stir among the people" deeply offensive.[71]

For his part, Lutheran pastor John George Schmucker (1771–1854), who had many warm contacts in the English-speaking religious world, characterized American revivalists as those who "storm, snort, clap hands, kick about, and in a repulsive way shout themselves hoarse; [while] the audience prays in thorough confusion at the top of their lungs" and individual worshipers "speak of the Savior of the World in an irreverent, shameless, and presumptuous manner." To his mind, it was all enough to make "frivolous people laugh, reasonable people take offense, and pious ones sigh over the dishonor which is done to the gospel through this fanaticism."[72] (Fig. 6.) "Enthusiast" soon became the harshest of sobriquets. Later, a disgruntled reader of the *Lutheran Observer* (the new periodical sympathetic to populist revivalism) could think of no stronger denunciation than labeling the publication a "*New Measure, Fanatical, Methodistical, Anti-Lutheran Engine, or Advocate of Screaming, Falling, Clapping of Hands, of Hypocrisy and Lies.*"[73] Other writers, such as Virginia Lutheran David Henkel (1795–1831), saw the threat of disorder on a more theological level, and in his published debate with "Mr. Joseph Moore, the Methodist," he contested the subjective basis of religious authority in popular evangelical revivalism.[74]

Attacks on traditional order occasionally came from more radical quarters as well. The theological innovations associated with Universalism, for example, found fertile soil in America, where egalitarianism quickly supported a popular brand of preaching that promised eternal equality. Small Pennsylvania German Universalist groups sprang up in several

Fig. 6 Interior of the Lutheran church in York, Pennsylvania, about 1800. John George Schmucker served as pastor here from 1809 to 1836. Watercolor by Lewis Miller. Courtesy of York County Heritage Trust, York, Pa.

communities. By 1829, Jacob Grosh (1776–1860) and Aaron B. Grosh (1804–83) of Manor Township, Lancaster County, were publishing *Der Fröhliche Botschafter,* an unorthodox paper carrying religious features and news from Pennsylvania German communities.[75] When a traveling New England Universalist preacher tried to fill a Lancaster Lutheran pulpit, however, "a body of Germans rushed into the house as the people were assembling, and shutting the doors threatened vengeance to any who should enter."[76]

Perhaps even more disturbing to traditional community order was the arrival, a few years later, of the radical perfectionist Theophilus "Battle-axe" Gates (1787–1846), who established a communal group that practiced "complex marriage." After its appearance in northern Chester County, Pennsylvania, the group attracted several Pennsylvania German members. On occasion, Gates's followers interrupted neighboring worship services, marching "through the aisles of Shenkel [German Reformed] Church, the scandalized brethren glowering at them from one side, the outraged sisters gasping on the other, the pastor in a fury in the pulpit."[77]

Such were the scenes of religious tumult and upheaval generated in the "spiritual hothouse" of the Early Republic.[78] Nevertheless, Pennsylvania German Lutheran and Reformed denominations survived the religious ferment of antebellum America. Notwithstanding the later complaints of anti-revivalist leaders such as John Nevin and Philip Schaff (1819–93), populist American evangelicalism never overwhelmed German-speaking America in the Early Republic. Lutheran and German Reformed confessional establishments continued to dominate the Pennsylvania German religious landscape. Ethnic demand never materialized to match fully the new American religious supply.[79]

That did not mean that Lutheran and German Reformed churches would be places of calm refuge. As congregational debates and the editorial sympathies in their publications demonstrated, religious struggles would continue within their boundaries. Yet that in itself was quite significant, for while the Anglican and Congregationalist intellectual and cultural leadership waned and Old School Presbyterianism failed to keep pace with its new competitors, the colonial-era denominations continued to be central institutions for the Pennsylvania German population. These bodies would provide the forum for negotiating ethnic identity—an identity that would have proven far different if members had largely opted for American evangelicalism and joined one of the republic's broader spiritual mainstreams.

The Lutheran and German Reformed traditions that Methodist leader Francis Asbury had condemned as "citadels of formality—fortifications erected against ... a more evangelical ministry" had not yielded completely to popular religious forces, and their members had not deserted them.[80] Evangelical enthusiasts such as James Patterson (1779–1837) of Philadelphia might worry over "the spiritual improvement of the German population" and even come to tears "thinking what is going to become of the Germans, there seem to be very few indeed who care about their souls," but most Pennsylvania Germans themselves found in traditional confessional membership the general parameters within which they would practice their ethnic habits and shape their identity.[81] Meanwhile, the popular evangelical rhetoric that they had resisted was becoming intertwined with a broader American discussion of national purposes and cultural promises, inviting Pennsylvania German church folk to define their loyalties further.

LIBERTY
AND ETHNICITY

The
German
Reformed
"Free Synod"
Schism

On the last day of September 1821, clergy and laity gathered for the annual synodic meeting of the German Reformed Church.[1] The atmosphere was tense. The normal routine of orderly business—licensing and ordaining ministers, listening to sermons, and transacting ecclesiastical correspondence—would not dominate the agenda. (Fig. 7.) Instead, the group faced the prospect of schism. A proposal to establish an American-style theological seminary threatened to tear the synod apart, and discussion became more animated and angry as the day wore on. Debate continued "until the feelings of several were wrought up to a high state of exasperation"; participants denounced each other, and one synod member publicly insulted a visiting New York Dutch Reformed observer who symbolized the distant ecumenical influences rocking the synod.[2] By the end of the day, threats and counterthreats had filled the air, and within several months, the synod had divided.

What had caused the "reverend synod" to lose its decorous composure and dance at the edge of denominational division? The late 1810s and early 1820s were hardly an "Era of Good Feelings" among German Reformed adherents. If the rest of the nation was finally experiencing a bit of collective relief in the aftermath of the War of 1812—confirmed in their independence from foreign power and influence—the Pennsylvania Germans had reason to be more anxious. They, too, were caught up in the expansive, energetic spirit of the times, increasingly at home in a world filled with the language of natural rights, the rhetoric of Columbian glory, and Washingtonian hagiography, all of which seemed to work against localized identities and cultural particularity. Yet if that world threatened the traditional ordering of their communities and churches, upsetting old balances of authority and deference, it also could provide new ways of constructing and defending the place of Pennsylvania Germans in the United States.

The autumn's tension did not divide cultural recalcitrants from ardent assimilationists; after a century on American soil, Pennsylvania Germans were not about to isolate themselves from the society that surrounded them. Instead, they drew on American notions of liberty to defend ethnicity— though they did not always agree on the content and meaning of either concept. The arguments that inflamed the synod of 1821 were not simply conflicts over church polity or personality clashes writ large, as denominational historians have interpreted them.[3] Rather, participants spoke in terms of republican ideals and American liberty. Fighting to remake their church, they acted in characteristically American ways in their efforts to defend German faithfulness.

Threatened Ethnicity, Threatened Liberty

Members of the German Reformed Church had reason to think of their denomination (despite its Continental title) as a proper American institution.[4] In several ways, the Reformed polity reflected the republican values of the young nation. Comprising ordained pastors and elected lay delegates, the synod's mixed membership combined hierarchical authority with popular representation—an orderly balance that granted the people a voice in

Fig. 7   The 1828 German Reformed Church Synod held in York, Pennsylvania. This watercolor by Lewis Miller is the only visual representation of a synod gathering from this period. Courtesy of York County Heritage Trust, York, Pa.

selecting leaders of merit, who in turn expected deferential cooperation.[5] Even within the synod itself, a system of ascribed rank regulated the group's operation. "According to an old custom, the ministers all sat in a row on the front seats" of the church sanctuary, one observer recalled, "arranged according to age, from the oldest to the youngest, and the elders sat behind in like regular order. The former did all the speaking, according to seniority of age, whilst the elders listened, but seldom, if ever, said anything."[6]

Yet despite the synod's formal authority, the German Reformed Church was remarkably congregational and local. The synod rarely acted on matters that meddled in congregational affairs, and the authority that church members granted their leaders—pastors as well as lay elders—was rooted in local power balances and Pennsylvania German ideals of peasant republicanism. Such a system placed subjects in the debt of their betters in the hierarchy, but it also championed liberty, eschewing intrusive interference with traditional custom. Adherents could simultaneously embody deferential social ideals and express populist democratic resistance when pressed. When the American dynamics of power, authority, and organization began to shift in the 1810s and 1820s, these contradictory impulses were set to react in quite different directions.

The American spirit of expansion and organizing drive during the new nation's first decades disrupted synod tradition. In 1818, for example, when clergy and elders gathered in Carlisle, Pennsylvania, for that year's synodic session, the increasing size of the denomination and the geographic scope of a seemingly unbounded country prompted some members to propose restructuring its organization and adopting a more complex and federal polity. The synod divided into eight regional classes, each of which was to meet annually and include the ministers and elders within its bounds.[7] The full synod, however, would be only a small delegate body, composed of a few representatives from each classis who would conduct business on behalf of their colleagues.[8]

Pennsylvania Germans borrowed their structural innovation from the model of the Dutch Reformed Synod, the Germans' anglicized theological kin from New York.[9] It was not the first contact the Germans had had with their Dutch coreligionists. In 1803 the German Reformed Synod, meeting in Lebanon, Pennsylvania, had received a letter from John H. Livingston (1746–1825), a theology professor at the Dutch Reformed seminary in New Brunswick, New Jersey.[10] Livingston suggested that the two groups begin regular fraternal correspondence. The Germans approved a resolution of cordial reply—and then promptly dropped the matter for a decade. Even then, it was the Dutch who pursued Reformed relations, sending two delegates to the German Synod in 1813 and again in subsequent years.[11] By 1820, eager to forge a broader Reformed Protestant vanguard in America, the Dutch church was proposing a sort of amalgamation of the two groups.[12]

Although the colonial-era German Reformed Coetus had reported to the Synod of Amsterdam and both groups shared the general outlines of Reformed faith, fraternal relations and even talk of union could be disconcerting to Pennsylvania Germans whose localist sensibilities inclined them toward fellowship with neighboring Lutherans. While theologically distinct, Lutherans and Reformed folk often shared meetinghouses and lived within a common Pennsylvania German cultural context that often meant more than their dogmatic differences.[13]

The Dutch Reformed Church, meanwhile, had become an exemplar of assimilation and anglicization and was already at the forefront of an emerging coalition of activist American evangelicals eager to claim responsibility for society as a whole and shape a common national culture. Their aims only prompted suspicion in the minds of peasant republicans, but proved attractive to those who looked to the wider Anglo-American evangelical world for direction.[14] Indeed, in 1806, a group of German Reformed members in Philadelphia lost in their effort to introduce English worship into their congregation; they promptly withdrew and joined the Dutch Synod, as later anglicizers would continue to do.[15] Ethnic controversy in the form of debates about language was resurfacing in Philadelphia (1817) and Baltimore (1818)[16] just as the latest Dutch ecumenical overtures arrived. Many in the German Reformed Church interpreted the aggressive advances of the more assimilated and geographically distant Dutch as a threat to their understanding of local liberty and their claims of ethnic identity.[17]

In the end, the Dutch Reformed institution that sparked the sharpest Pennsylvania German reaction was the theological seminary associated with Queen's College in northern New Jersey. The school represented a newly emerging style of ministerial training, one that efficiently centralized pastoral education and separated it from its community base. Traditionally, German Reformed ministerial students had received training through local apprenticeships to seasoned pastors,[18] with several acclaimed teachers attracting so many students that their homes became known as "Schools of the Prophets."[19] One of the best-known teachers was Lebrecht Frederick Herman (1761–1848), of Falkner Swamp, Pennsylvania, whose parsonage even received the appellation "Swamp College."[20]

German Synod members who admired the more formal seminary model, however, considered how they might begin such a program for their denomination.[21] Although the German Reformed Church was still an official sponsor of Lancaster's flagging Franklin College, that weak school held little promise of growth.[22] In 1819, seminary promoters received an open letter from John Livingston, who regretted that German churchpeople had "not found it convenient" to send their students to New Brunswick, but encouraged Pennsylvania Germans to begin their own school on the Dutch model.[23] Proponents enamored with the apparent Dutch success in creating the latest in organizational structure and efficiency drew plans for a German Reformed institution and brought them to the 1820 synodic meeting. That year's gathering took place in late September, in Hagerstown, Maryland. It was the first synod composed only of a small group of classis-appointed representatives: thirteen ministers and nine elders (delegates a step removed from local authority) conducted the church's business.[24]

With strong influence from their local hosts, the synod actually approved a five-article constitution for a denominational seminary to be established in Frederick, Maryland.[25] The delegate synod—not the more representative regional classes—would "have final power over the Theological Seminary, its officers, laws, and regulations," while trustees chosen by the synod would manage more immediate affairs. School finances would come from "an annual collection" in each congregation, or from subscriptions raised by para-church voluntary associations modeled after similar groups operating in the larger evangelical world. The synod also chose the school's first professor, Dutch Reformed pastor Philip Milledoler (1775–1852) of New York City, and granted him a salary of $2,000 per year.[26] Finally, the synod forbade the continuance of the local so-called Schools of the Prophets, resolving "that in the future no minister be allowed to receive a young man in order to educate him in theology; only in preparatory courses for entrance into the Seminary."[27]

The delegate synod's actions provoked sharp and immediate response.[28] Lay members and clergy cried out that Frederick was an English environment, that Milledoler was an English-speaking Dutch teacher not conversant with German culture, and that his salary was exorbitant.[29] Moreover, they questioned the synod's authority to pronounce the seminary's exclusive claims over local theological instruction. On 26 March 1821, in fact—preceding the meetings of the classes that spring—a group of seminary opponents met at Norristown, Pennsylvania, and drew up a protest petition. The Philadelphia Classis then endorsed the Norristown statement and sent three clergy to meet with the nascent seminary's board of directors, conveying a demand that, should the seminary actually materialize, they would insist (at the least) on its having an ethnically German professor.[30]

Seminary supporters found the mounting opposition deeply troubling. Lewis Mayer, a Maryland Classis pastor and member of the seminary board, wrote Bernard C. Wolff (1794–1870) that "the prospect before us was gloomy. A storm was gathering in the East among the German brethren, and threatened to burst upon us with destructive effect." In fact, when the three representatives of the Norristown remonstrants presented their demands, Mayer's fellow board members resorted to threats of schism and "assured them that if our [seminary] measures were defeated, both our congregations and we would secede from the German Reformed Church and go over to the Dutch Reformed." The threat only further linked the idea of ethnic betrayal and the anglicized Dutch in the minds of many Pennsylvania Germans.[31]

Seminary opponents now pursued a different strategy, prevailing upon Philadelphia Classis member Samuel A. Helfenstein (who had presided over the 1820 synod) to exercise his interim presidential prerogative and declare the upcoming 1821 synod an old-fashioned, all-inclusive convention synod, rather than a delegate gathering. They hoped that such a convention synod would translate grassroots opposition into effective voting power and restore the authority of local congregations.[32]

The 1821 convention-style synod met in Reading, Pennsylvania, and drew forty-three ministers, two ministerial candidates, and twenty-eight elders. It was an angry, raucous affair. In addition to the objections already raised against the proposed seminary, the remonstrants (who apparently constituted a majority[33]) added their opposition to the seminary's obtaining a state charter of incorporation. Many Pennsylvania Germans believed that incorporating religious institutions compromised the proper separation of church and state, because their ethnic conventional wisdom assumed that incorporation provided the synod with the legal and coercive right to extract money from congregations for institutional budgets.[34]

Seminary opponents demanded that professor-designate Milledoler present coursework and lectures entirely in German, even though, according to Mayer, it was "well-known that Dr. Milledoler would not accept the professorship of a merely German Seminary." When the resolution calling for exclusive German instruction passed by a wide margin, seminary supporters again threatened to secede from the church. After what Mayer considered a long and awkward silence, opponents conceded a dual-language institution, provided that all graduates would show themselves fluent in German before ordination.[35]

Having won approval for his seminary and professorial choice, Mayer left the synod believing that "[a] perfect cordiality now prevails" and that "the German brethren have generally pledged themselves to support the Seminary with all their influence."[36] However accurate his observations of the synod itself, he had greatly overestimated the goodwill that existed in the church.

Schism and the "Free Synod"

As word of the autumn synod's action spread, many Pennsylvania German lay members and clergy reacted with outrage and announced that the church was falling under the forces of foreign tyranny. Indeed, several months later, in January 1822, members of the German Reformed Church in Kutztown, Pennsylvania, reconsidered their relationship to a synod that had established an "English" seminary under Dutch direction. The secretary of the congregation, Ferdinand Bergenmeyer, noted that "[i]n accordance with the purpose of the meeting," those gathered read "the proceedings of the Synod of the years 1820 and 1821" and then listened to a report prepared by seven members. The report outlined their grievances, including their contention that "the Synod of North America in various sessions has made statutes and laws by which all congregations are to be compelled to maintain an incorporated seminary for preachers in Frederick, Maryland"— from which, they noted with a bit of sarcasm, the synod was supposed to obtain "their German preachers in the future."

Loss of local autonomy was also tied up with concrete economic concerns. Members complained that "already an English preacher from New York has been appointed with a salary of $2,000." Because "the delegates to the General Synod are getting too extravagant for our congregations in these pressing times,"[37] therefore, the group "resolved that we have declared our congregations from now on independent and free from the Synod of the Reformed Church in the United States of America." The group also requested that their pastor convene a consultation of "all free congregations in Pennsylvania and the adjoining states" and publish their decision in the *Reading Adler (Reading [Pa.] Eagle)*, a flagship newspaper for the Pennsylvania German population.[38]

The Kutztown church was not alone. By the time it took action, more congregations in Chester, Lancaster, and Berks Counties had also declared their independence.[39] Ten days after the Kutztown gathering, a similar secession meeting took place at the New Hanover (Falkner Swamp) congregation in Montgomery County. That group, too, reviewed synod actions and recorded similar dissatisfaction with the incorporated seminary and its "English" professor: "we consider such undertakings as aristocratic, robbing us of our liberty and [it] appears extravagant, [and] in it we see no benefit for the German congregations, but rather fear the loss of many members of our church."[40] The number of withdrawals mounted quickly as one congregation after another denounced the "extravagant and aristocratic" means of "depriving us our liberty."[41]

On 24 April, representatives of dissident congregations gathered at the Maxatawny, Pennsylvania, home of Charles G. Herman (1792–1861), a well-known pastor and leader of a circle of Reformed churches known as the Kutztown charge.[42] They drew up a constitution for the "Synod of the Free and Independent German Reformed Church of Pennsylvania," noting that they felt "themselves oppressed by the proceedings of the General Synod" and were prepared to "further the welfare of their congregations as Free and Independent Congregations." Yet they insisted that they were not the party of innovation, and wished it "understood ... that the same Catechism, Doctrine, and Symbols be retained as usual hereto-fore in the Reformed Church." Their constitution contained fourteen brief articles assuring members that the new synod would never become an indirect delegate body and that it would support historic local congregational rights and privileges.[43] By the time of the first regular meeting of the Free Synod on 7 September, its numbers had grown even larger, as more congregations in eastern Pennsylvania abandoned the old church.[44] (Fig. 8.)

Fig. 8   Kutztown Union Church (Lutheran-Reformed), dedicated 1791. The
Reformed congregation here was under the leadership of Charles Herman from
1810 to 1861, and in 1822, it stood at the center of Free Synod organizational
activity. Courtesy of St. John's United Church of Christ, Kutztown, Pa.

Many pastors supported the move toward independence, but not all. In response to a Northampton Classis demand that its members announce by 1 September 1822 "whether or not they desire to remain members of the German Reformed Synod," John Zülich (1796–1875) replied that he did "not desire to be a member of the so-called Free Synod," but his congregation had insisted on separation.[45] And the 25 June *Reading Adler* carried a notice by sixty-seven lay members—including elders, trustees, and deacons—of the Tulpehocken congregation: in it, they declared their refusal to have any pastor who supported the seminary. Although the Tulpehocken congregation never actually withdrew from the old synod, the pastor, seminary supporter William Hendel Jr., resigned.[46]

By 1826, so many congregations had withdrawn from the old church that two of its classes—Philadelphia and Northampton—were forced to combine into a new single Eastern Pennsylvania Classis. By 1832, in fact, the Free Synod minutes reported 101 churches and several dozen ministers and licensees.[47] (See Maps 4 and 5.) Meanwhile, in May 1822—in the midst of all the debate and schism—seminary professor-designate Milledoler, still living in New York, resigned his post at the not-yet-established seminary.[48] With Milledoler's announcement and the withdrawal of the congregations that constituted the Free Synod, the old church struggled for several years to stabilize itself and reorganize its efforts. Eventually, in 1825, it did open a small seminary department in Carlisle, Pennsylvania, on the campus of Dickinson College. But without the resources to attract an instructor from beyond its ranks, the synod settled for its own seminary proponent, Lewis Mayer, as professor.[49]

Did the old church consciously view its new seminary as a means of assimilation? Not according to its public pronouncements. In 1824, at the Bedford, Pennsylvania, meeting of the old church synod, delegates noted that "according to the view of the several members, as well as the entire Body," their seminary should be a German institution, lest "the German language shall die out in silence." Indeed, they feared that "the Germans in this country are in danger of forgetting their own language and thereby surrendering themselves to the influence of English literature."[50] Both the Free Synod remonstrants and the old synod loyalists saw themselves as faithful Pennsylvania Germans. Indeed, despite seminary opponents' charges to the contrary, it is unlikely that in 1820 even seminary-supporting German Reformed congregations in Maryland had English preaching.[51] The Free

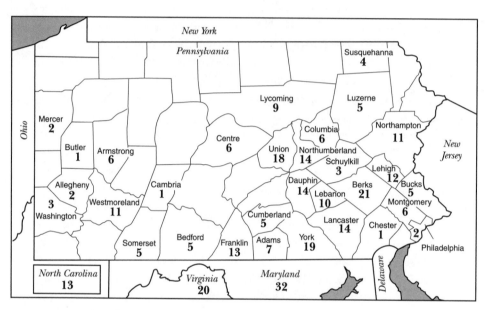

Map 4   German Reformed Eastern Synod congregations, 1831. Numbers indicate
congregations reported as being served by clergy from the Eastern Synod. Synodic
reports are invariably incomplete to some degree; 1831 was chosen because it is more
complete than many others of the period. Political boundaries are those of 1831.
SOURCE: *Proceedings of the Synod of the German Reformed Church . . . 1831* (Harrisburg:
George P. Wiestling, 1831).

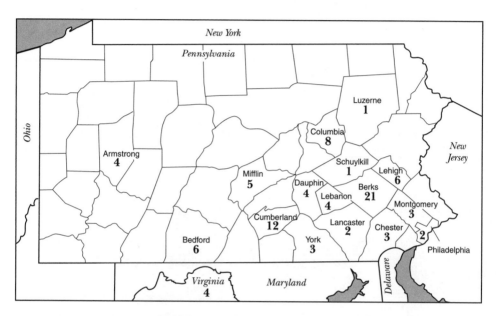

Map 5   German Reformed Free Synod congregations, 1832. Numbers indicate congregations reported as being served by clergy from the Free Synod. Free Synod reports are notably incomplete on such matters; 1832 was chosen because it is more complete than most others of the period. Political boundaries are those of 1831. SOURCE: William J. Hinke, ed., "Synodical Ordnung und Protocoll der Verhandlungen der Synode der Hochdeutschen Freyen Reformirten Gemeinden in Pennsylvanien Angefangen den 24sten Tag April, Anno Domini, 1822" (bound volume dated 1934), Evangelical and Reformed Historical Society, Lancaster, Pa.

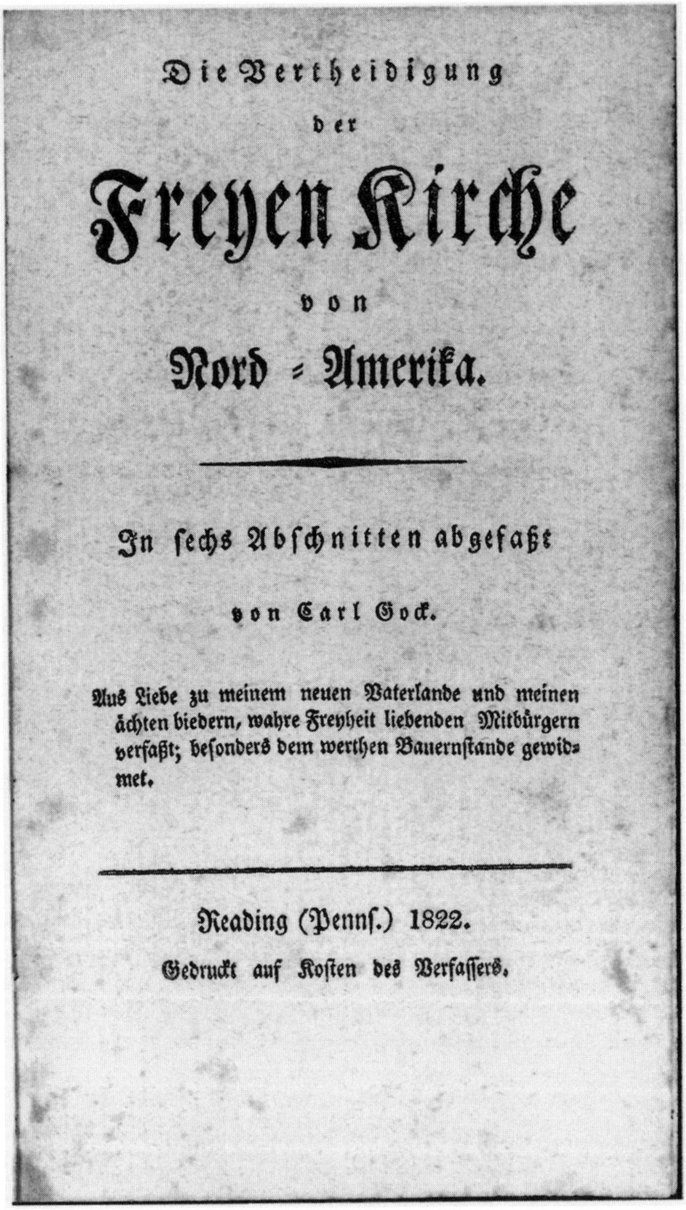

Die Vertheidigung

der

Freyen Kirche

von

Nord = Amerika.

In sechs Abschnitten abgefaßt

von Carl Gock.

Aus Liebe zu meinem neuen Vaterlande und meinen
ächten biedern, wahre Freyheit liebenden Mitbürgern
verfaßt; besonders dem werthen Bauernstande gewid=
met.

Reading (Pennf.) 1822.

Gedruckt auf Kosten des Verfaffers.

Fig. 9   The title page of Carl Gock's book, *Defense of the Free Church
of North America.* Courtesy of Evangelical and Reformed Historical
Society, Lancaster, Pa.

Synod controversy involved issues of ethnicity, but not ones simply pitting cultural assimilation against ethnic separation. Instead, the differences involved divergent streams of Americanization—different ethnic responses to life in the new nation.[52]

Literary Warfare and Rival Visions of America

In the months that followed the controversy over the seminary and Free Synod, several authors spelled out the ideas and issues at stake, giving voice to the fears and logic of both parties. Perhaps the first popular defender of the Free Synod was Carl Gock, who described himself as a farmer and schoolteacher in Berks County, Pennsylvania.[53] Apparently a Lutheran by baptism, he spoke for his Reformed neighbors as a Pennsylvania German immersed in the region's ethnoreligious cultural milieu for decades (no matter his claim of having been born in Europe).[54] Gock announced that his *Defense of the Free Church of North America* sprang from his "love of pure biblical religion following the words of Jesus [and of] ... sincere liberty."[55] The volume found a ready audience, and the German traveler and itinerant schoolteacher Jonas Heinrich Gudehus reported the book's circulation and importance among Pennsylvania Germans as far away as Ohio.[56] (See Fig. 9.)

For Gock, the issue that had sparked the formation of the Free Synod was quite simply one of true American liberty. "In what does our liberty exist, fellow citizens," he asked, "and what is the cornerstone of our liberty? I answer here what every other free American must also say: 'the right to vote!'" In place of this traditional exercise of popular opinion as a part of church government, he claimed, the old synod had proposed establishing layers of authority and complicated corporations—governed by indirectly selected boards of directors removed from the close influence of the local congregations—so as "to achieve complete control" of the church. Yet Gock was sure that "[e]very reasonable republican would agree" that there is no incorporation "that does not bring disadvantage to a free people in secular or spiritual matters" because of its separation of local opinion and effective power and its chartered right to collect funds from synod members.[57]

With such claims Gock brought together a powerful combination of sentiments linking local authority, community structure, and class. Civic voting rights in Pennsylvania were, after all, still linked to property holding.[58] Even if churchly voting was an entirely different legal matter, it did suggest ways in which the synod's actions were especially galling. A distant hierarchy was not only imposing an expensive educational institution that would burden the laity financially and thereby rob them of their property. It was also limiting the laity's ecclesiastical franchise, thus disregarding whatever standing common men of property had and upsetting the balance of peasant republicanism by subordinating them to a new class of distant clerics and educated anglophones.

Gock went on to detail the threat to liberty posed by the assertive synod itself and its institutional child, the seminary. Gock found ethnic mixing in the synod troubling, apparently reacting to the reciprocal inclusion of Dutch delegates who were, in his mind, English. "How is it that our reverend German preachers so generally unite and mix with the English clergy in a consistory?" Gock asked. "The religion is one thing!, but how do the two languages fit together: there is no earlier example at hand in the Old or New World."[59]

But while language and liberty were closely linked in Gock's mind, his concern was rooted in republican values, not ethnic romanticism. "[I]f we should send a [lay-elder] representative to General Synod, [and] the reverend pastor takes one who is a true German and who understands little or no English," Gock hypothesized, "and everything takes place in English, the [lay] deputies would then find themselves counting as less than nothing." Liberty was directly linked to lay representatives' comprehending the synodic proceedings. An English-speaking synod robbed Pennsylvania Germans of their republican rights. "O good German citizens," he cried, "what kind of morality will our overeducated reverend clergy teach us then?" Moreover, it would only get worse when younger seminarians came along who had been taught in English. "Although the way theology is taught in German is more thorough and basic and produces better pupils . . . than the English way," he opined, "nonetheless, the English theology is quickly and easily preferred [by seminary advocates] . . . because the worldly law is written in English and, yes, the reverend clergy (at least many of them) also like to mix in worldly matters."[60]

Gock predicted that the old synod would eventually arrogate to itself as much power as the ecclesiastical oppressors of Europe from whom he believed Pennsylvania Germans' ancestors had fled. Indeed, should the synod bureaucratize any further, "the sacred body would be too big and too powerful and it is not very hard to execute their plans as they fill the empty places with their [seminary] pupils." In such a setting the tradition of lay elders' acquiescence to clerical leadership would become a sort of tyranny in which deputy votes could be manipulated. With the growth of autonomous synodic power would come the censorship of religious books, Gock predicted, in a manner much like the Roman Inquisition. "[S]oon you would hear all the Lutheran and Reformed priests thunder from the pulpit and call everyone unchristian who does not say 'yes' and 'amen' to all that their constitution said, or who protests against it," he warned. Linking his attack to the highly charged contemporary issue of Freemasonry and its alleged antidemocratic principles, Gock insinuated that the synod was becoming a secret society for the clergy. Even the ministerial candidates remain uninitiated, he suggested, "until they are named as pastors, and [then] through a handshake and solemn vow, hold secret the particular way of life."[61]

Seminaries threaten liberty, too, Gock asserted, by centralizing power and removing ministerial training from the context of local churches whose pastors were directly accountable to them. Gock's rage against schools of higher learning at times took on an anti-intellectual air. Indeed, seminaries ran counter to Gock's brand of folk wisdom: "German farmers in Pennsylvania almost all have good Luther Bibles, with good interpretation from genuine theologians who lived according to Jesus' words," he claimed. "And so long as we have these, we will answer: let us alone in our darkness!" Gock believed that given English-language sermons of "high academic nonsense" and deprived of their German Bibles, he and his neighbors "would in the end become Christians in name only, reasonable animals in human form."[62]

In his book's last section, Gock delivered a detailed critique of the seminary charter, charging that it could only have come from a "monkish-synod-ministerium and consistory priests" who "take for themselves reverend titles" and constitute "an aristocratic spiritual Congress." The high costs of the school guaranteed that rural people would have to put up with repeated collections for funds, and they would likely be saddled with what amounted to a church-imposed tax enforced through laws of incorporation making members liable for the school's solvency. In the meanwhile, seminarians would have learned nothing but student pranks and "Yankee tricks."[63]

Yet Gock insisted that he was not opposed to proper order. On the contrary, "God is a God of order and a Synod free of all private and secret rules will we love and obey," he insisted. Thus, he could praise what he called the "republican synod in Pennsylvania" under Carl Herman's leadership.[64] "A free people love order," he wrote, but only order that is in accord with their liberty and not coerced. In contrast, corporations and associations amass power and destroy any true republic, and synods held in a language that the people cannot understand undercut their liberty.[65]

Gock's version of American liberty was not the only one afloat in Pennsylvania German circles of the time, however. Other voices in Gock's own neighborhood, in fact, responded quite differently, stressing obedience and criticizing populist revolt. Gock's pamphlet received a quick reply from Theodor Eylert, a schoolteacher from Berks County's Tulpehocken Township, near Rehersburg, who in January 1823 published *The Darkness in the Free Church of America*. Disparaging Gock's "coarse, false, twisted, tiresome, abusive, shallow, and empty contents," Eylert charged that Gock was simply "a vassal of pastor Rev. Herman and his followers." Eylert gave much of his pamphlet, with its occasional outbursts of romantic German nationalism, to criticizing Gock's disparaging remarks about European churches and clergy, insisting that American republican ideas could not be used as a measure for the Old World.[66]

When Eylert came around to Gock's immediate concern, however, he had little sympathy. "If at its center [Gock's] definition of liberty is, as I suspect, 'that one can do and allow, whatever we will'—then I do not speak to him," Eylert asserted. Whoever is a dutiful subject "is free whether he lives in a republic or a monarchical state." On the other hand, the one who detests civic law and order "is a slave even if he lives in America. Daily one hears the word liberty on all lips, and that God himself pities!" the teacher moaned. "If I must have unrestrained satisfaction of all my passion," Eylert cried, "and if I can do so because I live in the United States;—O noble liberty, how one has abused your name! It is lack of restraint that is the ruin of all over both the short and long term."[67]

Such a radical brand of populist liberty was, in fact, another form of tyranny, Eylert insisted. Should a single member dislike something a pastor preached, he could rely on demagoguery to have the pastor turned out. "Plenty of that liberty?" Eylert asked. "In that case it becomes a complete reversal. Here the citizen or farmer is the despot and the reverend pastor the slave; he must dance as we play the pipe." Eylert was all too familiar with such a definition of liberty among Americans. "One often has heard:

we will not have any nonlocal, none foreign; we can help ourselves." The teacher agreed that "[t]hat is noble, free, and respected republican language," but its speakers never practiced such professions. While praising independence, they aped European fashion and imported Continental goods—as any person going to a coastal port city would see.[68] Thus, Eylert concluded, if Gock's book represented the teaching of the Free Synod, "I am sorry for you ... because the liberty with which you pompously go about is none other than liberty-dizziness," and such liberty does not "square with the spirit of the teachings of Christ."[69]

Later in 1823, another reply to Gock's book appeared in Reading, Pennsylvania, under the title *Carl Gock's Slanders, or the Justification of the German Lutheran and Reformed Synods.*[70] The author was Johann C. Gossler (1798?–1831), whose work was more detailed yet less profound than Eylert's. Gossler was not one to grow romantic over American populist liberty; he had published a life of Napoleon only the year before.[71] But his effort against Gock was mostly given to personal attacks and point-by-point refutations of Gock's *Gewäsch* (twaddle). He did trace the history of the German Reformed Synod back to colonial days, when "deeply respected names such as Schlatter, Pomp, Helfrich, Helfenstein, Faber, Hendel, [and] Winkhaus" provided supervision for the church—and when good order prevented "anarchy that gets out of control."[72]

Gossler believed that the Free Synod resulted simply from fear-mongering among uneducated rural Pennsylvania Germans who did not understand constitutional law as well as they should have.[73] Gossler may have been partly correct, and yet such arguments only revealed the gulf that separated him from the impulses animating many of his neighbors. To Gossler, it was obvious that resolutions passed by religious bodies and even chartered church institutions posed no threat to public law or to anyone's civil liberty.[74] To his more reformist mind, church and state had legally distinct roles, yet supported one another in achieving common social goals. A state-chartered seminary was one result of such collaboration—and one to be appreciated. Gossler also found the fears of English-language influence to be exaggerated. He noted that "in our Reformed Synod no one may speak English without express permission." Moreover, anxiety over the influence of so-called English synods was misplaced, because they were all historically and theologically related.[75]

In his support of the theological seminary, Gossler most clearly revealed his commitment to vesting authority in a hierarchy of merit. "How can we practice virtue alone if we do not know what virtue is?" he asked. "How can we get clear the often dark places of the Bible if we do not have our men who have dedicated themselves exclusively to the study of the Holy Scriptures," and who can rebuke us if we choose some mistaken opinion? Gossler feared that the Free Synod had replaced external authority with local subjectivity—or the demagoguery of Free Synod leaders, or the likes of Gock. Turning some of Gock's primitivist-sounding arguments on their heads, Gossler suggested that the New Testament church had structure, organization, and even a treasury, much like the old synod. Thus, it was the Synod of the German Reformed Church that carried on apostolic tradition, while the Free Synod could claim nothing but human innovation.[76]

Behind and beside these arguments, Gossler also presented the Free Synod as a play for power on the part of the large Herman family, a clerical clan whose members had all left the old church.[77] Coincidentally, the 1821 synod that had debated the denominational seminary had also expelled pastor Frederick L. Herman (1795–1849), son of respected pastor and teacher L. F. Herman, for intemperance. When the aged Herman asked what his son's suspension involved, president Lebrecht Hinsch replied curtly, "In diesem Falle heißt das auf immer und ewig ausgeschlossen [in this case, it means exclusion forever]," and the elder Herman left the meeting in anger. Within a few months, a number of his kin had aligned themselves with the Free Synod movement.[78] Now, Gossler attacked the Free Synod and leveled a number of charges against L. F. Herman, accusing him of forging the name of Peter Miller (a pastor in Montgomery County, Pennsylvania) on a secession document and of giving only $5.00 to the synod treasury out of an 1818 Oley congregation contribution of $10.32.[79]

In the end, Gossler's book may have actually worked in favor of the Free Synod, since his personal attacks on the venerated senior pastor engendered a measure of defensive loyalty among the Free Synod faithful. Indeed, on 12 June 1823, thirty lay representatives from fifteen congregations—in Berks, Lancaster, Chester, and Montgomery Counties—met in Hereford Township, Berks County, to protest the attacks on the Free Synod and Gossler's ethical charges against L. F. Herman. They asserted that Herman had not started the Free Synod, insisting that it was the people's desire to leave the old church: Carl and L. F. Herman merely assumed leadership of the populist movement.[80]

Which "Galling Tyranny"?

With several decades of hindsight, German Reformed pastor and historian Theodore Appel (1823–1907) reflected on the bitter rancor surrounding the Free Synod schism, wondering if "it might be inferred that" during the 1820s "there could have been little or no Christianity ... among the German people" of Pennsylvania. In Appel's opinion, however, there was plenty of piety to go around. Rather, the problem stemmed from the fact that "the churches in Eastern Pennsylvania were badly constituted," because "the old order of things as brought from Germany still prevailed."[81]

But, in fact, it did not. Appel associated the Free Synod faction with reactionary opposition to a theological seminary and fear of interdenominational contact with English-speaking Christians; that faction, however, had acted in what was becoming a characteristically American way. Its members had mobilized, asserted their rights, drafted declarations of independence from authority they no longer considered legitimate, and published their actions in the popular press. In doing so, of course, they were striving to protect their understanding of what it meant to be faithful German Reformed people, but they had grounded their struggle in an American promise of liberty—a promise of freedom to manage their own affairs.

Meanwhile, supporters of the old synod could insist that they, too, were faithfully carrying on the German Reformed tradition in America (a tradition that was tied to their Dutch coreligionists since the colonial days) and championing synodic authority and respect for meritocratic leadership. Their notions of authority and American liberty showed signs of affinity with those of American evangelical crusaders, although their commitment to American-style democratic principles was perhaps less sure than they themselves realized. (Writers such as Eylert and Gossler could wax romantically eloquent when discussing Germany, Frederick the Great, or Europe in general, demonstrating that they had not embraced the American exceptionalism that marked the larger evangelical-republican coalition of their day.[82]) Moreover, most members of the old church—as much as their Free Synod counterparts—remained committed to staving off the inroads made by competing Anglo-evangelical revivalist groups.

Appel was correct, however, in suggesting that "many people imagined that they were in danger of losing some of their most precious rights—of being brought under a galling tyranny."[83] But what sort of galling tyranny was the most threatening to their liberty and faithfulness? The answers to that question demonstrated the particularly American quality of Pennsylvania German ethnic and religious identities.

That quality also suggested that Pennsylvania Germans had not faced the dilemma of American ethnicity for the last time. And as notions of American purpose gained currency in wider society, drawing on the language, labor, and quickened tempo of evangelical activism and assuming responsibility for society as a whole, Lutheran and Reformed adherents were bound to confront them more directly. Such confrontations and conflicts would both promote Americanization and further refine ethnic identity.

5

SOCIAL REFORM
OR CULTURAL TYRANNY?

Pennsylvania
Germans
and the
Public Role
of Religion

"The valley through which I traveled for nearly seventy miles is very beautiful and well cultivated, chiefly settled by the Germans," wrote a member of a British group touring eastern Pennsylvania in 1834. The delegation represented the Congregational Union of England and Wales and was especially interested in observing American religion and assessing the success of evangelical Protestantism on the western side of the Atlantic. However, the optimistic British scribe was troubled by the Pennsylvania Germans he encountered. While noting "their prosperous condition," he was quite perplexed by their spiritual sentiments. Although descendants of the Continent's great Reformation tradition, they seemed to him to "resemble the Roman Catholics more than the Protestant denominations." Specifically, the German church folk whom the Britons met had "hardly any share in the impulse that has been given to other sections of the Christian Church by revivals, and by the exertions of Bible, Missionary, and Sunday-school societies."[1]

As foreign travelers, the group's members likely missed many of the nuances that textured life in the United States. Yet they had noticed a striking thing about the Pennsylvania Germans they observed: in unmistakable ways, most Lutheran and even German Reformed faithful stood apart from the reformist impulse that animated much of American evangelical Protestantism.[2] They showed scant interest in assuming responsibility for the larger society's morality or its cultural direction. In fact, many interpreted such evangelical predilections as jeopardizing the religious and American liberties and identities that they saw as vitally linked.

This dissonance became especially clear as Lutheran and German Reformed opposition to the political activism and social reform efforts of a broad coalition of American evangelicals made headlines—even in cities beyond the ethnic communities of the Schuylkill, Lehigh, and Susquehanna valleys. During the summer of 1829, leading Protestant evangelical publications—such as the influential Presbyterian gazette, *New York Observer*—took Pennsylvania Germans to task for their reticence toward the larger project of national salvation. The *Observer* was astounded that any people who considered themselves loyal and true Americans would condemn religiously motivated reform efforts as "aggressions on the rights of liberty." Sensible mid-Atlantic clergy must face a daunting ministry in the region's German-populated districts ("doubtless the darkest spot within their pale"), the *Observer* concluded.[3]

The debates that marked 1829 and 1830 centered on the reformers' claims to be creating a better America. Yet such claims threw into bold relief the conflicting visions of American purpose and identity that set Pennsylvania German communities apart from the national mainstream and suggested that what passed for social improvement might be cultural tyranny. As Pennsylvania Germans perceived threats to their notions of liberty, they moved to defend publicly their understanding of America and their place within it, further committing themselves not simply to their own survival but also to the success of an American experiment with which they had come to identify. The controversy of these years points to the complex relationship between political and religious values in the Early Republic and the interaction of majority and minority cultures in a period often thought to have held little ethnic excitement.

Republican Order and Religious Reformism

As the social and intellectual implications of the American Revolution began to unfold, thoughtful Americans realized, as one commentator has put it, that "the democratic revolution did not solve problems; it posed dilemmas." During the first quarter of the nineteenth century, it became clear that "democracy could threaten cherished traditions, expectations, and institutions as much as aristocracy and establishment."[4] As the classical ideal of restrained civic virtue championed by the nation's Founders became untenable in a society increasingly driven by an aggressive, expansive, egalitarian spirit, Americans turned to other means of promoting social regulation and public order.

For many British-stock Protestants—especially those in the Reformed tradition, who were frequently near the center of national politics—theological norms and social constructs drawn from biblical mandates and models provided a counterweight to the mercurial nature of the new nation. They offered a stable basis for "all those things that were distinctly American—civil and religious liberty, and republican, if not democratic, government."[5] As Presbyterian pastor Gardiner Spring (1785–1873) put it, "Liberty without godliness is but another name for anarchy or despotism.... [T]he religion of the gospel is the rock on which civil liberty rests."[6] In the midst of societal upheaval, "the absolute necessity of religion to social order and national prosperity" became, in their eyes, even more acute.[7] For many northern Presbyterians, Congregationalists, and Dutch Reformed, for example, the virtues and values of evangelical Protestantism were essential to definitions of national destiny.

Yet given the constitutional principle of disestablishment embedded in national mythology and the ideology of republicanism, leaders of this activist "evangelical united front" pursued their goal of linking religious tenets and social policy in ways that respected the letter of the law separating church and state in America. They championed voluntary associations as the chief means of improving and securing society, and they spoke in nonsectarian terms, constructing a broad coalition of popular support as they aimed to redeem the republic and realize their hopes of national salvation. Insofar as simple demography (not to mention intellectual strength) gave members of the evangelical coalition a central place in the emerging shape of American life, their opinions and activities quickly assumed national proportions.[8]

Their wide range of activities—from establishing Sunday schools within reach of every American child to curbing alcohol consumption and stamping out poverty and vice—came with a comprehensive ideological promise to strengthen the republic by aligning its purposes and methods with divine interests, interests that its promoters interpreted to include such things as industry, frugality, and sobriety. The reformers hoped, as Presbyterian George Potts (1802–64) put it in a sermon on the fiftieth anniversary of the signing of the Declaration of Independence, to encourage "association between Religion and Patriotism." Indeed, the quest to complete the Revolution and secure the republic penetrated the rhetoric of reform, even if it sometimes contradicted social realities. By the 1820s, in an effort to overcome those stubborn realities more quickly, reformers often coupled their work with the energy of religious revivalism, which promised to speed the process of redemption through radical conversion.[9]

At first glance, such ideals and goals might seem potentially attractive to Pennsylvania German churchgoers, who had shown some unease with the disorderly nature of revolutionary, market-driven America and who still carried certain notions of a deferential and vertically structured society. The theological kinship between the German Reformed tradition in particular and large parts of the evangelical coalition might have proven especially significant in bringing those adherents into the united front of popular religious reform.[10] Yet such connections did not immediately materialize. Pennsylvania Germans may have yearned for social order, but theirs was a notion based on customary controls of extended family and social rank. In southwestern Germany, local villages and market towns, for example, had held the power to suppress immorality and disruptive ideas through traditional structures and local rights, not through broadly based voluntary associations or ideas of social contract.[11] Now, in America, Pennsylvania Germans embraced an idea of liberty that promised the sanctity of such locally regulated life.

The role of religion in guiding the nation and the related struggle over the meaning and extent of societal reform were not remote topics for Pennsylvania Germans, either; such questions increasingly impinged upon their immediate religious and political worlds. Evangelical reformers brought their message to the Pennsylvania backcountry in which many ethnic church folk lived. Tract societies were quite active in the region, employing peddlers and traveling evangelical ministers as *colporteurs* and even trying to recruit backcountry pastors as paid agents. Newspapers also filled their pages with reports from religiously based reform societies (and their boasts of size and influence). Subscribers to the new *German Reformed Magazine* read such reprinted articles—although one early historian believed that such publicity aroused as much suspicion as sympathy. Essays described, for example, American Bible Society receipts of $143,184, which "seemed enormous sums to many of the plain Pennsylvania German farmers with whom money was a scarce article."[12]

Yet it was the evangelical reformers' desire to shape national values and assume the role of cultural custodian that drew the sharpest Pennsylvania German criticism. Throughout the 1820s, that custodial attitude and program was clearly visible in Pennsylvania, which became the scene of some of the most public and discordant episodes in the debate over the connections between evangelical religion and civic reform. Attention centered on Ezra Stiles Ely (1786–1861), the well-known pastor of Third Presbyterian Church in Philadelphia, whose publications promoted an activist, religiously motivated program for the patriotic task of saving the republic.[13]

On 4 July 1827, Ely preached a widely cited sermon on *The Duty of Christian Freemen to Elect Christian Rulers,* in which he argued that each Christian voter had a divinely appointed obligation to vote for none but pious believers who supported the agenda of evangelical reformers. Ely went on to "propose, fellow-citizens, a new sort of union, or if you please, *a Christian party in politics.*" Presenting his argument in broadly evangelical terms, he did acknowledge that he "would prefer ... a sound Presbyterian" for any office and averred that "[t]he Presbyterians alone could bring half a million of electors into the field." While Ely may not have been advocating the establishment of a formally organized political party, his comments provoked heated debate in civic and church circles about the growing influence of Protestant activists in state and national politics. Ely's assertions were sharp enough to spark negative criticism in the state legislature toward the American Sunday School Union, with which Ely was closely aligned. The whole affair was not lost on Pennsylvania Germans.[14]

Other events added to the religious and political excitement of the late 1820s. For one thing, evangelical leaders were in the midst of establishing yet another high-profile campaign to shape public life around their religious convictions—this time by pressuring the U.S. Congress to stop the century-old practice of Sunday mail delivery. To that end, in 1828 an evangelical coalition founded the General Union for Promoting the Obser-vance of the Christian Sabbath, an elaborate organization that included leading politicians as honorary officers and represented reformers' hopes of harmonizing public policy and divine will. As its agents scoured the coun-try for petition signatures, Pennsylvania Germans could hardly have missed the flurry of activity, especially after January 1829, when the U.S. Senate backed continued Sunday delivery and Sabbatarians redoubled their efforts for another assault.[15]

Meanwhile, Pennsylvania's secular as well as religious newspapers had become caught up in debates over the politics of anti-Masonry and the pos-sibility that some voluntary associations might actually subvert the republic. Pennsylvania's first anti-Masonic newspaper appeared in June 1828 in the Lancaster County village of New Holland, and other such papers followed.[16] Pennsylvania German suspicion of political privilege and the nativist over-tones of Masonry may have fueled their sympathy for the anti-Masonic cause. In any case, it became yet another part of the environment in which church members discussed the relative merits and dangers of the power of private associations to direct the public life of others.

Into this highly charged atmosphere rode prominent New School Pres-byterian Charles G. Finney, eager to bring new measures revivalism and its associated notions of religiously based civic reform and national cultural renewal to churches in southeastern Pennsylvania. Personifying much of the evangelical social agenda in the Early Republic, Finney's arrival helped spark a Pennsylvania German backlash. While Philadelphia's Race Street German Reformed Church—recently weakened by the exodus of many parishioners in the wake of a debate over language—actually granted Finney the use of its sanctuary for a citywide campaign in August 1828, the move only contributed to the simmering debate among the synod's Phil-adelphia members over their relationship to the activities of the larger evan-gelical united front in their city.[17] More immediate outrage exploded in the winter of 1829, when Finney left Philadelphia and moved northwest to the Berks County borough of Reading, taking his methods and message into the heart of the nation's Pennsylvania German population.[18]

Although it had been Reading's Presbyterians who had invited the great revivalist to town, his appearance drew reactions from Pennsylvania Ger-man laity and clergy who feared the infusion of ideas and programs that Finney represented.[19] For his part, Finney was sure that his "opposition was emboldened by the attitude of the German ministers and church" who spoke "severely of those that forsook the way of their fathers," denouncing from the pulpit Finney's revivalism and attendant calls for moral reform backed by the rule of law.[20] Presbyterian elders tried to battle local criticism with a public statement in the *Berks and Schuylkill (Pa.) Journal* defending Finney's credentials and national acclaim, but their praise was immediately countered by one identified as "Luther" who attacked Finney as a disruptive interloper who "encourages children to *disobey* their *parents,* by telling them that what their parents do or have taught their children, will lead them to Hell!"[21]

Pennsylvania German Opposition

By the spring of 1829, many within the Pennsylvania German religious community were eager to respond publicly to the activist evangelicals' campaign to order American life—and they did so in a series of public protest rallies and petitions. While Finney's appearance sparked Lutheran and German Reformed gatherings, the list of grievances the remonstrants cited showed that their concerns stretched further than new measures techniques or Finney himself. For many, the Anglo-American evangelical program linking religion, social reform, and millennial hopes for the nation threatened their sense of America as a land of local liberty and of the proper relationship of church and state. They had come to embrace the young republic, its Constitution, and its ideological underpinnings, but their acceptance was predicated on their understanding that the state guarded cultural and religious freedom from grander schemes of homogenization. Pennsylvania German opposition, then, was more than reactionary; it also resulted from their growing attachment to an American homeland. As they came to identify with the republic, they feared having the state in the grip of those who conflated culture and ideology in defining America. In short, Pennsylvania Germans' growing Americanization spurred their mobilization as citizens to oppose efforts others billed patriotic.

On Thursday, 19 March 1829, at least 130 Lutheran and German Reformed lay members gathered at Benjamin Haberstich's Swan Tavern in Cocalico Township, Lancaster County, to protest the events and ideas that they claimed were invading and threatening their communities and churches.[22] This meeting set the stage for a slightly larger gathering on

21 May 1829 in Heidelberg Township, Berks County, where participants calling themselves "Freemen" denounced the assumptions and goals of evangelical reformism. This second convocation received coverage in the *Reading Adler* and the *Berks and Schuylkill Journal;* the latter reported that "a numerous and respectable meeting of citizens assembled at the house of George Gernand ... pursuant to public notice given by the committee of correspondence, appointed by the Committee in Cocalico township ... to deliberate and consult upon the causes and tendency of the religious excitement at present prevailing in the country."[23]

The group "unanimously accepted" a statement that diagnosed the problem. Fearing "that a religious excitement exists in many sections of the country," one that threatened "to abridge the civil and religious liberties of the people," they fixed the blame not on revivalist Finney himself, but more broadly on "the extraordinary conduct" of a cadre of activists "who appear to have undertaken a crusade for the spreading of particular religious opinions and the advancement of church establishments." In "a spirit of worldly ambition," such sponsors could be found "[p]ervading the country in every direction" where they "alarm the weak-minded and youthful part of the community with unusual and vehement denunciations of divine wrath." Moreover, the Pennsylvania Germans "observed with disaffection and alarm the establishment of opulent and influential societies," including Bible and mission societies and Sunday school unions that they judged "unnecessary burdens upon the church-going part of the community." The protesters' concerns quickly turned to the political purposes they saw behind the broader evangelical vision. The reformers and their associations actually threatened proper civic liberty and local order, the Pennsylvania Germans believed, since activist clergy used moralizing societies "to enable them to dictate to the conscience of their fellow-men; and to assume a right of interference in the direction of state affairs." Indeed, if anything demonstrated the reformers' power and ultimate designs, it was "the attempts recently made to induce the Congress of the United States to prohibit the transportation of the mail on Sunday." Such state-imposed religiosity "endeavors to procure legislative interference in matters of religion," they complained. The remonstrants condemned such efforts "as attempts to infringe upon the rights of conscience," and they similarly denounced "all measures adopted to compel particular observance of the Sabbath as incipient approaches to the establishment of spiritual tyranny."[24]

The group's members insisted that they "would shrink from proposing a single objection to the extension of the Christian Religion," and they affirmed their belief in orthodox, supernatural Christianity, with its "perfect system of morals." Yet in reviewing "the histories of bye-gone ages," they found themselves "admonished by the wails of nations and the groans of oppressed people" to oppose any mixing of ecclesiastical and governmental power.[25] In building their argument against the evangelical activists, the protesters drew on both the evolving myth of America (as contrasted with an oppressive Old World) and on their loyalty to the republic.

Backing their concerns with ten resolutions, the protesters marked their separation from the larger program of activist evangelical Protestantism. The document pronounced disapproval for voluntary associations (again, such as the religious reform societies and the Sunday school unions), labeling them "dangerous to the liberties of the people" and warning "that we will not assist in maintaining Clergymen who advocate them or are concerned in their support" or who are "engaged in distributing any so-called religious papers or Magazines." The group went on to oppose "the extraordinary zeal for religion" and the "erroneous opinions of over-heated enthusiasm" behind the ascetic impulse that repudiated "innocent amusements" outside Anglo-American evangelical social norms. Further, while the protesters could "appreciate the advantages of the Sabbath, considered as a day of worship and temporal repose," they saw Sabbatarianism as an attempt to consolidate political power by aggressive forces that threatened balanced republican order. Such power led only to arrogance—as seen in those reform association employees wearing "imported broad clothes" who "strut about our country, distributing tracts and asking money for Missionary purposes."[26]

In contrast to the activists' elaborate plans to employ large-scale revivalism and political influence in order to reform society and systematically redeem an entire nation, the Lutheran and German Reformed protesters presented a more local and modest gospel. They insisted that "our religious and moral duties are plainly set forth in the language of the holy Scriptures; that they consist in *visiting the sick, feeding the hungry, clothing the naked, rendering due honour to parents and the exercise of charity toward all men.*"[27]

The Cocalico and Heidelberg Township meetings were not isolated events. They preceded a similar rally on 27 June 1829 in Exeter Township, Berks County, at John Mellon's Inn; the rally drew at least 74 protesters.

Expressing sentiments like those sounded at Heidelberg, the Exeter group also called attention to Ezra Stiles Ely's recent remarks on religion and politics and warned against attempts "to gain the sanctions of the civil and national power." "As soon as the civil power interferes more or less," they contended, "so soon will church and state be united."[28] Nearly a month later, a group of 166 Germans assembled for similar reasons at Gicker's Hotel in Berks County's Bern Township.[29] Although their outrage seemed to peak that summer, by the following January, Pennsylvania German religious folk were meeting again, this time at the courthouse in Reading, Pennsylvania (Fig. 10.) Some 300 gathered to protest continued attempts to bar Sunday mail delivery, arguing that while the importance of Sunday worship and rest were "too obvious to be questioned," Sabbatarian efforts were "only incipient steps towards the attainment of an object fatal to religious freedom—the union of civil and ecclesiastical authority."[30]

News of the popular uprising among Lutheran and German Reformed Pennsylvanians quickly spread in religious newspapers, such as the Presbyterians' *Western Recorder* and the *New York Observer.* Some stories painted the Pennsylvania German denominations with a broad brush, treating the protesters as completely representative of their fellow ethnics' opinions. Yet differences also surfaced among German Protestants as Lutheran and German Reformed clergy and laity joined more fully in the debate now publicly associated with their people.

In some respects, the German remonstrants' words suggest an internal conflict between ordinary folk and church leaders, with the former challenging the latter's involvement with distant authorities and organizations. But the pattern of German reaction was more complicated. Only eight years earlier, the clergy themselves had played a leading role in fighting the establishment of a formal German Reformed seminary and of ecumenical ties with New York-based, anglicized groups. And while lay protesters certainly exhibited anti-institutional and at times even anti-intellectual tendencies, they were not, as a group, anticlerical, and they remained respectful of the traditional ministerial office.[31] Rather than replace reform-minded clergy with populist lay leaders, the remonstrants hoped to find trained clergy of a traditional bent. Should that prove impossible, they claimed that they would continue gathering for worship to sing, hear the scriptures, and listen to old sermons read from the published collections of respected divines.[32] Those most put off by the popular rallies were the editors of

Fig. 10 A reconstruction of the courthouse square in Reading, Pennsylvania, where anti-Sabbatarian rallies took place in 1830. The Berks County Courthouse, built in 1762, was razed in 1841. Courtesy of Historical Society of Berks County, Reading, Pa.

German church papers; they often saw themselves as mediators of innovative ideas from the Anglo-American religious press, and they were less
likely to think in localist terms. From western New York State, the editor of
The Lutheran Magazine confessed that his paper "had not intended to have
taken any notice of these Pennsylvania meetings because we supposed that
the disgrace attached to their proceedings would, in the judgement of every
reasonable man in the community, fall exclusively on the persons who were
engaged in them." Yet reports of the rallies had spread so as to "fix a stigma
upon the characters of the churches to which they profess to belong." For
example, a Presbyterian writer was going about claiming that "the mode in
which members are received into the [Lutheran] church" lay at the root
of their apostasy, because catechetical instruction did not demand "giving
any further evidence of piety." The Lutheran editor now felt constrained to
defend as authentic his coreligionists' anti-revivalist approach to faith, while
distancing himself from public political statements he felt imprudent.[33]

Closer to the center of the storm itself, in Chambersburg, Pennsylvania,
a German Reformed Church editor printed an article highly critical of the
protesters. The denomination's *Magazine* had generally looked with favor
on the efforts of the activist evangelical coalition and their brand of patriotism. Indeed, the writer sadly noted that the German protesters only too
well demonstrated "how much of heathenism is yet to be purged away in
our own country." Whatever the sincerity of those "persons who composed
this meeting," the writer asserted, "it is too manifest that they neither possess the spirit of Christianity, nor know what it is, and that their resolutions
strike with the most reckless violence" at "religious institutions which are
the glory of the present age."[34]

Nor was there any reason to fear that reformist clergy were compromis-
ing church-state separation. The *Magazine*'s version of patriotism shared
much with the quite narrow Reformed evangelical interpretation of disestablishment. "In the United States ministers of religion of all denominations possess no other than purely spiritual authority: they are officers of a
kingdom which is not of this world," the writer argued. Such influence could
not "possibly be dangerous to the liberties of the people." The essayist condemned traditional Pennsylvania German versions of liberty as libertarian
and opined, "If by liberty the Heidelberg *patriots* mean licentiousness, the
whole matter is very clear: that sort of liberty is in much danger from such
influence." But, he continued, if they meant "the unrestrained enjoyment

of the rights which God has given us"—presenting the now-standard evangelical activist definition of American liberty—"it is a thing which can only be safe where the people are intelligent and truly virtuous."[35]

Taking a quite different, more tactful approach, synodic gatherings of clergy also entered the fray, employing softer rhetoric that balanced support for the lay protesters' concerns with a desire to avoid public offense. Like some Baptists and Campbellites, the German church leaders were skeptical of the evangelical united front's political influence. But Lutheran and Reformed clergy also were concerned about the welfare of their local communities and wary of interdenominational programs that could weaken them and dilute group solidarity.[36] When the Lutheran Synod of Pennsylvania met in mid-June, the protest rallies that had occurred within their jurisdiction were still current events. So when pastor Benjamin German (1790–1848) "asked permission of the Synod to direct their attention to an occurrence of the day," he surprised no one by pointing to "symptoms of considerable commotion amongst the people in many places, on account of the religious operations" drawing public attention. Specifically, many Lutherans believed "that associations for unavowed purposes, hostile to civil and religious liberty, have been in some instances formed," and members had expressed "a deeply rooted suspicion towards the churches most active in these societies." After some consideration, the synod appointed a committee of five ministers and six lay deputies to formulate an appropriate response.[37]

Perhaps unsure of their mandate, or fearful of stirring deep emotions, the committee reported only the most general of recommendations "to promote tranquility and Christian feelings in the churches." Nevertheless, the benign report provoked considerable (though largely unrecorded) debate. Apparently some members of the synod tried to recall historical links between benevolent reform activity and their European heritage as Lutherans, noting that "particularly in Germany, the land of our forefathers," Bible, tract, and missionary societies had formed with the support of "thousands of Christians, as benefitted institutions for the advancement of Christianity." Sadly, however, the synod concluded that in America, the acquisitive nature of aggressive money making had tied "disputable and dishonourable motives" to otherwise noble efforts now carried on by those "advocating these institutions from secular and mercenary" bases. Such charges surfaced "in several of the congregations belonging to our Synod," the meeting reported, though it disclaimed any knowledge of impropriety on its part. Thus, the group's members hoped both to "tranquillize the minds of those in our churches" and to distance themselves from activities corrupted by conditions in the New World.[38]

The populist protests had also preceded the annual classis meetings of the German Reformed Synod. On 24–25 May 1829, eighteen members of the Classis of East Pennsylvania assembled at Trexlertown, Lehigh County, and issued an address to their coreligionists that subsequently appeared in several German newspapers. They reported that "much was said on the present condition of the church," and that they "learned with heartfelt sorrow, that the excitement in various churches within our bounds ... does not subside, but rather increases."[39]

Like their Lutheran counterparts, the members of the classis charted a mediating course, accepting the validity of much of the popular opposition, but issuing their concerns in softer terms, stating more precisely what they found objectionable. "We call Sunday Schools good, as institutions for education," they announced, so long as they were agents of tradition and community conservation. But "should the [interdenominational] design be cherished thereby to entice young members from their own churches to build up another denomination without regard to the one they are pulling down," then the ministers strongly rejected the Sunday school movement. They passed similar judgments on Bible and missionary societies and moved "therefore [to] declare ourselves opposed to those institutions which in their object may be good, but by their abuse become injurious." Certainly "we have in our Synod no Bible Society, and as a Synod are connected with none," they reminded their members. "We have a Missionary Society, but it belongs exclusively to ourselves, and its only object is to send traveling preachers to destitute places [where scattered German settlers live]." And if even this institution made parishioners nervous, the classis assured its members that it is "truly in a languishing condition." Acknowledging that the role of the church in shaping society was at the heart of the current uproar, ministers and elders moved from moderation to insistence: "Far be it from us to mingle our religious concerns with the affairs of the state" or "exercise lordship," they announced. "And least of all," they concluded specifically, "would we attempt to oppose the regulations and laws of our country, which deem it necessary that the mails should not be detained on the Sabbath." If other churches become so involved in politics, "we have a just right to censure them and to accuse them of designs upon the rights of liberty," the classis announced. "If other denominations do them, let it not be said the *Reformed* have done them."[40]

Church and State and American Liberty

Yet if the East Pennsylvania Classis protested its innocence, it hinted that it could identify the guilty party. "We all know that a respectable denomination in our country goes too far … [in] the exercise of its religious zeal, and thus gives cause of suspicion to the feeble-minded," it acknowledged. Readers likely suspected that the classis was referring to the Presbyterians, because that denomination epitomized evangelical united front activity in the early nineteenth century, especially in the mid-Atlantic region. The Presbyterians and the Germans who had gathered at Heidelberg represented the two largest religious camps in Pennsylvania at the time—and two strikingly different visions of American society and of church and state.[41]

The evangelical united front of the early nineteenth century saw its efforts as actually creating a new American culture out of disparate political, ethnic, and sectarian parts. After all, the voluntary associations brought together those whose "opinions upon political questions" and other matters were, "in many instances, as opposite as the poles," according to one sympathetic explanation. In an age of democratic uncertainty, economic transformation, and emerging geographic sectionalism, people could "be induced to unite in no other common object" than "the religion of Jesus Christ and … the happiness of mankind."[42] Promoters hoped that evangelical Protestantism would provide the basis for a national unity that both church and state could jointly pursue—a pursuit that could redefine American identity and purpose. For most Pennsylvania German Protestants, however, America provided the space to create and defend local particularity. The cooperation of church and state in any grand plan of cultural or religious unity contravened their notion of liberty. That a few notable Pennsylvania Germans seemed to appreciate the Presbyterian version made the ethnic debates of 1829 and 1830 more revealing.

The new editor of the *German Reformed Magazine*, for example, spoke for those who saw in the popular evangelical program something both religiously appealing and authentically American. The son of German immigrants, Daniel Young (1795–1831) had spent his early adulthood in Presbyterian circles. Only in 1829 had he transferred his credentials to the German Reformed communion. However, the well-educated Young possessed skills that landed him posts as a denominational editor and assistant professor at the church's fledgling seminary.[43] "Our lot is cast in an eventful period," Young had proclaimed at the beginning of 1829. "Invention, enterprise, and combined effort are swaying a resistless scepter over the minds of men," particularly in the areas of politics and religion. "The Christian patriot in this state of things," Young was sure, "will take his stand at the post of observation, prepared to embrace every opportune occasion to exert a Christian influence and diffuse a Christian spirit as far as practicable into the civil ... institutions of his country."[44]

Thus, Young was beside himself that summer as he read reports of the Pennsylvania German protest meetings and the supportive words of the East Pennsylvania Classis ministers and elders. "It was with no small degree of surprise and regret that we were informed that the respectable Classis of East Pennsylvania had taken such a stand," Young noted with a heavy heart. "We had hoped better things of those brethren." By granting the essential truth of the protesters' complaints, the classis had "tended to dampen the ardor and paralyze the exertions of the few pious individuals among them who were deploring the desolation of Zion and making every effort to check the torrent of iniquity which threatens to overwhelm the land." Moreover, the members of the classis had "imposed fetters upon themselves which must prevent exertions in the future to oppose the current of vice."[45]

From Young's perspective, the remonstrants were battling a futile war for particularity against the forces of national and evangelical convergence. If German church leaders refused to accept Sunday schools, for example, he was sure that they would "drive off the children and youth to other churches and in many cases the parents with them." Regardless of whether Young accurately gauged the pulse of his new denomination, he believed that "parents will no longer consent to deprive their children of them, and if they cannot obtain them in their own church or send them elsewhere without incurring the frowns of their pastor, they will forsake that church & abandon that pastor."[46]

Young had hoped to press his case further by contrasting his vision for the church with his own assessment of Pennsylvania German religious life in areas he had recently visited, though his planned article never made it into print.[47] Young was able, however, to publish a response to the

Pennsylvania German perception that Presbyterian-backed social reform amounted to an unholy union of church and state. Under anonymous authorship, the *Magazine of the German Reformed Church* printed an article on the subject of "Union of Church and State," which argued that "the excellency of the present [United States] constitution ... guarantees civil and *religious* liberty to every class of our citizens," even though many Pennsylvania Germans charged the "Presbyterian denomination" with secret designs of mixing ecclesiastical and religious authority. According to the author, "many virtuous and respectable individuals in our land" believed that although Presbyterians had "never *avowed* this to be their intention ... they are struggling to gain an ascendancy over every other denomination and in due time they will incorporate their Church with the State." Indeed, some wondered whether they were "scattering tracts in every part of the land and organizing Sabbath schools in every district so that, in a little while, they will have the whole country under their control."[48]

While conceding that preachers such as Ezra Stiles Ely may have uttered intemperate statements and that Presbyterians "are more active and contribute more to ... [reform society] funds than any other denomination," the author insisted that the group's benevolent actions were actually proof of its selflessness and devotion to America as a whole. Grand interdenominational work showed Presbyterians' lack of concern for building up their own group and their devotion to the larger cause of national redemption. Yet it was that very sort of generic, hegemonic definition of American culture that bothered many Pennsylvania Germans and made them fear the more subtle yet profound mingling of religious and civil influence.[49]

Those fears were articulated by Carl Gock, the spokesman who had voiced his fellow ethnics' concerns about liberty and traditionally defined local order during the Free Synod controversy. Gock's polemical and somewhat rambling book, *My Religious and Related Political Opinion of North America,* was published in 1830 and covered a variety of topics, but included portions devoted to the events and issues that had erupted in 1829. While he was still denouncing the "clergy-aristocracy" (who, he believed, had formed hierarchical synods that robbed the faithful of their proper freedom), he now expanded his concerns to include clerical attempts to "rule through union of church and state." The "truthful messengers of God and respected guardians of Zion of the German Church" needed to "unite hand in hand and drive out the English popular theologians" threatening the Pennsylvania German churches, he wrote. Only then will "true peace and unity [return], and the angel of peace which has flown out of many of the temples of the German church again make its home there." Gock was clearly a patriotic American: his writing was filled with exalted praise for Columbia and George Washington, and it rivaled the rhetoric of Ezra Stiles Ely. But for Gock, American liberty meant the freedom to create locally controlled German communities unencumbered by the meddling of denominations whose ecclesiastical polity and penchant for creating national societies threatened his people's version of liberty.[50] Social order was important, Gock asserted, but "godly order is not as they have done. Christ said my kingdom is not of this world." Gock advised his readers to follow the resolution of the Heidelberg gathering and dismiss any pastor who did not support the list of demands that guaranteed local liberty and opposed Anglo-American evangelical activism in public life. Gock presented his own list of nine resolutions that closely paralleled those of the 1829 protesters. These still included his complaints against centralized seminary study and a plea for separation from all "connections with [what he called] the English Reformed and English Lutheran Synods"—matters he and other Pennsylvania German laity and clergy had protested earlier in the decade. But he now also denounced the Christian campaigns of Bible, tract, and mission societies and Sunday school unions. Under no condition should a congregation "proclaim a collection" for a cause not chosen and controlled by local congregational elders, he contended.[51]

Gock contrasted his Pennsylvania German ideal with characterizations of other denominations, beginning with the Presbyterians. Given the amount of authority wielded by their hierarchy, he dismissed them both on biblical grounds and with respect to "our free North American laws." Historically, the group has been the "mother of all fanatics," he insisted. He speculated further that the Presbyterians must have somehow transported abundant European wealth to North American soil in order to hold such enormous power and maintain control of the nation's many reform societies.[52]

But in Gock's opinion, Presbyterians also posed a danger to Pennsylvania Germans because they threatened not only to assume control of the government, but also to exert intellectual control over German Christians. Prospective pastors at the new Lutheran and German Reformed seminaries studied under professors who themselves had been students in Presbyterian schools, Gock complained. The danger was all too clear: "such men are weak in the respected German evangelical theology," due to their "English and

Presbyterian" formation. Indeed, "[e]veryone must and will easily see that all students ... are better versed in the English Presbyterian theology than in the respected evangelical German theology." In only twenty years, English and Presbyterian perspectives would dominate the German churches, he predicted.[53] Gock summarized his treatise with a fictional conversation between two Pennsylvania German farmers "concerning religious and civil liberty."[54] The younger interlocutor mentioned the many evangelical reform societies that had appeared during the preceding twenty years, and then inquired of the older man whether people were not better off, more pious, or increasingly moral, given these evangelical efforts to Christianize the nation. The wise older man replied that, in fact, people had actually been more Christlike in the past, more neighborly, and less likely to sue one another or commit other crimes. Painting a picture of local communities free from undue meddling by outsiders, the aged speaker quoted the sayings of Jesus, which counseled the church to attend to its own affairs and shun the lures of political power. He compared the current anti–Sunday mail campaign with the pharisaical, human-derived law that scripture condemned; he even went so far as to characterize missionaries, traveling preachers, money collectors, and book and pamphlet sellers as "so like spiritual secret police."[55] They were hardly part of the free America in which Gock continually gloried. Indeed, the evangelical vision of a uniformly organized society was the antithesis of the widespread Pennsylvania German version of the American dream, which promised freedom to pursue locally governed and ordered life.

American Pursuits of Pennsylvania German Happiness

Both Daniel Young and Carl Gock thought of themselves as patriotic Americans concerned with their people's and their country's future well-being. But their visions of America diverged, and their convictions concerning church and state—as well as the place of public reform efforts—took different directions. Some Pennsylvania Germans argued for the utility and desirability of the evangelical Protestant vision, but for the most part, Lutheran and German Reformed adherents remained aloof from the sorts of projects and methods associated with the evangelical activists. The German Reformed Synod's fall 1829 report on the "state of religion" noted "that in many places prejudices are cherished by many against the institutions established by this synod—viz.: the Seminary, Missionary Society, &."[56] Moreover, when the denomination's two-year-old home mission association found its treasury empty, an appeal for funds drew little response. Its secretary reported that "the committee could not but indulge the belief that the ministers of our Reformed Zion would exert themselves by having collections made in their respective churches," yet they were "compelled to state that this address awakened scarcely any attention or respect."[57] A year later, activists still lacked hope that their vision would win the hearts and minds of the faithful.[58]

Lutheran support for religiously based civic reform societies also continued to be weak. When the Pennsylvania Synod met in 1830, it considered establishing a Missionary and Education Society. Lively discussion ensued after John Uhlhorn (1794–1834) inquired "whether such an association were necessary, or would be conducive to the prosperity of the Church." After due deliberation, the group resolved that the "Pennsylvania Synod considered the course pursued by our fathers the best; therefore could countenance no measure proposed which would burden the people, or introduce a spirit of proselytism into the Church." They "therefore determined by a large majority that no Missionary and Education Society should be formed amongst us."[59]

Pennsylvania German sentiment against any religious activism in the public sphere continued to be felt so strongly that in 1835, opponents of Pennsylvania gubernatorial candidate Joseph Ritner (1780–1869) sought ethnic votes by charging that in the 1820s, Ritner had voted for the incorporation of charitable religious institutions.[60] Though they chose to pursue the course established by their fathers, Pennsylvania Germans were also signaling their intent to defend cultural particularity in American terms. In a land of liberty that paradoxically seemed to demand conformity, they defended an alternative—and in their minds, a more authentic—American identity. Creating and upholding that identity required continual negotiation and produced regular conflict. But in such events Pennsylvania Germans began to think of themselves as ethnic Americans, full members of a young republic, whose visions of national purpose were equally worthy and worth protection. For their part, Pennsylvania German Lutherans would spend several decades sorting out the relationship between theology and ethnicity in Protestant America.

SEARCHING FOR
AMERICAN KINSHIP

Lutherans,
Liberty,
and
Ecumenism

"I am persuaded," pastor David F. Schaeffer (1787–1837) declared on 31 October 1817, that "were Christians more anxious to inform themselves as to past events, the gospel of our Lord Jesus Christ would be more generally experienced, appreciated, and supported, particularly in this land of liberty." Schaeffer was presiding over a Frederick, Maryland, tercentenary celebration of Martin Luther's posting of his "Ninety-five Theses" in Wittenberg, Germany, thus launching the Protestant Reformation. For Schaeffer and his Pennsylvania German Lutheran congregation, the festival evoked both ethnic and religious pride. The church choir even performed special anniversary hymns commissioned for the occasion.

Yet as Schaeffer's sermon also suggested, the anniversary was about more than Lutheranism's Old World past; it raised questions about the group's current place in a "land of liberty." One of the anniversary hymns sung at Frederick had proclaimed that "truth's radiant ray [had] beamed through the Reformation" and thereby "restored religious liberty" to contemporary society.[1] These Lutherans saw themselves as the original standard-bearers of one sort of freedom, heirs to a tradition that had rejected autocracy and distant absolutism in favor of more local religious authority and political nationalism. But what did such a legacy of liberty mean or imply in North America? Where did Lutherans fit in the religious panorama that had taken shape around them? Pennsylvania German Lutherans would repeatedly turn to the themes of liberty and freedom as they sought their religious bearings in a republic they now called home.

Old-fashioned filiopietistic sentiments remained, to be sure, and Lutherans of all stripes would long praise the "remarkably pure and elegant" language of Luther's Bible translation, comparing it to the English King James Version (which was "too rigidly literal to be entirely perspicuous").[2] But Old World ties steadily weakened in the Early Republic. The direct connections that did exist could even reverse historic relationships. In 1813, hearing of the devastation wrought by Napoleonic warfare, the Pennsylvania Ministerium forwarded $2,334.10 to the Francke Foundation at Halle, once headquarters of a Lutheran establishment that had provided pastors and ecclesiastical support to colonial churches.[3] No longer dependents of Halle, Pennsylvania German Lutherans would spend more time fashioning relationships with other American denominations. Indeed, it was in their search for spiritual kin in the New World that these Lutherans revealed their different understandings of America, liberty, and their place in the United States.

An American Protestant Festival

The 1817 Reformation tercentenary set the stage for a contest of claims that would fill the next twenty-five years. Steeped in the tradition of Continental Pietism—both of the Halle and southwestern German varieties—colonial Lutherans had "placed an emphasis on the practical application" of the historic confessions as "documents which were productive of piety and practical Christianity,"[4] while paying less attention to the actual theological conflicts of the sixteenth century or the immediate historical roots of their church.[5] The American clash with German-speaking, Methodist-inspired revivalists such as the United Brethren bolstered the Lutheran commitment to catechesis, but confessional consciousness, as it would later emerge among immigrants of the mid-nineteenth century, was not present among many adherents in the new nation.[6]

The three-hundredth anniversary of Luther's defiant actions, however, enlivened Lutheran historical sensibilities.[7] The festival afforded Lutherans the opportunity to claim a place as the New World's rightful representatives of the Reformation. They could glory in their distant heritage while carving a central place in the contemporary American religious scene. Hoping to cultivate widespread public interest in the anniversary, the Lutheran Ministerium of Pennsylvania even ordered that "notice of the Jubilee Festival ... be published at the proper time in the various newspapers."[8] The Reformation tercentenary, it turned out, would be Luther-centered, but construed in broadly Protestant terms. The ministerium "resolved that the German Evangelical Reformed Synod, the Moravians, the English Episcopal, and Presbyterian Churches shall [all] be invited by our President to celebrate the Reformation Festival with us." When Episcopal and Moravian bishops responded to the anniversary notice, "[t]he Synod rejoiced at the Christian fraternal affection and the high regard for the fathers of the Reformation which were manifest in both letters."[9] The German Reformed Church also resolved "to celebrate this festival with the Lutherans."[10]

Anniversary services, historical sermons, and commemorative hymns marked the October event and often tied it to various notions of American and religious liberty. In Northampton County, Pennsylvania, Johann A. Probst (1792–1844) used the occasion to celebrate New World religious freedom that was "a basic principle of the constitution of our happy nation."[11] Here was an image of the Lutheran Reformation as the vindication of local religious prerogatives opposed to distant authorities.

To the southwest, John George Schmucker presided over the festival in York, Pennsylvania, where he was less concerned than Probst with government interference in local life; instead, he presented Rome as the leading threat to Protestant liberty on a national scale. The York celebration, held in a "worthy manner" in accord with the ministerium's resolution, included the singing of specially commissioned festival songs. In his historical address, Schmucker dwelt at some length on Luther and his theology, but he also discussed the historical persecution of Protestants by Catholics, and the celebratory hymns blamed papal "deception and cunning" for exiling "the teaching of Jesus Christ."[12]

Anti-Catholicism long had been a staple of American Protestant thought, though Pennsylvania German Protestant and German-American Catholic relations were not always as antagonistic as they would become after 1817.[13] During the late eighteenth and early nineteenth centuries, in fact, as German-speaking Pennsylvania Catholics asserted their identity against an English hierarchy, they evinced sympathy from their Pennsylvania German Protestant neighbors, some of whom assisted Philadelphia German Catholics in constructing their own church building in 1789.[14] And as late as 1810, when Rev. John W. Beschter, S.J. (d. 1842) preached at the dedication of the Catholic chapel in Lebanon, Pennsylvania, the audience included six Lutheran and German Reformed pastors, who afterward took supper with Beschter in one of the Lutherans' homes, continuing a European practice of inviting local dignitaries to community celebrations and symbolizing the ongoing importance of such local customs.[15]

For a number of reasons, such Catholic-Protestant alliances waned,[16] and the stories, songs, and sermons prompted by the Reformation tercentenary only confirmed the notion that Pennsylvania German religion was a properly Protestant enterprise. Yet claiming to stand in the center of the American Protestant mainstream raised as many questions about Lutheran identity as it answered, and the church's place in the young nation's family of faiths remained unclear. For example, the anniversary publication— *A Comprehensive Account of the Rise and Progress of the Blessed Reformation of the Christian Church by Dr. Martin Luther* ... , by pastor Gottlieb Schober (1756–1838), a North Carolina Moravian turned Lutheran—celebrated the German reformer while criticizing Puritan and Presbyterian leaders. Yet it also proclaimed that "true Christians of all denominations as soon as they understand one another and meet ... are like David and Jonathan."[17] Schober had believed that promoting Reformation history would boost Lutheran visibility and status in America, and he hoped "that among the English also we may be recognized as an old Church, since there are many of them who hitherto hardly knew of us, and now are astonished to know that we are older than the Methodists and Baptists."[18] Yet Schober never specified what Lutherans actually contributed to American Protestantism or why their distinct presence was so important.[19] Similarly, the Reformation anniversary book issued by pastor Johann Georg Lochman

(1773–1826) of Harrisburg, Pennsylvania, entitled *The History, Doctrine, and Discipline of the Evangelical Lutheran Church,* presented a highly celebratory account of "the mother church of all Protestants," but lacked intellectual depth and concrete description of the denomination's future in light of its past.[20]

If American Lutherans were "the first born daughter of the Reformation,"[21] the group possessing an Augsburg Confession that was "the mother symbol of the Reformation,"[22] such familial imagery only begged the question of who their American religious relatives really were. Were they the first among Protestant siblings, as parts of the Reformation anniversary suggested? Or was their heritage one that expressed the highest elements of a German religious constitution in an American context? Nationalism and theological debate had often rested uneasily together in the sixteenth century; their tension would be at the heart of Lutheran ecumenical conflict during the quarter-century following the 1817 tercentenary as well.[23]

Complicating the picture was the fact that Reformation celebrations in German-speaking Europe had resulted in their own ecumenical experiment—the fusion of Lutheran and Reformed communions in Prussia and several other states.[24] By the mid-1820s, at least, such fraternal affairs were known in America. Pennsylvania Lutherans even received correspondence from "the eminent and learned G. J. Planck," a Prussian teaching at the University of Göttingen.[25] From New York, Frederick C. Schaeffer (1792–1831) wrote to Pennsylvania pastors to suggest "a closer union between the Lutheran and Reformed Churches in our States," following the "excellent example" of "our brethren in Germany."[26]

Some Pennsylvania German Lutherans needed no European encouragement to decide that their ethnic neighbors in the Reformed tradition were the proper objects of deeper ecclesiastical connection. The colonial practice of erecting Lutheran-and-Reformed union church buildings received a new burst of energy during the first half of the nineteenth century, and some sixty-seven jointly owned churches went up in the area covered by the Lutheran Pennsylvania Ministerium (in addition to those constructed beyond that body's bounds).[27] In a move that coincided with the Reformation celebration of 1817, a Baltimore press released a German hymnal for use in the groups' many common places of worship. Although not officially commissioned by either body, *Das Gemeinschaftliche Gesangbuch* proved enormously popular, going through numerous printings and netting endorsements from leaders of both communions.[28] And Lutheran and Reformed pastors took over one another's preaching responsibilities in times of need, as Lutheran John W. Richards (1803–54) did when he substituted for William Hendel Jr., the Reformed pastor near Womelsdorf, Pennsylvania.[29]

Indeed, many faithful had difficulty articulating where the two communions diverged. A Congregationalist minister from Portland, Maine, visited among Pennsylvania Germans in the early 1830s and reported, "To the question, In what do the Lutherans and the Reformed differ? I was told by one Lutheran clergyman that there was no material difference; by another that the disbelief of the doctrine of election was a distinctive characteristic of the Lutherans; and by a German Reformed that the Lutherans were Arminian."[30] Popular opinion suggested that the most salient distinction was that Lutherans began the Lord's Prayer *Vater Unser,* while the Reformed said *Unser Vater.* The Lutheran use of wafers and the Reformed use of bread at the Lord's Supper was as large a distinction as many made in the sacramental theology of both groups.[31] At the same time, their similar experiences as the targets of German evangelical revivalists had cemented another sort of commonality. If Lutherans were to uphold their historic Continental Reformation tradition, many believed that they should do so in the company of their German Reformed neighbors.

The anniversary of Protestantism, however, had also promoted another sort of ecumenical vision. In its rendering, Lutherans were the oldest sibling in a Protestant family of denominations that shared a sense of spiritual kinship. As the senior member of the family, the argument ran, Lutherans had a responsibility to foster such closeness. In 1812, the Pennsylvania Ministerium had approved inter-Protestant eucharistic communion "in *case of necessity,*" should a frontier community lack sufficient clergy, but after 1820 the ecumenical vision promoted by some Lutherans went further.[32] It assumed that the descendants of Wittenberg would lead all American Protestants in proclaiming and defending their common republican principles—principles that Martin Luther supposedly championed in the face of Catholic tyranny or infidelity.[33]

Chief among these tenets was the egalitarian claim of *sola scriptura*—the unfettered authority and interpretation of the Bible, a theme around which some Pennsylvania German Lutherans believed that they could rally fellow Protestants. Samuel S. Schmucker (1799–1873), the leader most closely associated with this position, later insisted that "as the eldest sister of the Reformation our church was the first to express the grand Protestant principle" of egalitarian biblicism; thus, he argued, Lutherans bore a historical responsibility to lead American Protestants in promoting such Reformation ideals.[34] In fact, this Lutheran ecumenical program was properly patriotic, Schmucker insisted, since it was to the Lutheran Reformation that he and all other Americans "owe[d] our liberty, civil and religious."[35] There was no need to limit Lutheran leadership to German-speaking, Continentally rooted denominations. The Reformation tradition was as wide as American Protestantism itself, even if that family of churches was often unaware of its lineage.

The sixteenth-century events celebrated in 1817, then, pointed in different ecumenical directions and assumed different understandings of Pennsylvania German peoplehood. Both programs—the broad Protestant alignment and the more specific Pennsylvania German Reformed connection—reflected possibilities for Lutheran Americanization: even the ethnically linked plan looked more to Pennsylvania German realities and colonial legacies than to events in far-off Prussia.

Fraternal Appeals

In the years immediately following the tercentenary celebration, Lutherans turned first to reorganizing themselves. The old Pennsylvania Ministerium had seen its North Carolina members separate from their northern co-religionists and create an autonomous synod in 1803. In 1817, when Ohio church members petitioned for self-governing status, the Pennsylvania fathers denied their request, so the Ohio group acted unilaterally the next year. Some denominational historians have suggested that the Pennsylvania Ministerium's initial support for an overarching national synod stemmed from its desire to influence or control these synodic stepchildren.

In any case, in 1818, the Pennsylvania Ministerium proposed forming a national General Synod, and Pennsylvania Germans in North Carolina, at least, responded favorably.[36] The 1819 proposal limited the power of the General Synod, granting it broad advisory status but no authority to serve as a final arbiter of disputes.[37] The plan required a minimum of three synodic members—a requirement more difficult to achieve than many first imagined. After some hesitation, the Ohio Synod rejected the idea, as did the New York Synod.[38] When the constituting convention met at Hagerstown, Maryland, on 22 October 1820, it gained the firm support of only the Pennsylvania Ministerium, the North Carolina Synod, and a two-week-old synod of Maryland and Virginia that had just separated from the Pennsylvania delegation.[39] The resulting constitution called for the establishment of a theological seminary to combat Unitarian deism—the sort of purpose that suggested other goals of the document and of several of its key supporters. Many of the new General Synod promoters, it turned out, hoped that the body would take up the cause of leading all orthodox denominations in battling problems common to American Protestantism.[40]

Members in ethnic strongholds of the Pennsylvania Ministerium soon grew suspicious of their new denominational creation, however. The ecumenical vision implicit in the constitution suggested ties they were not keen to draw. In May 1823, as the ministerium met in Lebanon, Pennsylvania, it received letters and protests from congregations in Lehigh County that opposed both the General Synod and its proposed theological seminary. The petitioners called on the Pennsylvania Synod to "withdraw and return to the old order of things." Under pressure from such quarters, the ministerium decided to abandon the General Synod and severed its ties.[41] Afterward, General Synod advocates John George Schmucker, Samuel S. Schmucker, and John Herbst Jr. (1791?–1834) convened a special conference at York, Pennsylvania, on 6–7 October 1823 to reconsider the decision, though they failed to sway the rest of the ministerium the next year.[42]

At this point, the General Synod tottered on the brink of dissolution with a membership of only two small synods (Maryland-Virginia and North Carolina). On 3 September 1825, just days before the next scheduled General Synod meeting, supporters in western Pennsylvania announced their withdrawal from the Pennsylvania Ministerium to organize the "Synod of the Evangelical Lutheran Church, West of the Susquehanna, in the State of Pennsylvania."[43] The new body had an admittedly small membership, but the General Synod now had a constituency of three regional synods and stood on somewhat firmer ground.[44] It quickly voted to establish a theological seminary the next year at Gettysburg, Pennsylvania, to be headed by Samuel Schmucker.[45] (Fig. 11.)

Though still a young man of twenty-six, Schmucker was already an important figure among Pennsylvania German Lutherans, and his ideas were

S. S. SCHMUCKER, D.D.

FIRST PROFESSOR OF THE THEOLOGICAL SEMINARY OF THE GENERAL SYNOD
OF THE LUTHERAN CHURCH IN THE UNITED STATES, GETTYSBURGH, PENN.

Fig. 11 Samuel S. Schmucker, Lutheran pastor, activist,
denominational organizer, and founder (in 1826) of the Lutheran
Seminary at Gettysburg, Pennsylvania. Courtesy of the Archives of
the A. R. Wentz Library at the Lutheran Theological Seminary at
Gettysburg, Pa.

at the center of the General Synod's vision of Lutheran ecumenism and the church's place in the American republic. Trained under the honored Philadelphia Lutheran pastor J. H. C. Helmuth and at Princeton Theological Seminary, Schmucker combined conversionist Pietist sensibilities (which were less given to dogmatics) with a broader evangelical agenda.[46] In an address presenting a "Portraiture of Lutheranism," Schmucker spoke of the "eldest member of the Protestant family" and its role in the young nation.[47] Despite his affection for "Germany, the mother of the Reformation, [and] the cradle of Lutheranism," Schmucker saw Lutheran history as having a more immediate connection to America, the place in which its ultimate purpose had unfolded. The Reformation was truly the "revolution ... to which, in the providence of God, these United States may clearly trace their liberties," Schmucker argued.[48] In fact, Luther and his associates had preached a gospel that "led our fathers to erect the standard of liberty on these Western shores."[49] As he and other West Pennsylvania Synod pastors had announced in 1826, Lutheranism "runs parallel with the government of our free and independent country."[50]

Lutheranism was not bounded by distant European events of the sixteenth century nor properly defined by strict adherence to every word of the Augsburg Confession. Rather, it was found in general Reformation principles such as biblicism and self-determination, which properly expressed themselves in North America.[51] In Schmucker's opinion, then, Lutherans served the nation by promoting Lutheranism's liberal tenets and battling the antirepublican forces of Catholicism.[52] In such efforts lay the meaning of liberty.

Another exponent of this vision of Lutherans' role in America was Benjamin Kurtz (1795–1865), a pastor and longtime editor of the *Lutheran Observer*.[53] In a book drawn from *Observer* columns—and entitled *Why Are You a Lutheran?*—Kurtz asserted that Lutherans had a responsibility to proclaim the Reformation tradition of *sola scriptura* and evangelical orthodoxy. If other Protestant denominations also espoused such principles, Kurtz was more than pleased: "[T]he Lutheran church is the one that first brought [these principles] to light from the dark depths of Romish corruption," and the denomination's mission in America had been their dissemination. Kurtz found in the historical story of Lutheran Pietism an example of Lutheranism leavening Protestantism as a whole. Members could recapitulate their success in contemporary society, he was sure.[54]

The General Synod's version of ecumenism was not just a means of internal self-understanding on the part of Lutherans; it was also a rationale for using Lutheranism as a vehicle for leading a latter-day Reformation against American infidelity and apostasy. Thus, its supporters welcomed the work of religiously based voluntary reform societies, and the General Synod went on record endorsing the work of several such agencies.[55] Samuel Schmucker himself even served for eight years as one of the honorary vice presidents of the American Tract Society and joined an American evangelical plan to proselytize Italy.[56] Schmucker encouraged his students to preach on public moral issues (though not on politics per se).[57] Yet sometimes Schmucker's Lutheran theology did check his support of popular religious reformism, and he declined an invitation from his friend Robert Baird (1798–1863) to become a traveling agent for the American Bible Society, choosing instead to focus his energy on serving his own denomination.[58] That commitment, of course, was the key to his construction of ethnic interests: he believed that Lutherans as a group bore the legacy of the Reformation and were especially charged with continuing the work of "leveling down the partition walls which are now separating Protestant from Protestant."[59]

With such ideas in mind, Schmucker dreamed of uniting all orthodox Protestant churches in a common federation against rationalism, Unitarianism, and Catholicism. Such a grand scheme could have no better leader than the Reformation's eldest child and potentially strongest voice.[60] So in 1837, Schmucker composed a *Fraternal Appeal to the American Churches, with a Plan for Catholic Union on Apostolic Principles,* which he issued the next year.[61] Built on postmillennial hopes and an ideal of American exceptionalism, Schmucker argued that now was the time and America was the place for the glorious Reformation begun by Martin Luther to find its proper fulfillment. Rather than merging denominational structures, Schmucker seemed to suggest, Protestants should view themselves as an extended family whose members agreed to recognize the validity of one another's household rules without necessarily appropriating all of them for themselves. The Apostles' Creed and a new "United Protestant Confession" that Schmucker compiled from existing Lutheran, Episcopal, Presbyterian, Reformed, Congregationalist, Baptist, and Methodist documents, would provide group boundaries.[62]

In 1839 he distributed the plan nationally for denominational consideration. For its part, the Lutheran General Synod meeting that year in Chambersburg, Pennsylvania, supported the idea.[63] Six years later, Schmucker circulated an "Overture for Christian Union" based on a second edition of the *Appeal*.[64] It garnered endorsements from forty-five American church leaders representing a range of denominations; nine were General Synod Lutherans.[65] In addition to the discussion it generated, the *Fraternal Appeal* provided an American point of connection with the later British-based Evangelical Alliance.[66] The vision and ideals behind the *Fraternal Appeal* represented the ultimate aim of one Lutheran search for spiritual kinship in America, one means of construing the role of a Continentally rooted church in an Anglo-American religious environment.

Pennsylvania German Religion

If some Lutherans heeded Schmucker's appeal and found solidarity among younger denominational siblings in an extended evangelical family, others believed that they had a different set of spiritual relatives. For many Pennsylvania German Lutherans, ethnic ties molded ecumenical concerns as the North American environment pushed their vision in another direction. By 1829, readers of the German press had already come across essays that questioned Schmucker's ethnic authenticity. That year J. Ernst Ludwig Brauns, of Braunschweig, Germany, published "Practical Advice for Emigrants to America," which was reprinted in the columns of the Philadelphia *Amerikanischer Correspondent*. Brauns charged that the Gettysburg Seminary produced culturally (and linguistically) English preachers, and that Schmucker was an "Irish-German"—a term of reproach suggesting that the professor wore only an ethnic veneer and was really the lowest sort of Briton.[67] Brauns's opinion was hardly an objective one, but letters in the *Allentowner Freibothen* about the same time also criticized Schmucker's German credentials and questioned his theological qualifications.[68]

Many Lutherans saw in their Reformed neighbors a Pennsylvania German religious kinship that contrasted with the more complex family system devised by Schmucker's associates. Members of the two communions had shared much in common since the colonial days.[69] Jointly administered Franklin College had proven rather disappointing as an educational institute, but its continuing charter provided one official link between the churches. Several other ties emerged, such as the 1812 Reformed Synod's endorsement of the Lutheran-originated *Evangelisches Magazin*.[70] That publication stressed the role of the German language in passing on the faith.

Historic doctrinal differences between the two major German bodies paled in the bright light of the *Magazin*'s praise of German speech and folkways. One author insisted, "The Lutheran and Reformed Churches are here so bound to one another and woven into each other that the small difference in their teaching is almost forgotten through the similarity of sentiment, church organization, and worship."[71] Hymnals and prayer books published and used by both groups also helped cement a common spirituality.[72]

But cooperation and parallel piety were not the end of Lutheran ecumenical concerns. In 1822, on the suggestion of its president, Christian L. F. Endress, the Pennsylvania Ministerium resolved to increase cooperation with the German Reformed Church, perhaps to the point of denominational union.[73] The next year, the group received a favorable reply from a Reformed Synod still stunned by the defection of Free Synod congregations angry over apparent ecumenical contact with the anglicized Dutch.[74] The Maryland-Virginia Lutheran Synod also wrote to the German Reformed Synod with similar intentions, although it is not clear whether the Lutherans on either side of the Mason-Dixon line were aware of the differences in polity and function of their respective organizations.[75]

Yet such details were never enough to derail Lutheran enthusiasts who favored the extension of their church along ethnic lines and the creation of a stronger Pennsylvania German religious voice in America. The Lutheran protesters from Lehigh County, Pennsylvania, and elsewhere, who had forced the Pennsylvania Ministerium's 1823 withdrawal from the General Synod, had been prompted in large part by their desire to refocus ecumenical energy. Tied up in opponents' demands to "return to the old order of things" was the desire to form primary ties not with all Protestant communions in general, but with their fellow Pennsylvania German neighbors in particular.[76]

One of the strongest advocates of an ethnically defined ecumenism was Johann A. Probst, an American-trained pastor who had studied theology in Lancaster.[77] Accepted into the Pennsylvania Ministerium in 1813, he served the Lutheran congregation in Strasburg, Pennsylvania, for two years before moving from Lancaster County to Northampton County and assuming the pastorate of the Mount Bethel parish and Forks Township congregations near Easton. (Fig. 12.) In 1826, Probst published a detailed and polemical book entitled *The Reunion of the Lutherans and Reformed*.[78] The volume was so popular that it appeared in a second edition two years later. The text received hearty endorsement in a preface written by Johann C. Jaeger, a

Fig. 12 Old Williams–St. Luke's Lutheran Church, Hellertown, Pennsylvania, built 1813. J. A. Probst was pastor here from 1815 to 1824, just prior to penning *The Reunion of the Lutherans and Reformed*. Other pastors included Johann C. Jaeger, 1792–1801, and Christian L. F. Endress, 1801–14. Courtesy of Michael L. Nolt.

native of York, Pennsylvania, who was then serving as a Lutheran pastor in Allentown.[79] Jaeger appealed to the New Testament, arguing that sectarian divisions had not existed in the apostolic church. But unlike the signatories to the *Fraternal Appeal,* Jaeger's ecumenical interests were tied to things German. While he mentioned the 1817 Prussian church union, he had a clear American orientation, noting that "here in our Fatherland [America] one has repeatedly heard the wish from our mutual Synods for a reunion of the Lutherans and the Reformed." Thankfully, "[t]he sectarian spirit of the church ... that has been an impediment, is more and more disappearing among Lutherans and Reformed," Jaeger announced, and he commended Probst's book to "our German public."[80]

In the bulk of the book, Probst detailed the background of both communions, along with their mutual antagonism and their common difficulties at the hands of Catholic overlords. Although at first glance Probst's plan may have appeared to be a simple scheme of ethnic isolationism, it was a very American creation. Like Jaeger, Probst could make restitutionist arguments then popular in a nation claiming to be "the new order of the ages," and he could insist that America was the proper place for this noble religious experiment. He gloried in the fact that denominational reunion would "hang completely on us, the people," because no government could compel faith in America. Any German church merger in the young nation would thus surpass that dictated in 1817 in Europe.[81]

While Old World-rooted confessional differences had once prohibited cooperation between the two bodies, conflicts over predestination and eucharistic theology were now hardly matters of debate: Probst asserted that it was hard to find a preacher who was prepared to be dogmatic over such points. The "old symbolical books" were important historically, but now served mostly to "interest scholars."[82] Life in a religiously disestablished America meant that the old debates were less critical and that no one needed "to subscribe to Luther's, nor Zwingli's, nor Calvin's opinions, human as they are in character," but rather to Christ and the Bible. On this point, Probst insisted, there were similar sentiments among all Pennsylvania German church folk.[83] They would agree, he was sure, that "Christianity stands not so much on opinion, custom, or ceremony, as on a fundamentally Christian outlook, and behavior that matches such an outlook."[84]

In practical terms, Probst called for the preparation of a common catechism, joint celebration of the Lord's Supper, and the formation of a single synod.[85] An important effect of such a union would be the realization of a long-held Pennsylvania German ideal: greater localizing of the church and closer relationships between congregations and pastors. Through the mathematics of denominational merger, parish sizes would dramatically shrink, because each locale would be served by a single pastor (thus eliminating the current duplication of Lutheran and Reformed clergymen in each community). Probst's plan promised to bring ministry closer to the people of a particular place and reduce the number of circuit-parish pastoral charges. Probst concluded his book with a poetic tribute to true Christian liberty that in turn guaranteed civil liberty and brought, among other things, "the success of the sciences, the growth of the arts, and the flowering of trades and crafts."[86]

Much of the impetus for a unified Pennsylvania German church seemed to come from the Lutheran side, although there was some response from the Reformed camp. In an 1833 issue of the *Messenger of the German Reformed Church,* a writer identified as "Unus" pointed to the two groups' common language, religious literature, and high incidence of intermarriage, calling the possibility of their merger "a subject of . . . thrilling interest to every German." Certainly the Heidelberg Catechism and the Augsburg Confession were "precious relics of our forefathers," but they should not "screw us down to" irreconcilable doctrinal positions in the present, Unus concluded. As "trophies of that splendid victory which our forefathers achieved" in the Reformation, such statements deserved a place of honor, but would also serve as first steps toward a "more *glorious confession of faith*" that all Pennsylvania Germans could place alongside their common customs and family ties.[87]

Into the 1830s, Lutherans within the bounds of the Pennsylvania Ministerium continued to make ethnically linked ecumenical overtures. In 1836, the Pennsylvania Ministerium again appointed delegates to approach the German Reformed Synod on the subject of denominational federation, believing that "a perfect union of the Evangelical Lutheran and of the Evangelical Reformed churches might be followed by the most blessed advantages."[88] Although the German Reformed Synod responded favorably, the proposal produced only the exchange of honorary synodic delegates.[89]

Had the Lutherans flagged in their struggle to find spiritual kin? Several events suggest that whatever the end of formal union talks meant, the members of the Pennsylvania Ministerium continued both to distance themselves from wider Anglo-American evangelical interests and to maintain their Pennsylvania German religious identity. In 1839, a proposal to rejoin the General Synod again failed in the ministerium, with opposition most intense in the ethnic strongholds that supported closer Reformed relations.[90]

By 1842, the emphasis on ethnicity as a denominational foundation proved too confining for a few Pennsylvania Ministerium members and their congregations. They issued a broadside entitled "Thoughts on the Formation of a New Synod in the Eastern District of Pennsylvania ..." that was sharply critical of the tie between Pennsylvania German identity and Lutheran church life.[91] The dissenters named several issues that increasingly separated them from their clerical brethren, including the majority's reticence in engaging the popular Protestant idea of religious reformism and national redemption operating in "the various instrumentalities or institutions by which the kingdom of God is to be maintained and extended in the world."

The protesters saw some good in conversionist preaching, though they rejected the charges of "wildfire, fanaticism, enthusiasm, and new measures" that other ministerium members hurled their way, and they insisted that they "have ever most faithfully instructed ... children and the youth of our churches by *catechisation*." They also objected to the binding nature of ministerium decisions and the singular use of German in synodic business meetings as "a great encroachment upon the rights of the people."[92]

Another of the minority group's complaints was that "certain foreigners [from Germany] are admitted to the privilege of membership in the Pennsylvania Synod, whilst native Americans, ordained by Lutheran Synods in this country are excluded, unless supported by a vote twice as numerous!" Indeed, according to the synodic constitution, "[a] majority of more than one half the ordained ministers present cannot introduce the minister born and educated in this country into Synod, but a *minority* of one more than one-third can compel Synod to give the right hand of fellowship to a stranger, educated in certain favored institutions of Germany!" Regardless of how few European Lutheran clergy actually arrived and served in Pennsylvania German congregations during the Early Republic, the very idea was repugnant to a certain sense of American republican logic. "For what minister," the remonstrants asked, "who has the spirit of a man, of an American, or of a Christian freeman, will submit to the invidious and disgraceful distinction that is here made? He is to be rejected if opposed by one-third of those who vote, but a *foreigner* is admitted unless twice as many oppose him!"[93]

Hoping for an amicable separation, the protesters met one day prior to the 1842 synodic and ministerium meeting, held that year in Lancaster. They presented a more subdued and polite memorial to the ministerium and cited issues in a less direct way, but highlighted "[d]ifferences of language": the "Synod having declared its determination to abide by the use of one language [German], there seems an obvious call for the organization of a body that will admit the indiscriminate use of the German and English."[94] The Pennsylvania Ministerium refused to allow the dissidents to leave cordially, forcing them to break with the parent body in a legal and emotional schism.[95] Bad feeling persisted, and as late as 1855, Pennsylvania Ministerium members opposed a plan for cooperation between the two bodies, with venerable Philadelphia pastor Charles R. Demme (1795–1863) announcing, "Ich bin dagegen; der Geist in der Ost-Pennsylvanischen Synode ist ein anderer [I am opposed; the spirit of the East Pennsylvania Synod is of another kind]!" Joshua Yeager (1802–88) of Hamburg, Berks County, declared, "Ich bin auch dagegen; dann wird alles Englisch [I am also opposed; then everything will be English]!"[96]

Americanists in Conflict

Denominational historians looked back on Lutheran affairs of the 1820s and 1830s as an uneventful time preceding the great confessional confrontation between later-arriving Lutheran immigrants to the Midwest and the Pennsylvania Germans who populated much of the East.[97] Yet these same colonial-stock Lutherans later charged with thoughtless Americanization were themselves sharply divided over the means and meaning of Americanization. They struggled bitterly over their role as an ethnic minority that was also part of the new nation's Protestant majority.

Ethnic identity provided a heritage and a cultural commitment that could supply resources for transforming their values into paradigmatic American experiences—thrusting Lutherans to the very forefront of evangelical ecumenism. On the other hand, they could also engage in the ethnic exercise of "making their own America": they could use the language and opportunity of American liberty and disestablishment to try to form a larger Pennsylvania German denomination in a setting marked by elements of culture, rather than doctrine. The opinionated regional commentator Carl Gock did not yet know about the later Lutheran confessional battles (nor the later Reformed struggle at Mercersburg) when, in 1830, he predicted that "the German evangelical church in the North American states will soon split themselves into old and new Lutherans, and into Zwinglian and Calvinist Reformed."[98] Yet he neatly described the conflict between alternative Pennsylvania German means of acclimating the church to life in the United States.

Eventually, word would filter across the Atlantic that the Prussian church union had achieved less than its backers had hoped,[99] and debate within the Gettysburg establishment itself would blur the focus of those Lutherans' evangelical ecumenical vision. By then, however, Pennsylvania Germans' commitment to America as their own land of liberty would be solidly in place, with patterns of ethnicization—as well as Americanization—shaping an Old World church into a New World tradition.

7

PENNSYLVANIA GERMANS AT MIDCENTURY

*Ethnic
Americans
in Their
Own Land*

In 1841, at a special synod gathering marking the hundredth anniversary of the German Reformed Church's organization in America, pastor Bernard C. Wolff expounded the group's history, tracing its story from the Rhine Valley to the settlements in Pennsylvania and the Appalachian backcountry. But rather than offering an image of lost refugees separated from their beloved ancestral land, Wolff painted a picture of a people more at home in the New World than they had been in the Old. In fact, listeners learned that their values and churches were the very models their British-stock neighbors were striving to imitate. From Germanic free-city republicanism to Reformed ecclesiology, Wolff believed that his people had "contributed more to the cause of civil and religious liberty" than any other Americans. Certainly, he conceded, Pennsylvania Germans possessed their own peculiar folkways, dreaded "the sprit of innovation," and protested "the substitution of modern inventions for our ancient, venerated customs."[1] In Wolff's mind, however, tradition and adherence to distinctly ethnic habits made his people Americans, and model ones at that.

During the previous half-century, Pennsylvania German church folk had made a place for themselves as feisty citizens in a nation engaged in an unfolding republican experiment. They had begun their journey as cultural outsiders noticeably set apart from the Anglo-American mainstream that in 1790 had dominated the country's political, religious, and social cultures. In the decades that followed, Pennsylvania German Lutheran and Reformed adherents had drawn on the language and ideology that animated the new nation, absorbed American notions of liberty and citizenship, and incorporated them into their group discourse and self-understanding. This process had produced its own tensions and led to internal arguments over group boundaries. But Pennsylvania Germans were also able to mobilize those ideas and that rhetoric to defend cultural particularism; in one sense, then, they turned the success of Americanization against those who had hoped that such a process would naturally lead to cultural assimilation. The result was the formulation of American ethnicity—a sense of peoplehood grounded in and fundamentally shaped by the American experience. Americanization had not meant complete assimilation, but the creation of an identity that defined and preserved peoplehood in New World terms.

By the time of Wolff's sermon, in fact, Pennsylvania German church folk were coming to realize just how American their ethnicity was. For the first time in decades, the forces of immigration were bringing large numbers of newcomers, primarily Irish and German, to the United States.[2] Many of these Continental arrivals ostensibly were the Pennsylvania Germans' kin and fellow church members. In his address, Wolf touched on the problems these immigrants faced in joining American society. The pastor argued that it fell to the descendants of eighteenth-century German immigrants—contemporary Pennsylvania German members of Lutheran and Reformed churches—to shepherd the new immigrants and "imbue this Foreign German population with the spirit of our American Institutions."[3]

If Wolff had correctly sensed the social changes that the rise of mass immigration would usher onto the national stage, his apparent faith in primordial affinity between people whose ancestors had roamed central Europe was misplaced. Despite the apparent links of language and religion,

Wolff's listeners had difficulty relating to the German immigrants of the 1840s and 1850s.[4]

For their part, German arrivals during those decades found the Pennsylvania Germans' culture puzzling even when their theological commitments might have brought them together. The "Old Lutherans" who settled in the Midwest, for example, had much in common with members of the highly confessional Tennessee Synod, a Pennsylvania German group centered in the North Carolina backcountry, Tennessee, and Kentucky. Old Lutheran leader Carl F. W. Walther (1811–87) praised Tennessee Lutheran doctrinal publications, yet the two groups were never able to achieve ecclesiastical unity due to cultural misunderstandings. In good Pennsylvania German style, the Tennessee Lutherans stoutly refused to have their churches or synod incorporated, believing such an action to be "a reprehensible co-mingling of state and church" that would eventually lead to the loss of civil liberty. They likewise abhorred theological seminaries, which, they argued, "tutored [men] in the principles of aristocracy." Missouri Lutheran confessionalists found such Tennessee opinions perplexing and the synod's sharp criticisms offensive, but Pennsylvania Germans had nursed their sentiments in the wake of the Revolution; during the early years of the republic, they had incorporated populist American notions of liberty into their cultural and theological identity.[5] Confessional agreement was not enough to bridge the cultural chasm.

American Identity at the Twilight of the Early Republic

The dramatic increase in immigration was one of the factors that prompted a shift in public discussion of national identity, marking another stage in the evolution of American social thought. A half-century of political maturity had not rendered the question of national unity and purpose less problematic. The country still lacked many common symbols of nationhood, such as a great capital city that showcased cultural achievements. The United States possessed no imposing public monuments and could not boast much in the way of literary and artistic glory.[6] In fact, the nation did not even share a common interstate currency—a practical commercial hindrance to the editor of the *Weekly Messenger of the German Reformed Church*. (He had to remind readers that subscriptions were payable in Pennsylvania,

Maryland, or Virginia currency, with other states' notes discounted or rejected.[7]) Indeed, it was obvious to one German Reformed writer in 1849 that "we cannot speak of an American nationality as a settled and given fact in the same way that we may speak of the nationality of England or France."[8]

While uniformly claiming allegiance to the ideals of the Revolution and the wisdom of the Constitution, Americans in the 1840s and 1850s continued to argue—often with a vigor that foreshadowed disunion—about the legacies and implications of that event and sacred document. In earlier decades, such debates had been weighted toward discussions of ideology and had suggested that citizenship and national identity could transcend differences in custom, material culture, or folkways.

The rise of mass immigration, however, prompted something of a cultural crisis, and many Americans began to conflate ideology and culture—extending a trend begun in the 1820s, as anxious citizens looked for ways in which to secure the republic in the midst of market revolution and social democratization. They argued, for example, that some "races" and religions were predisposed to republican responsibility, while others were not. Factors of national origins and Protestant religion began surfacing more often among the qualities that marked legitimate American-ness.[9] For Pennsylvania Germans who did not suffer from association with Catholicism or the Celtic "race," the question of culture and American identity was nonetheless still significant. As culture itself now combined with political ideology to measure fit citizenship, it became less an arena for negotiating ethnicity and more a standard for determining American identity. The impulse behind the establishment and spread of public education during these years sprang from the notion that proper Americans could be cast from a single cultural mold, and much of the intellectual sophistication behind such pedagogical enterprises looked to the Anglo-American Northeast and British-rooted Protestantism for cultural cues.

On another level, the mid-nineteenth-century shift in dialogue about American identity contributed to a larger pattern of regional identification and the rising awareness of geographic sectionalism. Regional cultural traditions vied for influence and position in a quest to affirm their legitimacy and shape national direction. In this context, Pennsylvania German identity became something of a sectional concern itself, a development that paralleled national fragmentation as ethnicity became a surrogate for geographic sectionalism. As midcentury approached, Pennsylvania Germans became more vocal about their status as legitimate Americans, and their ethnic identity grew more self-conscious, even prompting a measure of ethnic consolidation. Some older divisions, such as the split between the German Reformed "old church" and the Free Synod, mended. The impetus for that reunion came in the wake of the Free Synod's rejection of Dutch Reformed ecumenical overtures. Argued Free Synod pastor Joseph S. Dubbs (1796–1877), "After all we are *German* Reformed and not *Dutch* Reformed; therefore the logical step is to reunite with the old Synod."[10]

Ethnic pride surfaced even among those once considered advocates of greater assimilation. Samuel S. Schmucker, for example, had cultivated a warm familiarity with many Anglo-American Protestant leaders, yet he could also be the first to snipe that New Englanders cherish the "memory of the pilgrim fathers ... with an interest bordering on veneration." Schmucker himself, on the other hand, would "hesitate not to affirm that in regard to piety and zeal, [Lutheran] father [Heinrich M.] Muhlenberg, and [Peter] Brunholtz, and [John F.] Handschuh, and [Martin] Bolzius were by no means inferiors to [John] Cotton, [Thomas] Hooker, [John] Davenport, or the Mathers." In fact, Schmucker contended, when it came to learning and erudition colonial Lutheran clerics "were their superiors."[11]

"An American German from Head to Foot"

Perhaps the figure who best exemplified midcentury ethnic self-consciousness among Pennsylvania German church folk was Henry Harbaugh (1817–67), the pastor, poet, professor, and promoter of the Pennsylvania Dutch dialect who, at his death, was remembered as "an American German from head to foot.... In all his moral and religious instincts he was one of [them]."[12] (Fig. 13.) Reared in a south-central Pennsylvania German community, he imbibed a culture that taught him aversion "to all excitement in politics, all wild speculation in business, and all fanaticism in religion."[13] After trying his hand at farming and spending several years on the Ohio frontier in an area populated by Yankee pioneers, Harbaugh returned to Pennsylvania and prepared for the German Reformed ministry—a vocation that occupied the rest of his life in Lewisburg, Lancaster, Lebanon, and Mercersburg. Despite association in his later years with denominational controversialists at the church's Mercersburg Theological Seminary, Harbaugh was not primarily a theological polemicist, but rather a pastor and writer who influenced and spoke for a spectrum of Pennsylvania Germans.[14] He preached and wrote in a vein of Pennsylvania German folk spirituality that drew on religious and cultural themes to give moral shape to an overarching sense of peoplehood.[15]

Although Harbaugh supported the goals of a few Anglo-American evangelical reform causes,[16] he was often a vigorous opponent of evangelical betterment efforts such as public schools, which he saw as a means of cultural assimilation. "Shame on him who will know nothing of his parentage," Harbaugh thundered from the pulpit during one memorable sermon. "Shame on him who disowns his ancestry.... Both shame and sin on him who is ashamed of his countrymen [i.e., fellow ethnics]; he brands himself as a hypocrite in the eyes of all nations!"[17] He also condemned those who shrank from bilingualism, as if it were "evidence of ignorance, to be able to speak *two* languages instead of one!"[18]

Yet Harbaugh was never simply an advocate of preserving and perpetuating ancient tradition. Perhaps more than any other midcentury Pennsylvania German leader, he was at the forefront of the self-conscious creation and promotion of American ethnicity through his composition and publication of Pennsylvania Dutch dialect poetry.[19] Especially in the context of rising levels of immigration from Germany, the American-derived dialect set its speakers apart from newer arrivals and European Germans.[20] Much of Harbaugh's verse took the form of narrative description of Pennsylvania German home and community life. As a churchman, Harbaugh "devoted himself specifically to ... the German church planted in America" and wrote several works on colonial and early-nineteenth-century American German Reformed history.[21] Religion and Pennsylvania German religious values, in fact, were always constituent parts of Harbaugh's understanding of ethnicity, perhaps best illustrated in one of his long-remembered toasts: "There are seven learned languages, English and German, Latin and Greek and Hebrew, these are five. The sixth is called Pennsylvania German, the seventh is German Reformed!"[22]

Passing on a Pennsylvania German Identity

Harbaugh was an active agent in the effort to forge and pass on a coherent and religiously linked Pennsylvania German ethnicity. In 1850, he launched *The Guardian,* a magazine targeting Pennsylvania German youth with the

Fig. 13 Henry Harbaugh, German Reformed pastor, poet, professor, and promoter of the Pennsylvania Dutch dialect. Courtesy of Evangelical and Reformed Historical Society, Lancaster, Pa.

aim of fostering spiritual devotion and ethnic identity. (Fig. 14.) The publication circulated widely and developed a loyal readership.[23] In some ways the magazine reflected the Victorian romanticism of the day: its literary features offered idyllic visions of rural life, testimonies to self-education, and didactic pieces on frugality, respect for authority, and love of the church.[24] But *The Guardian* was also an unmistakably Pennsylvania German periodical that included healthy doses of German church history and was committed to the heritage whose "blood fills up our veins, and whose language is on our tongues."[25]

Harbaugh urged readers to appropriate and "vindicate" the "rich inheritance of associations and principles" that they possessed.[26] This inheritance included a ritual culture that promoted tradition, piety, and localist political sensibilities. Harbaugh promoted ethnic devotional literature and the Pennsylvania German celebration of the church year. He was a special advocate of Christmas, and *The Guardian* was filled with holiday stories and explanations of "very beautiful and significant customs." *The Guardian* also included articles by nineteenth-century Pennsylvania German historian I. Daniel Rupp (1803–78), who linked religious and ethnic themes of immigration with church and community history. Readers found warnings against marriages to members of other denominations and dismay over the confusion caused by evangelical revivalism. Harbaugh provided essays on Reformation-era and colonial American German church leaders, and for Reformed subscribers, he recommended Lewis Mayer's *History of the German Reformed Church* to understand the difference between their denomination and the Dutch Reformed.[27]

Harbaugh also devoted himself to countering what he considered the "reproach . . . upon Pennsylvania, and especially upon the Germans" that circulated among Anglo-conformists who structured definitions of American identity with cultural precision. Schoolchildren throughout the country learned that "there was no such a thing as ignorance at all among the descendants of the Puritans," *The Guardian* claimed, while "ignorance was confined to the Germans of Pennsylvania," and textbooks sounded the "glory and honor of every thing that is English."[28] His contentions rested on evidence such as public school literary exercises in which Pennsylvania German students read original compositions on "Our Forefathers," but then discussed only English history. "*Our English* forefathers!" *The Guardian* gasped. The schoolhouse was filled not with Yankee New Englanders or

The Guardian.

VOL. V.—JULY, 1854.—No. VII.

NEW ENGLAND SUPERSTITION.

BY THE EDITOR.

"I'll tell the tale as it was told to me."

"SUPERSTITION.—The Boston Post says that the following took place in Jewett city, Connecticut. About eight years ago, Horace Ray died there of consumption; since then two of his sons have died of the same disease; and another son being sick with the same disease, his friends, under the belief that the dead brothers were feeding on the living, went to their graves on the 8th, dug them up, and burned the corpses! This is an instance of superstition such as missionaries tell us of among 'the heathen.'"

The above paragraph, which met our eye the other day in a paper, attracted our attention. We commend it to the consideration of all such as have been taught to believe that there are none but wise men in the east. While we are willing to confess to much darkness reigning in the middle States, we protest against that affectation and credulity which assents to the idea that there is no superstition and ignorance in New England, while reproach is cast, in this respect, upon Pennsylvania, and especially upon the Germans. Yea, we go farther, and say that in superstition, intolerance and childishness, especially in public, civil and ecclesiastical acts, New England has always gone far ahead of German Pennsylvania. To say the contrary is slanderous, or betrays an ignorance of history too gross to be endured.

We appeal to history.

1. Upon no page of the history of German Pennsylvania are there to be found such silly and childish laws as are to be found among the "blue laws" of Connecticut. We have them not now at hand, and cannot quote instances; but having met them in a small volume several years ago, the impression is yet fresh in our memory.

2. In regard to intolerance and religious persecution, show me one act of public religious intolerance, sanctioned by law and authority, in the whole history of Pennsylvania.

Now, look to New England. In 1635, Roger Williams was

Fig. 14 A title page from Harbaugh's magazine, *The Guardian.*
Courtesy of Evangelical and Reformed Historical Society,
Lancaster, Pa.

British-stock southerners, but "by the descendants of settlers who never saw Albion's shore."

History books "legislated into the hands of our children" might claim to be national in scope, *The Guardian* charged, but in truth, "they are sectional," and in a "thoroughly *mixed* nation like ourselves" were sure to offend the "ancestry . . . religious opinions . . . habits of life and modes of thought" of many citizens. "Over and over again have we seen children recite that which boldly suppressed facts of dearest interest to them, while in place thereof some empty husks were substituted," the essayist complained.[29]

Yet damaged pride was only part of editor Harbaugh's concern. Essentially, he was eager to show readers that Pennsylvania German values and culture meshed with American republican principles—indeed, that they were a better fit than those of the nation's other contenders for the role of cultural caretaker—and that his people could be both model citizens and culturally distinct. In a lead article entitled "New England Superstition," Harbaugh criticized what he termed Yankee "intolerance and childishness" that had "always gone far ahead of German Pennsylvania." Nor were such flaws unrelated to one another or of minor significance, he argued, since irrational superstition bred intolerance of the sort that had produced the Salem witch trials and other examples of bigotry and despotism that ran counter to true American political principles. As self-appointed arbiters of culture, Anglo-conformists conflated the "is" and the "ought" of national purpose, leading them down the road to tyranny. In contrast, Harbaugh claimed, "persecuted brethren from Virginia and New England" had often sought refuge among tolerant Pennsylvania Germans who understood that American identity rested on local authority, custom, and religious liberty, not cultural uniformity.[30]

Ultimately, the crusading spirit of Anglo-conformism spawned nervousness and innovation, Harbaugh believed, and produced social extremism that Pennsylvania Germans noted with alarm. From Joseph Smith and the rapping Fox sisters to Millerites and Universalists, Anglo-American evangelical efforts at moral ultraism had resulted in half-baked fanaticism. All boded ill for the ongoing stability of the nation. Schemes "for the renovation of the world" offering "some sovereign balm for the wants and wounds of human nature" contrasted with Pennsylvania German commitment to tradition, moderation, and quiet piety that prudently refrained from the "wickedness of making 'blue laws,' burning witches, and cutting off people's heads because they would not be as pious as we ourselves ... [nor] be religious in the same way." *The Guardian* preached the practice of public piety, but condemned the impulse to link church and state in any way, terming such efforts not only "silly and childish," but also actually threatening to the nation's republican principles and to American liberty.[31]

In previous decades, Pennsylvania Germans had debated not the merits but the *means* of Americanization. Most had taken up democratic populist rhetoric to defend local cultural particularity and ethnic separatism; some others had wedded Whiggish notions of reform and national purpose to their traditions of clerical authority and the virtues of German piety. These streams merged in the pages of *The Guardian*. Harbaugh and other writers defended local custom and ethnic culture in terms of public good and republican virtue, but cooled the populist rhetoric that seemed too closely associated with demagogic instability.[32] "There is nothing more true and more significant than the common phrase, 'This is a great country,'" *The Guardian*'s editor noted, but sadly added, "[i]n nothing is our country greater than in its everlasting restlessness."[33] At the same time, *The Guardian* stood for the authority of virtue and character, but with little confidence in the success of its public promotion. "Just look at our common elections and see how matters are conducted there," contributor "J. E. G." of Ephrata, Pennsylvania, sighed, "going from house to house, ... [with] a hardy press of the hand, or long strains of flattering talk," so that a politician's success does not depend upon his constituents' asking "how respectable his character or how sound his principles." "Respect for civil authority and the laws framed by our government, is too much wanting in our free America," J. E. G. concluded.[34]

Yet in a society increasingly under the intellectual sway of Anglo-conformists, the writer tempered Whiggish political sentiment. Readers found not a call for a custodial state to resurrect, inculcate, or guard morality, but fears of intrusive government. "I mean no apology for bad government or public extravagance," J. E. G. asserted, but explained that he "was very much amused" when discussion turned to "'hard times and heavy taxes'" and people offered political solutions to the nation's ills. "Now I do not in the least doubt" that those who believe such sentiments "were all upright and sincere in their protestations," the author wrote, "and I would by no means despise their simplicity; but according to my opinion they do greatly err" in placing confidence in legislated social reform.[35]

Ethnic Americans

Pennsylvania German Lutheran and Reformed adherents at midcentury believed themselves to be Americans despite—and perhaps even because of—the growing chorus of Anglo-conformist voices suggesting that Americanization required cultural assimilation. Henry Harbaugh, among others, sensed that ethnicization was itself a process of Americanization and that ethnic faithfulness was possible for a people who had become American.

Clergy such as Harbaugh were in a good position to judge just how American those faithful were. The 1850s witnessed the eruption of a new set of conflicts within Pennsylvania German churches—though ones that involved lay members to a lesser degree than the boisterous contests of the 1810s, 1820s, and 1830s. Often summarized under the shorthand appellations of the "Mercersburg debate" among German Reformed and the "Americanist controversy" in Lutheran churches, the conflicts included a range of specific issues and ideas that have warranted their own substantial studies.[36] German Reformed adherents and thinkers at the group's seminary in Mercersburg, Pennsylvania, struggled with issues of religious authority, seeking ways to ground themselves in a nation and culture that they now called home, but that offered little support for notions of transcendent tradition. Likewise, Lutherans debated the place and relative merits of several different Reformation-era formulations of faith for a contemporary American context.

The opinions of more recent European arrivals complicated the controversies, but what is significant is the fact that by the time these conflicts surfaced, Pennsylvania German opponents actually held much in common as ethnic Americans. In fact, the timing of these controversies was far from coincidental, because they centered on new sets of problems having to do with tradition and the authority of times and places that now seemed far away, indeed, to American faithful. Pennsylvania Germans disagreed about the best way to accomplish that mixing of paradigms, and they produced competing answers that drew on romanticism, idealism, primitivism, and denominationalism. In any case, they were diverse solutions to a problem posed by the success of Americanization, a problem facing people determined to be active participants in the New World's social and political experience. Interpreters have often mistaken these conflicts for battles over the possibility or promise of Americanization, rather than properly seeing them as the *product* of successful Americanization—a view only attained by taking seriously the events of the preceding decades.[37]

The relationship of religion, ethnicity, and American identity continued to be close during the second half of the nineteenth century and even into the twentieth. Again, the processes of Americanization and ethnicization were linked. In the wake of the battles that rocked Lutheran and Reformed churches in the 1850s and 1860s—battles predicated upon their participants' common stake in asking New World questions of Old World traditions—exhausted clergy and parishioners "began to turn back upon themselves," cultivating an "upswelling of ethnic feeling" that, as Don Yoder has suggested, "bridged the gulf between the theological parties that were dividing the church by pointing up the church's part in the overarching Pennsylvania German culture." Yoder best illustrated his point with German Reformed examples, noting the many ways in which that denomination's Pennsylvania German members rallied around ethnic institutions in the second half of the nineteenth century even as they moved closer to the nation's dominant commercial, political, and educational centers.[38]

Among Lutherans, as well, Pennsylvania German members held their own interests against the ethnic approaches of Scandinavian and more recently arrived German coreligionists. Educator and pastor Samuel K. Brobst (1822–76) of Lehigh County, Pennsylvania, for example, played a role similar to Harbaugh's; after 1847, he published a youth magazine entitled *Jugend Freund Aller Christlichen Benennungen*.[39] Ordained the year he launched his magazine, Brobst assumed the posture of culture bearer in the pulpit as well as in the classroom. Bowing to the inevitable establishment of public education even in rural areas, he worked to found, in 1866, the Keystone Normal School in Kutztown, Pennsylvania, as an institution to train teachers sensitive to Pennsylvania German culture—who would then prove suitable for placement in ethnic communities. He also presented eloquent pleas for bilingual education for all students and offered strikingly modern-sounding arguments for cultural diversity.[40]

Both Pennsylvania German communions remained carriers and promoters of ethnicity and institutional sources of differentiation from the German-American identities that blossomed among later European immigrants.[41] Nor did the postbellum centralization of denominational bureaucracy—with its tendency to dissolve local expressions of faith—fully succeed in limiting ethnic attachments. In 1891, clergy and lay leaders founded the

Pennsylvania German Society as another forum for promoting their own story.[42] Predictably, its gatherings and publications stressed the American character of this still easily identifiable and distinct people.

Religion, Ethnicity, and American Culture

"Was this great nation descended from a ship-load of settlers landed in 1620 on Plymouth Rock?" *The Guardian* asked in 1855.[43] The answer, despite what the writer may have believed, has always been both "yes" and "no." The experience of making and remaking one's identity in a new land has been recapitulated innumerable times since 1620, and acculturation to some Anglo-American patterns of life has often been part of a successful effort to resist actual assimilation. Among American ethnic groups, religious identities have frequently helped provide stability and structures for negotiating ethnicity amid the stress of cultural conflict.

Religion was a peculiar factor in the Pennsylvania German experience, even though it might strike later observers as a poor servant of ethnic differentiation. As northern European Protestants descended from the mainstream and magisterial Reformation, German Reformed and Lutheran adherents might have seemed to blend easily into the American religious scene and could hardly, at first glance, be saddled with the worldview that theologian H. Richard Niebuhr labeled "Christ against culture."[44] Yet in the context of the Early Republic, their position on the cultural margin gave even their religious sensibilities a different cast, transforming them into resources for mounting an ethnic defense. In the Early Republic, religion was not simply the ideological servant of a single American culture; it was an agent in the process of cultural creation. Religion was also more than a simple symbol of ethnicity: it provided the intellectual resources, community setting, and public arena for sorting out the claims of culture and ideology that emerged in the often disorienting days of the early nineteenth century. Pennsylvania German religion did much more than reflect the times. It mediated and managed them.

That process promised an interesting—even novel—mixture of cultural interaction, ethnicization, and formation of national identity. A nation that defined itself in ideological terms eventually faced the question of whether its ideology produced, transcended, or was limited by culture. Initially, the question nearly went unnoticed in a land whose enfranchised members in overwhelming numbers shared British political and religious legacies. The presence of a sizable and geographically concentrated cultural minority near the new nation's center, however, ensured that the matter never became merely academic. Pennsylvania Germans explored the relationship of ideology and culture throughout the period, eventually discovering that republican principles could be marshaled to defend cultural particularism as much as to fuel the universalizing impulse to invent a new society in a "New World."

In that combination of transcendent ideology and local culture, Pennsylvania German ethnicity took shape. As Kathleen Neils Conzen has written, ethnicity defined by common cultural folkways is not enough to sustain a sense of peoplehood. What groups living in a society built on competition need are common interests.[45] While Conzen suggested interests tied to economic class or labor opportunities, Lutheran and German Reformed adherents made local culture itself their interest, defending it in terms of republican ideology. In the process, of course, their culture changed, absorbing assumptions from its new context and separating elements once tightly fused. The result was ethnicization and Americanization. That combination and its outcomes would be repeated by others in the years to follow. It would confound those who believed that cultural assimilation and cultural separatism were stark and singular choices, but it also suggests why a nation could accept plurality without necessarily sorting out the details of pluralism. In another age of mass immigration and cultural debate, the dilemma of those details persists, but so does the claim of the Early Republic's Pennsylvania Germans that the politics of liberty is bound not by culture, but by commitment.

NOTES

INTRODUCTION

1. Johann G. Kohl, *Reisen in Canada und durch die Staaten New York und Pennsylvanien, von J. G. Kohl* (Stuttgart: J. G. Cotta, 1856), 528: "schien es mir, wenn sie von den 'Yankees,' den 'Neuengländern,' den 'Eirschen' (Irländern) u. redeten, und sich dann wieder, 'Amerikaner' nannten, als wenn sie das Wort für sich im prägnanten Sinne nähmen, und sich für die Amerikaner ausgeben wollten."

2. Heinz Kloss, "Fünf Stationen einer Reise in Pennsylvanien," *Der Auslanddeutsche: Halbmonatsschrift für Auslanddeutschtum und Auslandkunde. Mitteilungen des Deutschen Ausland-Institutes, Stuttgart* 14 (1931): 2–4. From a linguistic standpoint, see Heinz Kloss, "German-American Language Maintenance Efforts," in *Language Loyalty in the United States: The Maintenance and Perpetuation of Non-English Mother Tongues by American Ethnic and Religious Groups*, ed. Joshua A. Fishman (The Hague: Mouton, 1966), 215–23.

3. Don Yoder, "The 'Dutchman' and the *'Deitschlenner'*: The New World Confronts the Old," *Yearbook of German-American Studies* 23 (1988): 1–17; R. Laurence Moore, *Religious Outsiders and the Making of America* (New York: Oxford University Press, 1986), ix, xi, xiii.

4. This study uses the term "adherents" to describe Pennsylvania Germans associated with Lutheran and Reformed churches. Exact membership numbers are difficult to obtain; see Charles H. Glatfelter, *Pastors and People: German Lutheran and Reformed Churches in the Pennsylvania Field, 1717–1793* (Breinigsville, Pa.: Pennsylvania German Society, 1981), 2:177. Lutheran and Reformed clergy often reported annually the number of active communicants (those who participated in eucharistic communion) in their charges, but the number of baptized members was significantly larger. Then, too, some pastors did not send reports every year, so even annual totals taken from synod or ministerium records are almost always incomplete and undercounted.

5. This study uses the term "Anglo-American" to refer to the British-stock Americans (English and British borderland Scots and Irish) who constituted the demographic majority white population in the American colonial era and Early Republic. While these people did not represent a wholly unified culture, one can speak broadly of concepts such as Anglo-American notions of law or an Anglo-American Protestant heritage (even if highly contested) that drew on the common experiences of the English and Scottish Reformation. The related term "anglophone" refers not so much to the actual English speech of Anglo-Americans, but to the culture and society—broadly construed—that Anglo-Americans developed. In some cases, particularly those involving early-nineteenth-century evangelical Protestant reform movements, the term "Anglo-American" is an adjective describing the transatlantic, international character of such movements.

6. The next largest (though much smaller) non-British-stock white population in colonial British America comprised the Dutch of New York, who had begun settling in the seventeenth century. During the eighteenth century, however, they had experienced an extensive process of anglicization—in contrast to Americanization—and never underwent the sort of ethnicization discussed here. By the time of the Revolution and the founding of the republic, Americans of Dutch descent were largely part of the cultural mainstream to the extent that their experience of coming to think of themselves as Americans during and after the Revolution proceeded apart from ethnicization. See Randall Balmer, *A Perfect Babel of Confusion: Dutch Religion and English Culture in the Middle Colonies* (New York: Oxford University Press, 1989), especially 155–56. Dutch identity persisted longer in the rural areas around Albany, though even here, there had been a great deal of Dutch-Puritan melding by 1800. See David G. Hackett, *The Rude Hand of Innovation: Religion and the Social Order in Albany, New York, 1652–1836* (New York: Oxford University Press, 1991); see also A. G. Roeber, "'The Origin of Whatever is not English Among Us,'" in *Strangers Within the Realm: Cultural Margins of the First British Empire*, ed. Bernard Bailyn and Philip D. Morgan (Chapel Hill: The University of North Carolina Press, 1991), 236–37. Joyce D. Goodfriend, *Before the Melting Pot: Society and Culture in Colonial New York City, 1664–1730* (Princeton: Princeton University Press, 1992), argues against the term "anglicization" with regard to the Dutch, but with good reason also resists calling the Dutch experience ethnicization. In any case, her study details an early colonial period: she reports that "[a]fter 1700 the ethnic basis of community life began to fracture" and agrees that by the mid-1700s "other forms of social identity superseded ethnicity" among New York's original residents (7).

7. See Philip Gleason, "American Identity and Americanization," and William Petersen, "Concepts of Ethnicity"; both appear in *Harvard Encyclopedia of American Ethnic Groups*, ed. Stephan Thernstrom (Cambridge: Harvard University Press, 1980), 31–58 and 234–42, respectively. Many historians cite sociologist Milton M. Gordon on this point: see his *Assimilation in American Life: The Role of Race, Religion, and National Origins* (New York: Oxford University Press, 1964), 23–25.

8. See, for example, definitions and discussion in George DeVos and Lola Romanucci-Ross, eds., *Ethnic Identity: Cultural Continuities and Change* (Palo Alto, Calif.: Mayfield Publishing, 1975). Anthropologist Fredrik Barth does, however, suggest a definition more akin to that employed by historians: "In some social systems ethnic groups co-reside though no major aspect of structure is based on ethnic inter-relations. These are generally referred to as societies with minorities.... [S]uch situations have come about as a result of external historical events; the cultural differentiae have not sprung from the local organizational context— rather, a pre-established cultural contrast is brought into conjunction with a pre-established social system and is made relevant to life there in a diversity of ways." Fredrik Barth, introduction to *Ethnic Groups and Boundaries: The Social Organization of Cultural Differences*, ed. Fredrik Barth (Boston: Little, Brown, 1969), 9–15, 30 (quotation from 30).

9. Dale T. Knobel, *Paddy and the Republic: Ethnicity and Nationality in Antebellum America* (Middletown: Wesleyan University Press, 1986), xi.

10. Jonathan D. Sarna, "From Immigrants to Ethnics: Toward a New Theory of 'Ethnicization,'" *Ethnicity* 5 (December 1978): 370–78. A study that stresses the social construction of immigrant group identity in a new American environment is Noel Ignatiev's *How the Irish Became White* (New York: Routledge, 1995).

11. Since no German nation-state existed at the time, these people's most obvious commonality to outsiders was language. This linguistic-ethnic ascription is somewhat like that experienced by Colombians, Hondurans, Mexicans, and others who, upon immigration to the United States, become "Hispanics"—a linguistically based ethnic designation. See Suzanne Oboler, *Ethnic Labels, Latino Lives: Identity and the Politics of (Re)Presentation in the United States*

(Minneapolis: University of Minnesota Press, 1995), 1–16. Ethnicization can, in fact, proceed to a point that meets anthropological understandings of ethnicity. The people who came to be labeled Pennsylvania Germans hailed from a variety of primarily Rhine Valley states, but in numbers and from locations too varied to constitute a discrete genetic group. Over time, however, the interplay of their self-identification and ascribed status in North America created a group sensibility that resulted in remarkable rates of endogamy and kinship. Victor Greene coined the term "ethnicization" in *For God and Country: The Rise of Polish and Lithuanian Ethnic Consciousness in America* (Madison: University of Wisconsin Press, 1975), 3–10.

12. Although the Lutheran and Reformed Pennsylvanians of this study at least controlled their own religious institutions, this was not the case for all Pennsylvania Germans; cf. the struggle for national parishes by Catholic Pennsylvania Germans in Vincent J. Fecher, *A Study of the Movement for German National Parishes in Philadelphia and Baltimore, 1787–1802* (Rome: Apud Aedes Universitatis Gregorianae, 1955).

13. Constitution of the Commonwealth of Pennsylvania [1790], art. 9, sec. 3, in *Pennsylvania Archives*, 1st ser. (Philadelphia: Joseph Severns, 1856), 12:22. Historian Leslie Woodcock Tentler suggested this idea in a response to a paper on Pennsylvania Germans that I presented at the 1999 American Historical Association annual meeting in Washington, D.C.

14. Kathleen Neils Conzen, David A. Gerber, Ewa Morawska, George E. Pozzetta, and Rudolph J. Vecoli, "The Invention of Ethnicity: A Perspective from the U.S.A.," *Journal of American Ethnic History* 12 (Fall 1992): 3–63; Werner Sollors, ed., *The Invention of Ethnicity* (New York: Oxford University Press, 1989). See also Kathleen Neils Conzen, *Making Their Own America: Assimilation Theory and the German Peasant Pioneer* (New York: Berg Publishing, 1990), 1–33; idem, "The Paradox of German-American Assimilation," *Yearbook of German-American Studies* 16 (1981): 156–57; George J. Sánchez, *Becoming Mexican American: Ethnicity, Culture, and Identity in Chicano Los Angeles, 1900–1945* (New York: Oxford University Press, 1993); Jon Gjerde, *The Minds of the Middle West: Ethnocultural Evolution in the Rural Middle West, 1830–1917* (Chapel Hill: The University of North Carolina Press, 1997); and David A. Gerber, *The Making of an American Pluralism: Buffalo, New York, 1825–1860* (Urbana: University of Illinois Press, 1989). Rob Kroes, *The Persistence of Ethnicity: Dutch Calvinist Pioneers in Amsterdam, Montana* (Urbana: University of Illinois Press, 1992), 7–11, offers some helpful words with regard to the use of "invention" when speaking of the "invention of ethnicity." Cautioning against a slippery postmodern understanding of "invention," he explains how the concept can be useful and held in balance with other historical criteria.

15. For historiographic context, see Russell A. Kazal, "Revisiting Assimilation: The Rise, Fall, and Reappraisal of a Concept in American Ethnic History," *American Historical Review* 100 (April 1995): 437–71.

16. Timothy L. Smith suggested a reason for this difference in the self-understanding of Catholics and Protestants in "Religious Denominations as Ethnic Communities: A Regional Case Study," *Church History* 35 (June 1966): 217–18. Henry F. May's pronouncement of "The Recovery of American Religious History," *American Historical Review* 70 (October 1964): 79–92, and the 1965 founding of the University of Minnesota's Immigration History Research Center signaled the twin emergence of these historical subfields.

17. Walter Nugent, *Structures of American Social History* (Bloomington: Indiana University Press, 1981), 59.

18. But see several pages of an exceptional essay by John Higham, "Integrating America: The Problem of Assimilation in the Nineteenth Century," *Journal of American Ethnic History* 1 (Fall 1981): 10–14. See also chapter 3 of Thomas J. Archdeacon, *Becoming American: An Ethnic History* (New York: Free Press, 1983), 57–84, although it dwells largely on events after the 1830s.

19. Although today "Pennsylvania Dutch" is often considered a misnomer (i.e., an assumed

corruption of Pennsylvania *Deutsch*), it was actually the correct eighteenth-century term for Rhine Valley immigrants. "Dutch," according to the *Oxford English Dictionary*, was the proper English term for the Rhine Valley inhabitants the whole way to Switzerland. Thus, the English spoke of "Dutch" and "Switzer" immigrants where sources today would speak of the Germans and Swiss. (The English also spoke of the "Holland Dutch" or "Low Dutch" to refer to those today known as Dutch.) Nevertheless, this text will generally use "Pennsylvania German" instead of "Pennsylvania Dutch"—not because it is a more correct term, but rather to avoid possible confusion. The text will use "Pennsylvania Dutch" to denote the dialect spoken by the Pennsylvania Germans. See Don Yoder, "Palatine, Hessian, Dutchman: Three Images of the German in America," in *Ebbes fer Alle–Ebber Ebbes fer Dich: Something for Everyone–Something for You*, ed. Albert F. Buffington (Breinigsville, Pa.: Pennsylvania German Society, 1980), 107–29.

20. Many historical sources, however, are catalogued in Emil Meynen, comp. and ed., *Bibliography on German Settlements in Colonial North America, Especially on the Pennsylvania Germans and Their Descendants, 1683–1933* (Leipzig: Otto Harrassowitz, 1937), which contains eight thousand titles. Most of these are late-nineteenth- and early-twentieth-century secondary sources of somewhat limited value.

21. Marianne Wokeck, *Trade in Strangers: The Beginnings of Mass Migration to North America* (University Park: The Pennsylvania State University Press, 1999); Wolfgang Splitter, *Pastors, People, Politics: German Lutherans in Pennsylvania, 1740–1790* (Trier: Wissenschaftlicher Verlag Trier, 1998); Aaron S. Fogleman, *Hopeful Journeys: German Immigration, Settlement, and Political Culture in Colonial America, 1717–1775* (Philadelphia: University of Pennsylvania Press, 1996); A. G. Roeber, *Palatines, Liberty, and Property: German Lutherans in Colonial British America* (Baltimore: The Johns Hopkins University Press, 1993); and idem, "In a German Way? Problems and Potentials of Eighteenth-Century German Social and Emigration History," *William and Mary Quarterly*, 3d ser., 44 (October 1987): 750–74.

22. Frederick C. Luebke's thirty-page bibliographic and historiographic essay on "Three Centuries of Germans in America" jumps over this period: see *Germans in the New World: Essays in the History of Immigration* (Urbana: University of Illinois Press, 1990), 160–61. Despite the advent of Canada's 1971 multicultural policy, Canadian historiography has also largely ignored Pennsylvania German Canadian subjects; see Gerhard Bassler, "German Immigration and Settlement in Canada: English-Canadian Perspectives," in *Emigration and Settlement Patterns of German Communities in North America*, ed. Eberhard Reichmann, LaVern J. Rippley, and Jörg Nagler (Indianapolis: Max Kade German-American Center/Indiana University–Purdue University at Indianapolis, 1995), 325, 333–34.

23. The last lengthy study of the German Reformed Church in the Early Republic can be found in the opening sections of James I. Good, *History of the Reformed Church in the U.S. in the Nineteenth Century* (New York: The Board of Publication of the Reformed Church in America, 1911). Until recently, Lutherans lacked any similar study apart from introductory sections of works on the 1850s confessionalist debates (debates over the place and role of historic Lutheran theological statements in the context of contemporary church life). See, however, Paul A. Baglyos, "In This Land of Liberty: American Lutherans and the Young Republic, 1787–1837" (Ph.D. diss., University of Chicago Divinity School, 1997), though it is heavily weighted toward the experiences of those involved in what would become known as the "Americanist" camp.

24. Manfred S. Zitzman, trans. and ed., "William Helffrich, Horse and Buggy Preacher," *Historical Review of Berks County* 47 (Summer 1982): 118.

25. For an example of cultural factors in the persistence of hand technology among Pennsylvania German artisans in one community, see Thomas R. Winpenny, *Bending Is Not Breaking: Adaptation and Persistence Among Nineteenth-Century Lancaster Artisans* (Lanham, Md.: University Press of America, 1990), xiv–xv, 75–81. Striking studies of perpetuated cultural values with

regard to land use among Germans in the Midwest—and continuing cultural differences separating them from their Yankee or Irish neighbors—is presented in Sonya Salamon, *Prairie Patrimony: Family, Farming, and Community in the Midwest* (Chapel Hill: The University of North Carolina Press, 1992). See also the work of historian Kathleen Neils Conzen, "Peasant Pioneers: Generational Succession Among German Farmers in Frontier Minnesota," in *The Countryside in the Age of Capitalist Transformation: Essays in the Social History of Rural America*, ed. Stephen Hahn and Jonathan Prude (Chapel Hill: The University of North Carolina Press, 1985), 259–92.

26. Curiously, Catherine L. Albanese, *Sons of the Fathers: The Civil Religion of the American Revolution* (Philadelphia: Temple University Press, 1976), 15, suggests that Continental ethnics would have had limited interest in the ideas of collective American national myths. Baglyos, "In This Land of Liberty," also finds Lutheran interest in American exceptionalism rather surprising. On the optimistic hopes of German-speaking immigrants to British America in the first half of the eighteenth century, see Fogleman, *Hopeful Journeys*.

27. Stanley Nadel, *Little Germany: Ethnicity, Religion, and Class in New York City, 1845–80* (Urbana: University of Illinois Press, 1990), especially 160–61.

28. Dale B. Light, *Rome and the New Republic: Conflict and Community in Philadelphia Catholicism Between the Revolution and the Civil War* (Notre Dame: University of Notre Dame Press, 1996), 3–93; Jay P. Dolan, *The Immigrant Church: New York's Irish and German Catholics, 1815–1865* (Baltimore: The Johns Hopkins University Press, 1975), 68–98.

29. Kathleen Neils Conzen, *Immigrant Milwaukee, 1836–1860: Accommodation and Community in a Frontier City* (Cambridge: Harvard University Press, 1976).

CHAPTER 1

1. Benjamin Rush, *A Letter by Dr. Benjamin Rush Describing the Consecration of the German College at Lancaster, in June, 1787*, ed. Lyman H. Butterfield (Lancaster: Franklin and Marshall College, 1945), 16–17. The original 19 June 1787 letter is housed in the Franklin and Marshall College Archives, Shadek-Fackenthal Library, Lancaster, Pa.

2. Ibid., 21.

3. Benjamin Rush, *An Account of the Manners of the German Inhabitants of Pennsylvania by Benjamin Rush*, ed. Theodore E. Schmauk (Lancaster, Pa.: Pennsylvania German Society, 1910), 113. Benjamin Franklin was also anxious about the Pennsylvania German population. See, for instance, Franklin to James Parker, 20 March 1751; Franklin to Peter Collinson, 9 May 1753; "Observations Concerning the Increase of Mankind," in Benjamin Franklin, *The Papers of Benjamin Franklin*, ed. Leonard W. Labaree (New Haven: Yale University Press, 1959–), 4:120, 477–86, 234; and John B. Frantz, "Franklin and the Pennsylvania Germans," *Pennsylvania History* 65 (Winter 1998): 21–34.

4. For an account of Rush's life and thought, see Donald J. D'Elia, *Benjamin Rush: Philosopher of the American Revolution* (Philadelphia: American Philosophical Society, 1974).

5. Fogleman, *Hopeful Journeys*, 6, 28–34.

6. Wokeck, *Trade in Strangers*, 1–58; Aaron S. Fogleman, "Migrations to the Thirteen British North American Colonies, 1700–1775: New Estimates," *Journal of Interdisciplinary History* 22 (Spring 1992): 691–709.

7. Yoder, "Palatine, Hessian, Dutchman," 107–29.

8. Fogleman, *Hopeful Journeys*, 36–65; Wokeck, *Trade in Strangers*, 1–36.

9. *Colonial Records, or Minutes of the Provincial Council of Pennsylvania* (Harrisburg, Pa.: Theodore Fenner, 1851), 4:508.

10. Thomas L. Purvis, "The Pennsylvania Dutch and the German-American Diaspora in

1790," *Journal of Cultural Geography* 6 (Spring/Summer 1986): 81–99; Dieter Cunz, *The Maryland Germans: A History* (Princeton: Princeton University Press, 1948); Klaus G. Wust, *The Virginia Germans* (Charlottesville: The University Press of Virginia, 1969), 1–57; Susanne M. Rolland, "From the Rhine to the Catawba: A Study of Eighteenth-Century Germanic Migration and Adaptation" (Ph.D. diss., Emory University, 1991). The term "Greater Pennsylvania" is drawn from Carl Bridenbaugh, *Myths and Realities: Societies of the Colonial South* (Baton Rouge: Louisiana State University Press, 1952), 127–33. Wust, *Virginia Germans*, 36, says that colonists in the Shenandoah Valley used Pennsylvania currency in the eighteenth century. See also Parke Rouse Jr., *The Great Wagon Road from Philadelphia to the South* (New York: McGraw-Hill, 1973).

11. Don Yoder, "Pennsylvania Germans," in *Harvard Encyclopedia of American Ethnic Groups*, ed. Stephan Thernstrom (Cambridge: Harvard University Press, 1980), 770.

12. Fogleman, *Hopeful Journeys*, 77. For some context on the reassertion of traditional village communal rights, see David Warren Sabean, *Power in the Blood: Popular Culture and Village Discourse in Early Modern Germany* (New York: Cambridge University Press, 1984).

13. James T. Lemon, *The Best Poor Man's Country: A Geographical Study of Early Southeastern Pennsylvania* (Baltimore: The Johns Hopkins University Press, 1972).

14. Thomas L. Purvis, "Patterns of Ethnic Settlement in Late Eighteenth-Century Pennsylvania," *Western Pennsylvania Historical Magazine* 70 (April 1987): 107–22. Nadel, *Little Germany*, 29–61, also discovered especially dense and segregated ethnic settlement patterns and strikingly high rates of endogamy among German settlers of a later period in New York City. Fogleman, *Hopeful Journeys*, 149 and 215–16, cites several marriage studies—including, for example, M. Walter Dundore, "A Population Study of the Pennsylvania Germans in Berks and Neighboring Counties," *Historical Review of Berks County* 28 (Autumn 1963): 113–16.

15. Fogleman, *Hopeful Journeys*, 93–99. In contrast, Lemon, *Best Poor Man's Country*, assumed a high level of mobility on the part of colonial Pennsylvanians, and his work has influenced much of the subsequent scholarship accordingly.

16. Though there is no comprehensive synthesis of Pennsylvania German folkways, representative specific studies include William Woys Weaver, *Sauerkraut Yankees: Pennsylvania-German Foods and Folkways* (Philadelphia: University of Pennsylvania Press, 1983); Tandy Hersh and Charles Hersh, *Samplers of the Pennsylvania Germans* (Birdsboro, Pa.: Pennsylvania German Society, 1991); Beatrice B. Garvan, *The Pennsylvania German Collection* (Philadelphia: Philadelphia Museum of Art, 1982); Scott T. Swank et al., *Arts of the Pennsylvania Germans* ([New York]: Norton, 1983); and Susan M. Burke and Matthew H. Hill, eds., *From Pennsylvania to Waterloo: Pennsylvania-German Folk Culture in Transition* (Kitchener, Ontario: Friends of the Joseph Schneider Haus, 1991).

17. Julian U. Niemcewicz, *Under Their Own Vine and Fig Tree: Travels Through America in 1797–1799 and 1805, with Some Further Account of Life in New Jersey*, trans. and ed. Metchie J. E. Budka (Elizabeth, N.J.: Grassmann Publishing, 1965), 112. Although Niemcewicz was not describing Pennsylvania German sectarians (none lived there at the time), one can still see elements of the costume he described among the most traditional of Old Order Amish groups—the so-called Nebraska Amish of Mifflin County, Pa. Their members have preserved several eighteenth- and early-nineteenth-century Pennsylvania German clothing styles, including large, flat, almost crownless straw hats worn by women working outside. Nearly three decades after Niemcewicz, British visitors in eastern Pennsylvania were able to identify visually Pennsylvania Germans "sitting in the porches of their dwellings." Among the "many ancient customs of their fathers" was their manner of dress, "which was quite foreign, [and] at once pointed out their origin": see Andrew Reed and James Matheson, *A Narrative of the Visit to the American Churches by Deputation from the Congregational Union of England and Wales* (New York: Harper and Brothers, 1835), 2:302. More recent students of material culture have also documented the

different clothing patterns that existed among ethnic Americans of the time; see, for example, Ellen J. Gehret, *Rural Pennsylvania Clothing, Being a Study of the Wearing Apparel of the German and English Inhabitants ... [of] Southeastern Pennsylvania in the Late Eighteenth and Early Nineteenth Centuries* (York, Pa.: Liberty Cap, 1976). Pp. 261–68 contain primary source references on Pennsylvania German clothing.

18. The government-ordered 1757 census of Pennsylvania's Roman Catholics revealed only 949 German Catholics, male and female, aged twelve and older. There were an additional 416 Irish or English adherents to Rome. The entire group of 1,365 was under the care of four priests. See *Pennsylvania Archives*, 1st ser., 3:144–45.

19. Gottlieb Mittelberger, *Gottlieb Mittelberger's Journey to Pennsylvania in the Year 1750 and Return to Germany in the Year 1754*, trans. Oscar Handlin and John Clive (Cambridge: Harvard University Press, 1960), 48; see also 45–47. Stephen L. Longenecker, *Piety and Tolerance: Pennsylvania German Religion, 1700–1850* (Metuchen, N.J.: Scarecrow Press, 1994), 27–70, introduces many of the sectarian groups.

20. On the German Reformed Church in the Rhine Valley that produced most of that body's eighteenth-century American immigrants, see Henry J. Cohn, "The Territorial Princes in Germany's Second Reformation, 1559–1622," in *International Calvinism, 1541–1715*, ed. Menna Prestwich (Oxford: Clarendon Press, 1985), 135–66. Roeber, *Palatines, Liberty, and Property*, 27–94, provides background on the Lutheran communities of the German southwest, as well as the influential center at Halle.

21. Membership figures are difficult to establish, but John B. Frantz, "The Awakening of Religion Among the German Settlers in the Middle Colonies," *William and Mary Quarterly*, 3d ser., 33 (April 1976): 270 n. 19, calculates sixteen thousand communing and/or baptized Lutheran and German Reformed Pennsylvanians in 1740. These figures come from William J. Hinke, *The Life and Letters of the Rev. John Philip Boehm, Founder of the Reformed Church in Pennsylvania, 1683–1749* (Philadelphia: Publication and Sunday School Board of the Reformed Church in the United States, 1916), 83–84. Hinke estimated that there were likely thirty thousand residents with Lutheran and Reformed connections in 1740, but only sixteen thousand were communing and/or baptized. On membership numbers and records, see Glatfelter, *Pastors and People*, 2:177.

22. Glatfelter, *Pastors and People*, 2:161–70. On the Herborn school, see J. Steven O'Malley, *Pilgrimage of Faith: The Legacy of the Otterbeins* (Metuchen, N.J.: Scarecrow Press, 1973), 54–60, 98–109.

23. Fogleman, *Hopeful Journeys*, 86.

24. Gotthardt D. Bernheim, *History of the German Settlements and of the Lutheran Church in North and South Carolina ... to the Close of the First Half of the Present Century* (Philadelphia: Lutheran Book Store, 1872), 148–54, 175–273; *Historic Sketch of the Reformed Church in North Carolina by a Board of Editors Under the Classis of North Carolina* (Philadelphia: Publication Board of the Reformed Church in the United States, 1908), 13–49; and Fogleman, *Hopeful Journeys*, 92.

25. Frantz, "Awakening of Religion," 266–88; Martin E. Lodge, "The Crisis of the Churches in the Middle Colonies," *Pennsylvania Magazine of History and Biography* 95 (April 1971): 195–220; Dietmar Rothermund, "Political Factions and the Great Awakening," *Pennsylvania History* 26 (October 1959): 317–31; idem, *The Layman's Progress: Religion and Political Experience in Colonial Pennsylvania, 1740–1770* (Philadelphia: University of Pennsylvania Press, 1961), 37–56; Longenecker, *Piety and Tolerance*, 71–104; and Jon Butler, *Awash in a Sea of Faith: Christianizing the American People* (Cambridge: Harvard University Press, 1990), 118–27.

26. Muhlenberg's journals attest to the disorganized state of Lutherans before the Awakening's organizing efforts. See, for instance, Heinrich M. Muhlenberg, *The Journals of Henry Melchior Muhlenberg*, trans. Theodore G. Tappert and John W. Doberstein (Philadelphia:

Evangelical Lutheran Ministerium of Pennsylvania and Adjacent States, 1942), 1:66–67, 88. See also Marthi Pritzker-Ehrlich, "Michael Schlatter (1716–1790): A Man-in-Between," *Yearbook of German-American Studies* 20 (1985): 83–95, and Leonard R. Riforgiato, *Missionary of Moderation: Henry Melchior Muhlenberg and the Lutheran Church in English America* (Lewisburg: Bucknell University Press), 1980. Muhlenberg's influence extended especially among the Germans of Greater Pennsylvania; his work in organizing the ministerium contrasted with that of William Christopher Berkenmeyer (1686–1751), who kept his New York and northern New Jersey Lutherans separate from those in Pennsylvania and more closely tied to Europe.

By 1776, about 45 percent of these denominations' congregations met under union arrangements—see Glatfelter, *Pastors and People*, 2:161–70. (The term "union churches" is commonly understood to refer to jointly constructed and maintained buildings overseen by trustees appointed by both groups. Some writers draw a more narrow definition and limit the label to those few congregations that shared not just a building and cemetery, but also liturgy and pastoral oversight.) There was some precedent to union church practice in the Palatinate *Simultankirchen*, in which Catholic and Reformed congregations shared common buildings. See Don Yoder, "The Palatine Connection: The Pennsylvania German Culture and Its European Roots," in *Germans in America: Retrospect and Prospect*, ed. Randall M. Miller (Philadelphia: German Society of Pennsylvania, 1984), 98.

See also Adolph Spaeth, Henry E. Jacobs, and George F. Spieker, eds., *Documentary History of the Evangelical Lutheran Ministerium of Pennsylvania and Adjacent States. Proceedings of the Annual Conventions from 1748 to 1821* (Philadelphia: Board of Publication of the General Council of the Evangelical Lutheran Church in North America, 1898); *Minutes and Letters of the Coetus of the German Reformed Congregations in Pennsylvania, 1747–1792. Together with Three Preliminary Reports by Rev. John Philip Boehm, 1734–1744* (Philadelphia: Reformed Church Publication Board, 1903); and William J. Hinke, *Ministers of the German Reformed Congregations in Pennsylvania and Other Colonies in the Eighteenth Century* (Lancaster, Pa.: Historical Commission of the Evangelical and Reformed Church, 1951).

27. Frantz, "Awakening of Religion," 288.

28. The German Reformed Church regarded its own singular adherence to the Heidelberg Catechism—in the German language—as a critical mark of distinction. In contrast, the Presbyterians used the Westminster Confession, and the Dutch Reformed used several other Dutch doctrinal formulations. See *Acts and Proceedings of the Coetus and Synod of the German Reformed Church in the United States from 1791 to 1816, Inclusive* (Chambersburg, Pa.: M. Kieffer, 1854; rpt., 1930), 68, 70. See also such claims of Heidelberg exclusivity in the *Weekly Messenger of the German Reformed Church*, 11 January 1837, 287, and 10 April 1839, 746. Indeed, as late as the 1850s, when southern Old School Presbyterians attempted to win over North Carolina German Reformed congregations, "so strong was their unalterable attachment to the doctrines of the Heidelberg Catechism, that union ... was an impossibility": see *Historic Sketch of the Reformed Church in North Carolina*, 72.

29. E.g., Laura Becker, "Diversity and Its Significance in an Eighteenth-Century Pennsylvania Town," in *Friends and Neighbors: Group Life in America's First Pluralist Society*, ed. Michael Zuckerman (Philadelphia: Temple University Press, 1982), 196–221.

30. Fogleman, *Hopeful Journeys*, 127–48. More background is found in Alan W. Tully, "Englishmen and Germans: National-Group Contact in Colonial Pennsylvania, 1700–1755," *Pennsylvania History* 45 (July 1978): 237–56, and Sally Schwartz, *"A Mixed Multitude": The Struggle for Toleration in Colonial Pennsylvania* (New York: New York University Press, 1987), 159–291.

31. Roeber, *Palatines, Liberty, and Property*. The study deals with regions beyond Greater Pennsylvania.

32. Paul A. W. Wallace, *The Muhlenbergs of Pennsylvania* (Philadelphia: University of Pennsylvania Press, 1950), 274–302. The Muhlenbergs were an unusually politically active clan; at

one time or another between 1789 and 1949, six family members held seats in Congress representing districts in Pennsylvania and Ohio. On the limited Pennsylvania German Lutheran participation in politics, see Splitter, *Pastors, People, Politics*, 66–86, 135–254.

33. One must take critically works such as that by Willi Paul Adams, "The Colonial German-Language Press and the American Revolution," in *The Press and the American Revolution*, ed. Bernard Bailyn and John B. Hench (Worcester, Mass.: American Antiquarian Society, 1980), 151–228, which assumes that Pennsylvania Germans of the Revolutionary era shared Anglo-American political opinions, assumptions, and goals.

34. Gordon S. Wood, *The Creation of the American Republic, 1776–1787* (Chapel Hill: The University of North Carolina Press, 1969).

35. On the early history of Franklin College, see Joseph H. Dubbs, *History of Franklin and Marshall College* (Lancaster: Franklin and Marshall College Alumni Association, 1903), and Frederic S. Klein, *The Spiritual and Educational Background of Franklin and Marshall College* (Lancaster: Franklin and Marshall College, 1939). For a number of reasons, Franklin College—though well endowed—languished during the first half of the nineteenth century. In 1853, it merged with the academically respectable but financially insolvent Marshall College to create Franklin and Marshall College. On Franklin College's place in a larger educational scheme, see Benjamin Rush, "Of the Mode of Education Proper in a Republic," and "Education Agreeable to a Republican Form of Government," both in Benjamin Rush, *The Selected Writings of Benjamin Rush*, ed. Dagobert D. Runes (New York: Philosophical Library, 1947), 87–100, especially 98.

36. The design included a shield containing the coats of arms of England, Scotland, Ireland, France, the Dutch Republic, and the Holy Roman Empire. This composite emblem was flanked by Liberty and her pileus on one side and a rifle- and tomahawk-carrying American soldier on the other. The design is described by John Adams (who sat on the Congress's Great Seal design committee) to Abigail Adams, 14 August 1776, in Lyman H. Butterfield, ed., *Adams Family Correspondence* (Cambridge: Harvard University Press, 1963), 2:96.

37. Joseph Galloway tied American Revolutionary and republican ideology to the legacies of the English Reformation and English Civil War; see his *Historical and Political Reflections on the Rise and Progress of the American Revolution . . .* (London: G. Wilkie, [1780]), 3, 24–42.

38. David Hackett Fischer, *Albion's Seed: Four British Folkways in America* (New York: Oxford University Press, 1989).

39. This is the basic thesis of Hans Kohn's *American Nationalism: An Interpretive Essay* (New York: Macmillan, 1957). Kohn's work remains valuable, though its insights should be combined with those of later works, such as Bernard Bailyn's *The Ideological Origins of the American Revolution* (Cambridge: Harvard University Press, 1967) or David Waldstreicher's *In the Midst of Perpetual Fetes: The Making of American Nationalism, 1776–1820* (Chapel Hill: The University of North Carolina Press, 1997). See also Wilbur Zelinsky, *Nation into State: The Shifting Symbolic Foundations of American Nationalism* (Chapel Hill: The University of North Carolina Press, 1988).

40. Waldstreicher, *Perpetual Fetes*, 53–173; see 1–14 for a recent review of the literature on the concept of nationalism in the Early Republic. See also Albanese, *Sons of the Fathers*, especially 143–81.

41. Paul C. Nagel, *This Sacred Trust: American Nationality, 1798–1898* (New York: Oxford University Press, 1971), xii. Eric Foner, *The Story of American Freedom* (New York: Norton, 1998), provides an overview of the predominant definitions of liberty in American history.

42. Gleason, "American Identity and Americanization," 31–33.

43. While historians of ethnicity in the later nineteenth and twentieth centuries have appropriately dispensed with the notion that perceptions about ethnic diversity are tied necessarily to the presence of many immigrants of different backgrounds, the situation in the Early Republic was somewhat different. Aaron S. Fogleman's persuasive argument about the

relationship between the shifts in immigration and national self-understanding suggests that immigration was a factor in American thinking about ethnicity and the ideological foundations of national identity in the Early Republic. See Aaron S. Fogleman, "From Slaves, Convicts, and Servants to Free Passengers: The Transformation of Immigration in the Era of the American Revolution," *Journal of American History* 85 (June 1998): 43–76.

44. Many anglophone national political leaders assumed the demographic dominance of British-stock Americans, as in the *Federalist* no. 2, which claimed that the population of the United States was descended from a common British ancestry and that all Americans shared language, religion, customs, and political assumptions and outlook in common. See Jacob E. Cooke, ed., *The Federalist* (Middletown: Wesleyan University Press, 1961), 1:9.

45. Peter D. McClelland and Richard J. Zeckhauser, *Demographic Dimensions of the New Republic: American Interregional Migration, Vital Statistics, and Manumissions, 1800–1860* (Cambridge: Cambridge University Press, 1982), 38, 100–101, calculates 121,655. A study that specifically documents German-speaking arrivals in the United States gives greater totals, though it covers a somewhat different period. It counts 31,700 German immigrants during 1783–1819, compared with 87,700 English and Scots (combined) and 199,300 Irish. In each case, about half of the people came during 1810–19; see Hans-Jürgen Grabbe, "Besonderheiten der europäischen Einwanderung in die USA während der frühen nationalen Periode, 1783–1820," *Amerikastudien/American Studies* 33 (1988): 276.

46. Certainly the prominent place of race-based slavery was one symbol and reality of the conflicted nature of the ideological discussions surrounding American identity.

47. John M. Murrin, "A Roof Without Walls: The Dilemma of American National Identity," in *Beyond Confederation: Origins of the Constitution and American National Identity*, ed. Richard Beeman et al. (Chapel Hill: The University of North Carolina Press, 1987), 333–48. See also Higham, "Integrating America," 13, for a good description of a young nation "scantily endowed with the outward trappings of power and social connection."

48. Washington's "Farewell Address," for example, exemplified the mix of pride and anxiety common among many who commented on American nationality at the time.

49. Robert E. Shalhope, "Republicanism in Early America," *William and Mary Quarterly*, 3d ser., 39 (April 1982): 334–56, surveys the literature on this theme. Historiographic background can be found in Daniel T. Rodgers, "Republicanism: The Career of a Concept," *Journal of American History* 79 (June 1992): 11–38.

50. Simon P. Newman, *Parades and the Politics of the Street: Festive Culture in the Early Republic* (Philadelphia: University of Pennsylvania Press, 1997), illustrates the unity and divergence of thought that was present in the use and meaning of public celebrations during this time. The patriotic material, symbols, and historical allusions were common, but political opponents used them to different ends. Newman's study deals only with mainstream, British-stock American political culture.

51. Joyce Appleby, *Capitalism and a New Social Order: The Republican Vision of the 1790s* (New York: New York University Press, 1984). For another look at the intellectual connections and the differences among emerging American ideological positions, see James T. Kloppenberg, "The Virtues of Liberalism: Christianity, Republicanism, and Ethics in Early American Discourse," *Journal of American History* 74 (June 1987): 9–33.

52. Gordon S. Wood, *The Radicalism of the American Revolution* (New York: Alfred A. Knopf, 1992). Shifts in immigration and demography also played an important role in this social development. See Fogleman, "From Slaves, Convicts, and Servants," 60–66.

53. Alfred F. Young, *The Shoemaker and the Tea Party: Memory and the American Revolution* (Boston: Beacon Press, 1999), 1–84.

54. Alan Taylor, "From Fathers to Friends of the People: Political Personas in the Early Republic," *Journal of the Early Republic* 11 (Winter 1991): 465–91.

55. Alan Taylor, *Liberty Men and Great Proprietors: The Revolutionary Settlement on the Maine Frontier, 1760–1820* (Chapel Hill: The University of North Carolina Press, 1991).

56. Charles G. Sellers, *The Market Revolution: Jacksonian America, 1815–1846* (New York: Oxford University Press, 1991), develops this theme, the roots of which predate 1815. A more balanced and generally excellent discussion of these issues also appears in Daniel Feller, *The Jacksonian Promise: America, 1815–1840* (Baltimore: The Johns Hopkins University Press, 1995).

57. Nagel, *Sacred Trust*, 23–26.

58. Robert H. Wiebe, *The Opening of American Society: From the Adoption of the Constitution to the Eve of Disunion* (New York: Alfred A. Knopf, 1984), xiii, and 110–67. See also Simon Newman, *Parades,* for a comparative look at how promoters of this sort of American vision could also use a populist "politics of the street" to further their ends.

59. John M. Kloos Jr., *A Sense of Deity: The Republican Spirituality of Dr. Benjamin Rush* (Brooklyn: Carlson Publishing, 1991), and Robert H. Abzug, *Cosmos Crumbling: American Reform and the Religious Imagination* (New York: Oxford University Press, 1994), 11–29.

60. Daniel Walker Howe, *The Political Culture of the American Whigs* (Chicago: The University of Chicago Press, 1979), 1–42.

61. Of course, as Canadian historian George A. Rawlyk has shown in his studies of early Canadian evangelicals, such sentiments could be present in areas that had not experienced political revolution, but they did not have the lively continuance or attachment to national meaning that they held in the United States: see *The Canada Fire: Radical Evangelicalism in British North America, 1775–1812* (Montreal: McGill-Queens University Press, 1994).

CHAPTER 2

1. Fischer, *Albion's Seed,* 560–66, 743–47, though the less pious backcountry folk maintained Old Christmas (January 6) as a holiday.

2. *Der Volksfreund,* 27 December 1808, [2], bound copies at the Lancaster County Historical Society, Lancaster, Pa. For general background on Christmas in America, see Stephen Nissenbaum, *The Battle for Christmas* (New York: Alfred A. Knopf, 1996), and Penne L. Restad, *Christmas in America: A History* (New York: Oxford University Press, 1995). See Don Yoder's Introduction to *Christmas in Pennsylvania: A Folk-Cultural Study,* ed. Alfred L. Shoemaker (Kutztown, Pa.: Pennsylvania Folklife Society, 1959), 6 and 11–13, for a discussion of Christmas in the mid-Atlantic states. Nissenbaum, *Battle for Christmas,* 195–98, presents a persuasive argument for the relatively recent vintage of American Christmas traditions among British-stock Americans, although in his zeal to deconstruct the forms of later traditions he likely does not pay enough attention to Christmas as a significant and legitimate cultural marker in periods preceding those on which he focuses (as the 1808 legislative debate cited above illustrates). Decorated Christmas trees made their first recorded American appearance in 1821 in Lancaster, Pa., in the home of Matthias Zahm (1789–1874), but years later neighboring Lancaster residents still would not countenance holiday trees, believing "such a symbol of the christmas tide was too Germanic for [their] Scotch-Irish appreciation." See Matthias Zahm, "Matthias Zahm's Diary," ed. Robert H. Goodell, *Proceedings of the Lancaster County Historical Society* 47 (1943): 64; Robert Blair Risk [1848–1926], "Noted and Observed," *Lancaster Examiner,* 21 December 1912. See also Shoemaker, ed., *Christmas in Pennsylvania,* 52–58. James L. Morris, "Diary, or Daily Notes of the Weather together with the Events of the Neighborhood, etc., etc." (microfilm roll 74, vols. 1–2), Historical Society of Berks County, Reading, Pa., 25 December 1842, believed that Christmas played the same role among his Pennsylvania German neighbors that Thanksgiving (generally also a December holiday at that time) did among New Englanders;

on 21 December 1843, Morris reported that Thanksgiving Day was legally observed in Pennsylvania for the first time. See also the late-eighteenth-century Christmas and Good Friday sermons by German Reformed pastor J. C. Albertus Helfenstein, *A Collection of Choice Sermons by the Rev. J. C. Albertus Helfenstein . . . translated from the German by I. Daniel Rupp* (Carlisle, Pa.: George Fleming, 1832), 47–59 and 71–80.

3. *Der Volksfreund,* 27 December 1808, [2]; the vote in favor of a Christmas recess was 56 to 37. On the Pennsylvania German "Second Christmas," see Shoemaker, ed., *Christmas in Pennsylvania,* 102–3. *Der Volksfreund* believed that the recess's extra expense to the state of $4,000–5,000 was not excessive.

In High Church Anglican settings, 26 December was marked as the Feast of St. Stephen, although its celebration at the time was rare in America. The association of the day with gift giving and its designation as "Boxing Day" were later, Victorian-era developments that subsequently spread to other parts of the British Empire but not, by then, to the United States. The *Oxford English Dictionary* gives a mid-nineteenth-century origin for Boxing Day.

4. Stephanie Grauman Wolf, "Hyphenated America: The Creation of an Eighteenth-Century German-American Culture," in *America and the Germans: An Assessment of a 300-Year History,* ed. Frank Trommler and Joseph McVeigh (Philadelphia: University of Pennsylvania Press, 1985), 1:66. To earlier generations, the English word "ethnic" held the connotation of "pagan" or "heathen."

5. Indeed, the terms "German" and "Dutch" held different meanings prior to the nineteenth century than those commonly associated with the words after that time. "Dutch" was not an American corruption of the word *Deutsch;* it was, in fact, the general English designation for the inhabitants of the Rhine Valley from Rotterdam to Basel. See Yoder, "Palatine, Hessian, Dutchman" (though observers from William Penn to Benjamin Rush also made reference to the "German" language).

6. Fischer, *Albion's Seed,* 419–782.

7. Susan Klepp, "Five Early Pennsylvania Censuses," *Pennsylvania Magazine of History and Biography* 106 (October 1982): 504.

8. Zitzman, trans. and ed., "William Helffrich," 143; Niemcewicz, *Under Their Own Vine,* 110; "English Pronunciation," *Berks and Schuylkill (Pa.) Journal,* 11 July 1829, [3]. Anne Newport Royall, *Mrs. Royall's Pennsylvania, or Travels Continued in the United States* (Washington, D.C.: by the author, 1829), 105, reported that Pennsylvania Germans referred to all non–Pennsylvania Germans as "the English." In their ecclesiastical correspondence, German Catholics in Pennsylvania and Maryland also referred to English-speaking Catholics as simply "the English." See Fecher, *Movement for German National Parishes,* 94.

9. Even in the late 1700s, the well-educated German traveler Johann David Schoepf (1752–1800) was appalled by the Pennsylvania Dutch dialect. See Johann David Schoepf, *Travels in the Confederation* [1783–84], trans. Alfred J. Morrison (New York: Bergman, 1911), 1:106–10, 194. See also the comments of Jonas Heinrich Gudehus, "Journey to America," trans. Larry M. Neff, in *Ebbes fer Alle—Ebber Ebbes fer Dich: Something for Everyone—Something for You,* ed. Albert F. Buffington (Breinigsville, Pa.: Pennsylvania German Society, 1980), 209, 225–26, and 298–300; and Philip Schaf[f], *Anglo-Germanism, or the Significance of the German Nationality in the United States . . .* (Chambersburg, Pa.: Publication Office of the German Reformed Church, 1846), 10. For their part, many Pennsylvania Dutch speakers contended that the speech of later immigrants was difficult to understand, even when those newcomers protested that they spoke the most proper and pure German language. See, e.g., Carl G. Koch, *Lebenserfahrungen von Carl Koch, Prediger des Evangeliums* (Cleveland: Verlagshaus der Evangelischen Gemeinschaft, 1871), 234–35.

10. The oral dialect thrived, in part, because High German sources were relatively rare. The early nineteenth century represented "the low water mark of supply and demand" in

German-language publishing in the United States. See Robert E. Cazden, *A Social History of the German Book Trade in America to the Civil War* (Columbia, S.C.: Camden House, 1984), 21; also 33, 41. Churches remained the focus of spoken High German, and thus conflict often accompanied any shift to English as an ecclesiastical language. New York's Lutheran Synod switched to English record keeping in 1807, but those in Greater Pennsylvania retained their language longer; see Henry E. Jacobs, *A History of the Evangelical Lutheran Church in the United States* (New York: Christian Literature, 1893), 327. Armin G. Weng, "The Language Problem in the Lutheran Church in Pennsylvania, 1742–1820," *Church History* 5 (December 1936): 359–75, surveys events in several congregations, although it stops well before the transition was accomplished in most places.

11. Bernheim, *History of the German Settlements*, 148–49. While still spoken among "a few aged persons" a decade after the Civil War, Bernheim said that the dialect had largely fallen out of use in North Carolina. In 1881, another writer reported that while Pennsylvania Dutch had "almost ceased to be heard on our streets [of Salisbury, N.C.] . . . the accent and the idiom still lingered on many tongues": Jethro Rumple, *History of Rowan County, North Carolina, containing Sketches of Prominent Families . . .* (Salisbury, N.C.: J. J. Bruner, 1881; rpt., n.p.: Elizabeth Steele Chap., D.A.R., 1916), 57. Gudehus, "Journey to America," 247, reports easy conversation in Pennsylvania Dutch with a black servant of an elderly Pennsylvania German woman in eastern Pennsylvania.

12. Entry for 20 May 1780, Christopher Marshall, *Extracts from the Diary of Christopher Marshall, kept in Philadelphia and Lancaster during the American Revolution, 1774–1781*, ed. William Duane (Albany, N.Y.: Joel Munsell, 1877), 242. See also the early-nineteenth-century memory of a Presbyterian pastor in Harrisburg, Pa., regarding Pennsylvania German holidays, quoted in Charles A. Hay, *Memoirs of Rev. Jacob Goering, Rev. George Lochman, D.D., and Rev. Benjamin Kurtz, D.D., LL.D.* (Philadelphia: Lutheran Publication Society, 1887), 64, and Johann Georg Lochman, *The History, Doctrine, and Discipline of the Evangelical Lutheran Church* (Harrisburg, Pa.: John Wyeth, 1818), 159–60. For broader context, see Alfred L. Shoemaker, "Whit-Monday: Dutch Fourth of July," *The Pennsylvania Dutchman* 5 (May 1953): 5, 12. Although Whit Monday was seen as the more popular and ethnically linked holiday among Pennsylvania Germans, some did participate in July Fourth ceremonies (as lists of participants, including those with German surnames, demonstrate). See, for instance, reports for Reading and Lebanon, Pa., *Berks and Schuylkill Journal*, 18 July 1829, [2].

13. Entry for 1 June 1846 in James Morris, "Diary," original vol. 3, Historical Society of Berks County, Reading, Pa. Also in the Morris "Diary" (microfilm roll 74), for Christmas 1844: "This day is not so strictly kept [by English neighbors]. . . . Many work at their callings or do errands. The Germans mostly abstain from work." On Easter Monday 1837, Morris reported that the Pennsylvania Germans were virtually alone in observing the day as a holiday.

14. Joseph H. Dubbs, *Historic Manual of the Reformed Church in the United States* (Lancaster, Pa.: Inquirer Printing, 1885), 302, quoting a document from 1837.

15. Fischer, *Albion's Seed*, 199–205, 410–18, 595–603, 777–82, 815.

16. Jack P. Greene, *Pursuits of Happiness: The Social Development of Early Modern British Colonies and the Formation of American Culture* (Chapel Hill: The University of North Carolina Press, 1988); see especially 139–41 on this theme among British-stock residents of the middle colonies.

17. Among the secondary works that explore these notions of liberty as preservation of traditional privileges and freedom from external interference in a customary way of life are Mack Walker, *German Home Towns: Community, Estates, and General Estate, 1648–1871* (Ithaca: Cornell University Press, 1971), 34–142, 185–279; Thomas Robisheaux, *Rural Society and the Search for Order in Early Modern Germany* (New York: Cambridge University Press, 1989), especially 8, 11–12, and 257–63; and John G. Gagliardo, *Reich and Nation: The Holy Roman Empire*

as Idea and Reality, 1763–1806 (Bloomington: Indiana University Press, 1980). An important collection of six Württemberg village case studies of the social relationships of power *(Herrschaft)* in these local settings can be found in Sabean, *Power in the Blood;* Sabean offers an outline of traditional power relationships on 16 and 21–24. Of course, mid-eighteenth-century British notions of rights and citizenship were of relatively recent origin themselves, though in any case they differed from those held by German-speaking immigrants. See Michael P. Zuckert, *Natural Rights and the New Republicanism* (Princeton: Princeton University Press, 1994), on the development of Lockean citizenship ideas. For the broader context of German political discourse (including European regions with no connection to Pennsylvania Germans), see Diethelm Klippel, "The True Concept of Liberty: Political Theory in Germany in the Second Half of the Eighteenth Century," in *The Transformation of Political Culture: England and Germany in the Late Eighteenth Century,* ed. Eckhart Hellmuth (New York: Oxford University Press, 1990), 447–66.

18. Roeber, *Palatines, Liberty, and Property,* 77, 94, 179–80, 325–26, and Martin Brecht and Klaus Deppermann, eds., *Der Pietismus im achtzehnten Jahrhundert,* Geschichte des Pietismus, vol. 2 (Göttingen: Vandenhoeck and Ruprecht, 1995), 198–318. On competing views of liberty among German Moravians in North Carolina, see Elisabeth W. Sommer, *Serving Two Masters: Moravian Brethren in Germany and North Carolina, 1727–1801* (Lexington: The University Press of Kentucky, 2000).

19. Ralph B. Strassburger and William J. Hinke, *Pennsylvania German Pioneers: A Publication of the Original Lists of Arrivals in the Port of Philadelphia from 1727 to 1808* (Norristown, Pa.: Pennsylvania German Society, 1934), 1:3–6.

20. Splitter, *Pastors, People, Politics,* 87–109; Samuel E. Weber, *The Charity School Movement in Colonial Pennsylvania* (Philadelphia: William J. Campbell,1905; reprint, New York: Arno, 1969); Whitfield J. Bell Jr., "Benjamin Franklin and the German Charity Schools," *Proceedings of the American Philosophical Society* 99 (December 1955): 381–87; and Schwartz, *"Mixed Multitude,"* 187–93. See also Frederick G. Livingood, *Eighteenth-Century Reformed Church Schools* (Norristown, Pa.: Pennsylvania German Society, 1930); Charles L. Maurer, *Early Lutheran Education in Pennsylvania* (Norristown, Pa.: Pennsylvania German Society, 1932); and A. G. Roeber, "The von Mosheim Society and the Preservation of German Education and Culture in the New Republic, 1789–1813," in *German Influences on Education in the United States to 1917,* ed. Henry Geitz, Jürgen Heideking, and Jurgen Herbst (New York: Cambridge University Press, 1995), 157–76.

21. Brecht and Deppermann, eds., *Pietismus im achtzehnten Jahrhundert,* 319–57. The differences in understandings between clergy and laity did create their share of local arguments. Roeber, *Palatines, Liberty, and Property,* traces the many Lutheran congregational conflicts that resulted from this tension.

22. Splitter, *Pastors, People, Politics,* 66–86, 135–254. While Pennsylvania Germans were better represented at the level of county government, their general level of political participation did not change significantly during the course of the Revolution. Note that Splitter significantly corrects contentions in Wayne L. Bockelman and Owen S. Ireland, "The Internal Revolution in Pennsylvania: An Ethnic Religious Interpretation," *Pennsylvania History* 41 (April 1974): 125–60, and Owen S. Ireland, *Religion, Ethnicity, and Politics: Ratifying the Constitution in Pennsylvania* (University Park: The Pennsylvania State University Press, 1995). Don Yoder has written that "[i]t would be a neat correlation with the theories about European types of Protestantism if one could prove that the Reformed—in a sense following their Calvinist counterparts in the Anglo-American world, the Presbyterians and the Dutch Reformed—showed more activist pro-Revolutionary attitudes than did Pennsylvania's Lutherans, but their records appear actually quite similar." See "The Pennsylvania Germans and the American Revolution," *Pennsylvania Folklife* 25 (Spring 1976): 4.

23. Note, though, that the Revolution was not a sharp turning point with regard to *public* participation; Pennsylvania Germans remained underrepresented and underinvolved in the years following the Revolution. See Wolfgang Splitter, "The Germans in Pennsylvania Politics, 1758–1790: A Quantitative Analysis," *Pennsylvania Magazine of History and Biography* 122 (January/April 1998).

24. Wood, *Radicalism of the American Revolution*. These developments are illustrated biographically in Alfred Young, *Shoemaker and the Tea Party*, 1–84.

25. *Minutes and Letters of the Coetus*, 406. In the following years, their views became more optimistic (see 411–12, 428, 439, 445, and so on). A coetus is a governing church body dependent upon a foreign synod. The American German Reformed Coetus relied on the Reformed Synod of Amsterdam until 1793; that year, the German Reformed Church in the United States became a freestanding synod.

26. John M. Vincent, *Costume and Conduct in the Laws of Basel, Bern, and Zurich, 1370–1800* (Baltimore: The Johns Hopkins University Press, 1935), 1, 19, 37–39, 74–95, 133. Fogleman, "From Slaves, Convicts, and Servants," 57–59, notes the visible changes in the American population and its system of social rank in the wake of the Revolution—changes that drew observers' notice.

27. See Henry J. Young, "The Treatment of the Loyalists in Pennsylvania" (Ph.D. diss., The Johns Hopkins University, 1955), 352–53, for naturalization figures; see also the discussion in Fogleman, *Hopeful Journeys*, 131–37. During the period 1694–1773, only 6,909 Continental Europeans (almost all Germans) were naturalized in Pennsylvania. About 40 percent of those naturalizations occurred in a single year (1765), when Germans became involved in the struggle to defeat efforts to make Pennsylvania a royal colony instead of a proprietorship. Pennsylvania Germans mobilized, fearing the loss of their traditional proprietor-client relationship. See James H. Hutson, *Pennsylvania Politics, 1746–1770: The Movement for Royal Government and Its Consequences* (Princeton: Princeton University Press, 1972).

28. Splitter, *Pastors, People, Politics*, 255–314, 323.

29. Among the original arguments and evidence against such an assumption is Robert E. Lane's *Political Life: Why People Get Involved in Politics* (Glencoe, Ill.: Free Press, 1959), 235–55.

30. Heinrich M. Muhlenberg, *Journals*, 2:200.

31. On initial Pennsylvania German support for the Federalist Party, see Philip S. Klein, *Pennsylvania Politics, 1817–1832: A Game Without Rules* (Philadelphia: Historical Society of Pennsylvania, 1940), 38–39, 50.

32. A. G. Roeber, "J. H. C. Helmuth, Evangelical Charity, and the Public Sphere in Pennsylvania, 1793–1800," *Pennsylvania Magazine of History and Biography* 121 (January/April 1997): 77–100. In addition to Helmuth, one of the last major exponents of a Halle-inspired Pietism was G. Henry Ernst Muhlenberg (1753–1815), Lancaster pastor, master of Franklin College, and son of the patriarch Heinrich Muhlenberg. The younger Muhlenberg was better known for his biological and botanical studies than for theological polemics, and he corresponded on scientific matters with leading Anglo-American intellectuals. See Wallace, *The Muhlenbergs of Pennsylvania*, 308–19.

33. A. G. Roeber, "Citizens or Subjects? German-Lutherans and the Federal Constitution in Pennsylvania, 1789–1800," *Amerikastudien/American Studies* 34 (1989): 49–68. Roeber shows how Helmuth and Endress derived their views from the ecclesiastical history of Johann Lorenz von Mosheim (1694–1755). Helmuth tried to fill the gap that existed in Pennsylvania German knowledge of revolutionary American political thought. See A. G. Roeber, "'Through a Glass, Darkly': The Changing German Ideas of American Freedom, 1776–1806," in *Transatlantic Images and Perceptions: Germany and America Since 1776*, ed. David E. Barclay and Elisabeth Glaser-Schmidt (New York: Cambridge University Press, 1997), 19–40.

34. Daniel Hertz, "A Catechism on Church Government," unpaginated [manuscript book of notes]; last page with text dated 18 February 1823, Philadelphia. Evangelical and Reformed Historical Society, Lancaster, Pa. Quotations are from chapter 4.

35. Outside church circles, the secular German Republican Society of Philadelphia, founded in 1793, also advocated democratic republican ideals. It should be noted, however, that unlike its parallel English-language Democratic Republican Societies, it was not sparked by the American visit of French "Citizen" Edmond-Charles Genêt, but grew out of local Pennsylvania German community concerns. See Harry M. Tinkcom, *The Republicans and Federalists in Pennsylvania, 1790–1801: A Study in National Stimulus and Local Response* (Harrisburg, Pa.: Pennsylvania Historical and Museum Commission, 1950), 84.

36. Roeber, "J. H. C. Helmuth," 97. Roeber points out that the new group did not immediately establish a fund for poor relief—an organization that suggested benevolent management of others.

37. Henry Harbaugh, *The Fathers of the German Reformed Church in Europe and America*, 2d ed. (Lancaster, Pa.: J. M. Westhaeffer, 1872), 2:214. Mahnenschmidt continued to work among Ohio German settlers, later publishing a combination catechism, hymnal, and prayer book for these communities: *Der kleine Heidelbergische Catechismus, oder: kurzen Unterricht Christlicher Lehre, für die Jugend, in der Reformirten Kirche* . . . (Canton, Ohio: Peter Kaufmann, 1834).

38. Preston A. Laury, *The History of the Allentown Conference of the Ministerium of Pennsylvania* (Kutztown, Pa.: Kutztown Publishing, 1926), 240. Dill served in Bucks County, Pa., from 1791 to 1806.

39. A comprehensive study of the revolt is Paul Douglas Newman's "The Fries Rebellion of 1799" (Ph.D. diss., University of Kentucky, 1996).

40. Ethan A. Weaver, "*The American Eagle:* The First English Newspaper Printed in Northampton County, Pennsylvania," *Pennsylvania Magazine of History and Biography* 23 (January 1899): 69–70. On Pomp, see Theodore Appel, "Biography of Rev. Thomas Pomp (1773–1852)," manuscript, Evangelical and Reformed Historical Society, Lancaster, Pa.

41. Testimony given at the trial of Eyerman, in John Sneider, *The Two Trials of John Fries on an Indictment for Treason* . . . (Philadelphia: William W. Woodward, 1800), 222–23. Eyerman also appealed to his status as an educated clergyman, insisting that he would not respect any tax collector who could not read his French, Latin, Hebrew, or Greek texts. He was convicted (225). In *Rural Politics and the Collapse of Pennsylvania Federalism* (Philadelphia: American Philosophical Society, 1982), Kenneth W. Keller lists him as a German Reformed pastor (see 27), although I have been unable to locate a clergyman with that name in the records of the Evangelical and Reformed Historical Society in Lancaster, Pa.

42. A wider political atmosphere is sketched in Simon P. Newman's "The World Turned Upside Down: Revolutionary Politics, Fries and Gabriel's Rebellions, and the Fears of the Federalists," *Pennsylvania History* 67 (Winter 2000): 5–20. Terry Bouton, "'No Wonder the Times Were Troublesome': The Origins of the Fries Rebellion, 1783–1799," *Pennsylvania History* 67 (Winter 2000): 21–42, argues that opponents saw the tax as a real economic hardship in addition to their ideological concerns.

43. Keller, *Rural Politics,* 26–27. Pennsylvania's revolutionary government had disenfranchised Pennsylvania German sectarians beginning in 1777. They (along with Quaker pacifists) returned to the political sphere in 1790 under the allowances of the conservative regime and new state constitution of 1790. For the next decade or so, Moravian, Mennonite, and other ethnic sectarians generally supported their Federalist-oriented political patrons, which in some cases—notably that discussed here—put them at odds with fellow Pennsylvania German neighbors.

44. Ibid., quoting 1798–99 depositions in the Rawle Papers, Insurrection manuscripts, vol. 2, Historical Society of Pennsylvania, Philadelphia.

45. Theodore G. Tappert, trans. and ed., "Helmuth and the Fries Rebellion in 1799," *Lutheran Quarterly* 17 (August 1965): 266–68.

46. *General Advertiser,* 18 October 1799, quoted in Keller, *Rural Politics,* 32.

47. Even before 1799, Pennsylvania Germans had been petitioning outgoing governor Thomas Mifflin (1744–1800) to appoint more local magistrates from their own ranks: see Keller, *Rural Politics,* 17–19, 29–32, and 36–38. For an introduction to ethnoreligious interpretations of politics, see Paul Kleppner, *The Cross of Culture: A Social Analysis of Midwestern Politics, 1850–1900* (New York: Free Press, 1970), 37–51, 69–91.

48. Keller, *Rural Politics,* 56. A. G. Roeber has even contended that Helmuth's style of political thought was swept away by the events that followed 1800. See Roeber, "Citizens or Subjects?" 67.

49. Kenneth W. Keller, "Cultural Conflict in Early Nineteenth-Century Pennsylvania Politics," *Pennsylvania Magazine of History and Biography* 110 (October 1986): 529.

50. Cf. the various ways (discussed in Hackett, *Rude Hand*) in which national traditions and ethnic assumptions shaped groups such as the Dutch Reformed, Puritans, and Presbyterians— groups that otherwise held similar Reformed theology. The German Reformed Church was at least sure that sacred and political vocational callings were mutually exclusive, discussing and then declaring that ministers of the gospel could not hold public office. See *Verhandlungen der General-Synode der Hochdeutschen Reformirten Kirche . . . 1820* (Hagerstown, Md.: Johann Gruber and Daniel May, 1820), 13–19.

51. Other counties formed during this period, as well, but they were new jurisdictions on the frontier that were added to keep up with population expansion (e.g., Susquehanna [1810], Union [1813], Perry [1820], Juniata [1831], and so on). Lehigh and Lebanon Counties were cut from the counties of Northampton and Dauphin, which were historically German but now increasingly English-dominated.

52. Arthur D. Graeff, "Pennsylvania, the Colonial Melting Pot," in *The Pennsylvania Germans,* ed. Ralph Wood (Princeton: Princeton University Press, 1942), 22. On the Amalgamation Party's turn toward Jackson as a symbol, see Philip Klein, *Pennsylvania Politics,* 119, 125; Robert V. Remini, *The Election of Andrew Jackson* (Philadelphia: J. B. Lippincott, 1963), 104, 144; and "Andrew Jackson," *The Guardian* 5 (September 1854): 280–82. Lutheran pastor Gottlieb F. J. Jaeger from Berks County, Pa., translated the Jackson campaign biography for Pennsylvania German consumption: see *Leben des Generals-Majors Andreas Jackson, enthaltend eine Geschichte des Kriegs in Süden . . .* (Reading, Pa.: Johann Ritter, 1831).

Jackson won Pennsylvania German sympathy as a privately religious man who nevertheless resisted evangelical Protestant attempts to co-opt governmental activity and power, e.g., refusing an 1832 Dutch Reformed request to declare a national day of prayer and fasting. See the Dutch Reformed letter in *Niles Weekly Register,* 7 July 1832, 338, and Jackson's reply in Andrew Jackson, *Correspondence of Andrew Jackson,* ed. John S. Bassett (Washington, D.C.: Carnegie Institution, 1929), 4:447. On Pennsylvania German attraction to the conservative Democratic Party, see Nathan Sargent, *Public Men and Events: From the Commencement of Mr. Monroe's Administration, in 1817, to the Close of Mr. Fillmore's Administration, in 1853* (Philadelphia: J. B. Lippincott, 1875), 1:42; and Julius Friedrich Sachse, *The Wayside Inns on the Lancaster Roadside Between Philadelphia and Lancaster* (Lancaster, Pa.: Pennsylvania German Society, 1914), 76.

53. David Hackett Fischer, *The Revolution of American Conservatism: The Federalist Party in the Era of Jeffersonian Democracy* (New York: Harper and Row, 1965), 47. Some additional election data specific to Pennsylvania during this period are found in Sanford W. Higginbotham, *The Keystone in the Democratic Arch: Pennsylvania Politics, 1800–1816* (Harrisburg, Pa.: Pennsylvania Historical and Museum Commission, 1952), but the interpretation is outdated in almost every case. See also Philip S. Klein and Ari Hoogenboom, *A History of Pennsylvania,* 2d ed. (University Park: The Pennsylvania State University Press, 1980), 125–35, for more context, and Philip

Klein, *Pennsylvania Politics,* 47–48, 211–18, 262. On party terminology, see William H. Crawford to Albert Gallatin, 23 April 1817, in Albert Gallatin, *The Writings of Albert Gallatin,* ed. Henry Adams (Philadelphia: J. B. Lippincott, 1879), 2:37.

54. *Intelligencer and Weekly Advertiser,* 26 October 1816, quoted in Philip Klein, *Pennsylvania Politics,* 80.

55. Steven Watts, *The Republic Reborn: War and the Making of Liberal America, 1790–1820* (Baltimore: The Johns Hopkins University Press, 1987).

56. Yost H. Fries, *Die Wahre Liebe eines republicanischen Helden, in einer Ermahnung, zu seinem Volk. Eine Predigt gehalten den 10ten September 1812, bey Zusammenkunft der Freywilligen zu Jungmanstaun in der Elias-Kirche* (New Bern, Pa.: G. N. H. Peters, 1845), 3. "Youngmanstown" was later renamed Mifflinburg.

57. Harry S. Stout, *The New England Soul: Preaching and Religious Culture in Colonial New England* (New York: Oxford University Press, 1986), 145–46, 287–89, 305–6.

58. Fries, *Die Wahre Liebe eines republicanischen Helden,* 3.

59. Ibid., 11; 15 ("keiner war frey von Monarchie, Aristocratie oder Despotismus, und die mehrsten waren im strengsten Sinn des Worts Erz Tyrannen"); 17. He came back to Washington and a comparison with Christ at the close of the sermon (22–23).

60. Cf. Victor A. Sapio, *Pennsylvania and the War of 1812* (Lexington: The University Press of Kentucky, 1970), which argues for the war's popularity in Pennsylvania, but ignores ethnic communities. Cunz, *Maryland Germans,* 192, reports that Pennsylvania Germans in western and central Maryland were not enthusiastic supporters of the 1812 declaration of war. Baglyos, "In This Land of Liberty," 67–79 and 114–15, discusses several Lutheran wartime sermons, a few apparently quite patriotic, though others served as more conventional repentance sermons that simply used the crisis of war as a backdrop (e.g., Heinrich A. Muhlenberg, *Busstags-Predigt* . . . [Reading, Pa.: Johann Ritter, 1812]). Baglyos also notes that Lutheran pastors in the Early Republic did not normally preach specifically patriotic sermons on July Fourth, even when the day was a Sunday (167–68).

61. Fries, *Die Wahre Liebe eines republicanischen Helden,* 19, 21. Hartmut Lehmann, *Martin Luther in the American Imagination* (München: Wilhelm Fink Verlag, 1988), 77, suggests that the theme of German exceptionalism in Europe was noted by other German Americans as well and was expressed in an 1812 essay in the *Evangelisches Magazin.*

62. Fries, *Die Wahre Liebe eines republicanischen Helden,* 19, 20 ["daß er mit Weisheit und Verstand . . . seine Unterthanen regieren könnte"].

63. Philip Klein, *Pennsylvania Politics,* 6, 29–34. While there were a surprising number of nineteenth-century Pennsylvania governors of German extraction, Klein believes that their numbers resulted from the quirks of the caucus and nomination processes of the time. In any case, few of their fellows followed in their political footsteps. See also Cunz, *Maryland Germans,* 133, on the lack of Pennsylvania Germans in Maryland judiciary posts—even in heavily German communities.

64. Cazden, *German Book Trade,* 20.

65. Michael B. Katz, "From Voluntarism to Bureaucracy in American Education," in *Education in American History: Readings on the Social Issues,* ed. Michael B. Katz (New York: Praeger, 1973), 38, 40, 44–49. Katz uses the terms "paternalistic voluntarism" and "democratic localism." The editor of the *Weekly Messenger of the German Reformed Church* deemed the matter of such importance to his readers that he devoted space to it in the June 1836 and 22 August 1838 issues (pages 177 and 625–26, respectively), among other places.

66. Donald S. McPherson, "The Fight Against Free Schools in Pennsylvania: Popular Opposition to the Common School System, 1834–1874" (Ph.D. diss., University of Pittsburgh, 1977), especially 175, 343, and 365, offers tables and a map of resistance areas during the 1834–73 period. This is a comprehensive study of the subject, filled with hard data and political, ethnic,

and religious interpretation. See also Clyde S. Stine, "The Pennsylvania Germans and the School," in *The Pennsylvania Germans,* ed. Ralph Wood (Princeton: Princeton University Press, 1942), 112 and 115–18. For one contemporary description of a Pennsylvania German parochial school, see Daniel Miller, *History of the Reformed Church in Reading, Pa.* (Reading, Pa.: Daniel Miller, 1905), 33–34. North German schoolteacher Jonas Heinrich Gudehus (1776–1831) immigrated to Berks County, Pa., in 1822 and taught in a parochial school associated with Zion Moselem Lutheran Church for three years before he returned to Europe, believing that his services were underappreciated. See his negatively critical but detailed observations on Pennsylvania German attitudes toward formal education in Gudehus, "Journey to America," 226–33.

67. James P. Wickersham, *A History of Education in Pennsylvania ... to the Present Day* (Lancaster, Pa.: Inquirer Printing, 1886), 322, 331. A state commissioner of education, Wickersham had little patience with those who had opposed public schools.

68. McPherson, "The Fight Against Free Schools," 365. For one local example of the school controversy among Pennsylvania German religious folk in the Lancaster County village of Bowmansville in 1850, see Charles D. Spotts, "The People of Bowmansville," *Community Historians Annual* 9 (July 1970): 34–37. Supporters of common schools were forced out of Bowmansville's Mennonite and German Reformed churches, both of whose members generally opposed the introduction of such schools into the community that year.

Ethnic attachments to education could override even substantial doctrinal differences, as demonstrated by the late-eighteenth-century Baltimore German Catholics who sent their children to local German-run Protestant schools. See Fecher, *Movement for German National Parishes,* 95.

69. Wickersham, *History of Education in Pennsylvania,* 321. For contemporary observations by outsiders, see Reed and Matheson, *Narrative of the Visit,* 2:302, 307.

70. Reed and Matheson, *Narrative of the Visit,* 2:307, and Royall, *Mrs. Royall's Pennsylvania,* 1:262 and 1:152–55.

CHAPTER 3

1. Charles G. Finney, *Memoirs of Rev. Charles G. Finney, Written by Himself* (New York: A. S. Barnes, 1876), 267. Finney's allusion to "Dr. M——" was undoubtedly to Henry A. Muhlenberg (1782–1844), pastor of Reading's Trinity Lutheran Church from 1802 to 1828, and a grandson of Heinrich Melchior Muhlenberg. Anne Newport Royall (1769–1854), a travelogue writer and Washington, D.C., socialite who was no friend of evangelical enthusiasm, approved of Muhlenberg's preaching when she visited Reading in 1828. Although unable to understand a word of the German sermon, she was impressed with the fact that "he was free from that awkward bobbing up and down [which is] so common and so disgusting" among many contemporary preachers. See *Mrs. Royall's Pennsylvania,* 154.

2. Finney, *Memoirs,* 267–68.

3. In this text, the terms "evangelical" and "evangelicalism" describe a "discrete network of Protestant Christian movements arising during the eighteenth century in Britain and its Colonies," one characterized by emphases on biblicism, individual and experiential conversion, an energetic activism, and a belief that Christ's redeeming work is essential to Christianity. For more discussion of this definition, see Mark A. Noll, David W. Bebbington, and George A. Rawlyk, eds., *Evangelicalism: Comparative Studies of Popular Protestantism in North America, the British Isles, and Beyond, 1700–1990* (New York: Oxford University Press, 1994), 3–10. American evangelicalism was marked particularly by its popular (widespread) and populist (egalitarian) expressions, expressions that were characteristic of American culture in the

Early Republic. Certainly there have been other definitions of "evangelical" in certain times and places—not the least of which has been (and remains) its use by European German Lutherans as the designation for "Protestant" or "Protestantism."

4. The combative language and imagery in this chapter reflect the many primary sources that report the era's heated religious competition. Certainly there were also cases of quiet coexistence. For example, because there were no organized English-language churches of any denomination in the town of Easton, Pa., until at least 1811, some English and Irish residents were married or had children baptized by local German pastors (who perhaps used English rites on such occasions). See the many English and Irish names in the baptism and marriage records of the Easton German Reformed Church, published as Henry M. Kieffer, trans., *Some of the First Settlers of "The Forks of the Delaware" and their Descendants; Being a Translation from the German of the Recordbook of the First Reformed Church of Easton, Penna., from 1760 to 1852* (Easton, Pa.: [First Reformed Church of Easton], 1902), 16–17 and 81–225 (records).

5. Nathan O. Hatch, *The Democratization of American Christianity* (New Haven: Yale University Press, 1989); Jon Butler, *Awash in a Sea of Faith*, 225–88; and John H. Wigger, *Taking Heaven by Storm: Methodism and the Rise of Popular Christianity in America* (New York: Oxford University Press, 1998).

6. On the variety and development of these approaches to revival, see the typology in Walter H. Conser Jr., *Church and Confession: Conservative Theologians in Germany, England, and America, 1815–1866* (Macon: Mercer University Press, 1984), 231.

7. Gleason, "American Identity and Americanization," 34–38.

8. A tenet of the common scholarly interpretation of religion in the Early Republic is that the motor of evangelical revivalism propelled this revolution in faith in a supply-driven (rather than demand-initiated) fashion; that is, the presence of the populist message itself engendered fervent support and transformative power. See Hatch, *Democratization of American Christianity;* Terry D. Bilhartz, *Urban Religion and the Second Great Awakening: Church and Society in Early National Baltimore* (Cranbury, N.J.: Associated University Presses, 1986); Roger Finke and Rodney Stark, "How the Upstart Sects Won America: 1776–1850," *Journal for the Scientific Study of Religion* 28 (March 1989): 27–44; and Curtis D. Johnson, *Islands of Holiness: Rural Religion in Upstate New York, 1790–1860* (Ithaca: Cornell University Press, 1989). As the Pennsylvania German case discussed here illustrates, however, this supply-side model is limited in its explanatory power.

9. Don Yoder, ed., "A Letter to Bishop Asbury," *The Pennsylvania Dutchman* 1 (12 May 1949): 5. On Colbert, see his biographical sketch in George Peck, *Early Methodism Within the Bounds of the Old Genesee Conference from 1788 to 1828 . . .* (New York: Carlton and Porter, 1860), 272–75.

10. Indeed, their prior familiarity with it may have heightened their resistance to Colbert. For early Methodist contact with Pennsylvania Germans, see John B. Frantz, "Early German Methodism in America," *Yearbook of German-American Studies* (1991): 171–84.

11. For an overview of these two groups, see Longenecker, *Piety and Tolerance,* 105–40.

12. See Augustus W. Drury, *The Life of Rev. Philip William Otterbein, Founder of the Church of the United Brethren in Christ* (Dayton, Ohio: United Brethren Publishing House, 1884), 117–22. In what was perhaps the first formal Brethren conference, held in Baltimore in 1789, the group numbered eighteen preachers, including ten German Reformed, six Mennonite, one Amish, and one Moravian.

13. Otterbein letter, 15 June 1788, quoted in Hinke, *Ministers of the German Reformed Congregations,* 78. On American-style populist Arminianism, see Hatch, *Democratization of American Christianity,* 170–79. Technically, Otterbein never severed his formal ties to the Reformed Synod, but his work with and leadership of the United Brethren quickly made that denomination his *de facto* affiliation. For his part, Boehm had been expelled from his Mennonite

conference not for promoting revivalism so much as for his open support of the American patriot cause during the Revolutionary War.

14. But see Frantz, "Early German Methodism."

15. The group took the name Evangelical Association in 1816; it had previously been known as the "Albright Brethren." For a very early interpretation, see the brief biography published as George Miller, *Jacob Albrecht* (Reading, Pa.: Johannes Ritter, 1811), which contains an account of Albright's spiritual struggle, conversion, and ministerial calling. For the subsequent history of the United Brethren and Evangelical Association, see Bruce Behney and Paul H. Eller, *The History of the Evangelical United Brethren Church* (Nashville: Abingdon Press, 1979). The majority in each group merged in 1946 to form the Evangelical United Brethren, which in turn merged with the Methodist Church in 1968 to form the United Methodist Church. A portion of the old United Brethren in Christ denomination still exists today (mostly in the Midwest), while a remnant of the old Evangelical Association continues in Pennsylvania as the Evangelical Congregational Church.

16. J. Steven O'Malley, "A Distinctive German-American Credo: The United Brethren Confession of Faith," *Asbury Theological Journal* 42 (Spring 1987): 51–64.

17. Newcomer's autobiography offers an important window onto the German evangelical experience. See Christian Newcomer, *The Life and Journal of the Rev'd Christian Newcomer, Late Bishop of the Church of the United Brethren in Christ. Written by Himself* (Hagerstown, Md.: F. G. W. Kapp, 1834). On Newcomer's travels with Dow, see 132 (7, 15–17 April 1805) and 286 (20 February 1823). On Dow himself, see Charles C. Sellers, *Lorenzo Dow: The Bearer of the Word* (New York: Milton, Balch, 1928).

18. The minutes of the Association demonstrate required itinerancy, prohibition of pastoral settling (except for old age), and reservations about licensing married men. See, for example, Sylvanus C. Breyfogel, ed., *Landmarks of the Evangelical Association, Containing all the Official Records of the Annual and General Conferences ... to the Year 1840; and the Proceedings of the East Pennsylvania Conference together with Important Extracts from ... the General Conference from 1840 to the Present Time* (Reading, Pa.: Eagle Book Printers, 1888), 28, 33, 38, 51, 54, 56–57, and 79.

19. Newcomer, *Life and Journal,* 232 (1 April 1815), 240 (1 May 1816), 252 (12 October 1817), and so on. After 1809, the United Brethren and Methodist Episcopal Church even discussed organic union. See Augustus W. Drury, trans., *Minutes of the Annual and General Conferences of the Church of the United Brethren in Christ, 1800–1818* (Dayton, Ohio: United Brethren Publishing House, 1897), 24ff., and especially 45–63 (reproducing correspondence from the period 1809–1814). The United Brethren also considered union with the Evangelical Association in 1813 (31). This story is traced in Donald K. Gorrell, "'Ride a Circuit or Let It Alone': Early Practices That Kept the United Brethren, Albright People, and Methodists Apart," *Methodist History* 25 (October 1986): 4–16.

20. Ezra Grumbine, "Stories of Old Stumpstown," *Papers and Addresses of the Lebanon County Historical Society* 5 (1909–12): 169.

21. J. Steven O'Malley, *Touched by Godliness: Bishop John Seybert and the Evangelical Heritage* ([Independence, Mo.]: Granite Publications, 1984), discusses the importance of dreams in the early Evangelical Association (151–67) and healing, prophecy, glossolalia, and miracles (183–204). John H. Wigger, "Taking Heaven by Storm: Enthusiasm and Early American Methodism, 1770–1820," *Journal of the Early Republic* 14 (Summer 1994): 167–94, discusses these phenomena among early Methodists.

22. Henry A. Thompson, *Our Bishops: A Sketch of the Origins and Growth of the Church of the United Brethren in Christ as Shown in the Lives of Its Distinguished Leaders* (Dayton, Ohio: United Brethren Publishing House, 1904), 132. See also Don Yoder, *Pennsylvania Spirituals* (Lancaster, Pa.: Pennsylvania Folklife Society, 1961), and Terry Heisey, "*Singet Hallelujah!* Music in the Evangelical Association, 1800–1894," *Methodist History* 28 (July 1990): 237–51.

23. Richard Kern, *John Winebrenner: Nineteenth Century Reformer* (Harrisburg, Pa.: Central Publishing, 1974), and John Winebrenner, *A Brief View of the Formation, Government, and Discipline of the Church of God* (Harrisburg, Pa.: Montgomery and Dexter, 1829). Winebrenner was expelled from the German Reformed Eastern Synod in 1828. See Hatch, *Democratization of American Christianity*, 68–81, 167–70, for the parallel anglophone story.

24. See, for instance, Breyfogel, ed., *Landmarks of the Evangelical Association*, 34. Appeals to plain dress were significant during this period, which was (paradoxically) a time of gentrification among the middling classes emancipated from hierarchical social authority. See also Richard L. Bushman, *The Refinement of America: Persons, Houses, Cities* (New York: Alfred A. Knopf, 1992).

25. By midcentury, both groups had followed the Methodists in bourgeois gentrification, allowing preachers to settle and founding colleges. The United Brethren began Otterbein College, Westerville, Ohio, in 1847. However, the 1866 founding of Lebanon Valley College in Annville, Pa.—in the ethnic Pennsylvania German heartland—provoked a schism and the formation of a dissenting "primitive" United Brethren group known as the United Christians (or Hoffmanites), much in the style of the "croaker Methodists." For its part, by 1850, the Evangelical Association was building a large, two-story church edifice to honor the memory of Jacob Albright, and in 1858 it urged congregations "to have their parsonages furnished." See Breyfogel, ed., *Landmarks of the Evangelical Association*, 130, 159. For the parallel story among English-language evangelicals, see Hatch, *Democratization of American Christianity*, 201–6.

26. Spaeth et al., eds., *Documentary History*, 190; Thompson, *Our Bishops*, 104–19. See also *Acts and Proceedings*, 37–40 (1804).

27. Henry Harbaugh, *Fathers of the German Reformed Church*, 2:68.

28. Reber journal (no longer extant), quoted in Henry Harbaugh, *Fathers of the German Reformed Church*, 3:433–35. Several decades later, Reber published a critique apparently aimed at the United Brethren: see Joel L. Reber, *Ein Ernsthaftes Wort über den Secten-Geist und das Sect-Wesen* (Chambersburg, Pa.: Moses Kieffer, 1850). The copy housed at the Evangelical and Reformed Historical Society, Lancaster, Pa., is bound with a response from two United Brethren ministers.

29. Yoder, *Pennsylvania Spirituals*, 60, reprinting a lengthy portion of Russell W. Gilbert, ed., "The Unpublished Autobiography of Ernst Max Adam, M.D. [1801–1880], Settler in Dunker Blooming Grove," *Susquehanna University Studies* 5 (May 1953): 35–37. See also O'Malley, *Touched by Godliness*.

30. John G. Morris, *Fifty Years in the Lutheran Ministry* (Baltimore: James Young, 1878), 579. The Lutheran storyteller delighted in the fact that lightning had subsequently also struck the Association's local meetinghouse.

31. Henry Harbaugh, *Fathers of the German Reformed Church*, 3:62–63.

32. This event is discussed in light of recently discovered documents in R. H. Baur, "Paul Henkel and the Revivals," *Concordia Historical Institute Quarterly* 63 (Fall 1990): 113–22.

33. John Morris, *Fifty Years*, 565.

34. Henry Harbaugh, *Fathers of the German Reformed Church*, 3:84–93. Similar examples include Henry Wiegand (1810–72); Thomas Winters (1777–1863) in Ohio, 4:138–41; and Conrad Saure (1820–73). See Daniel Y. Heisler and Henry Harbaugh, *The Fathers of the German Reformed Church in Europe and America, continued by D. Y. Heisler* (Lancaster, Pa.: J. M. Westhaeffer, 1872; Reading, Pa.: Daniel Miller, 1881–88), 5:31–32; 4:138–41; and 5:65. See also John Morris, *Fifty Years*, 600–601.

35. John George Butler, 1 September 1805 entry in "Diary of Journey to Knoxville, Tenn., 27 July–27 September 1805" [composed 1806], Lutheran Archives Center at Philadelphia, Lutheran Theological Seminary at Philadelphia, Philadelphia, Pa. For more on Butler, see

William B. Sprague, *Annals of the American Lutheran Pulpit; or Commemorative Notices of Distinguished Clergymen of the Lutheran Denomination* ... (New York: Robert Carter and Bros., 1869), 72-77.

36. Spaeth et al., eds., *Documentary History*, 231.

37. Stories told in Henry Harbaugh, *Fathers of the German Reformed Church*, 3:250-51, and *Historic Sketch of the Reformed Church in North Carolina*, 41-44. "Herr Reily," whose mother was Pennsylvania German and father was Irish, moved in several ethnic worlds. He also represented the German Reformed Church to European theological faculties in an 1825-26 tour to solicit books. See his "Diary of Trip to Europe, 1825-26," Evangelical and Reformed Historical Society, Lancaster, Pa.

38. These new western synods were not the product of later-arriving German immigrants, but were formed by descendants of colonial-stock Germans in the South and Pennsylvanians moving west. See Clarence V. Sheatsley, *History of the Evangelical Lutheran Joint Synod of Ohio and Other States, from the Earliest Beginnings to 1919* (Columbus, Ohio: Lutheran Book Concern, 1919), 103 and 106-8, on their confessionalism and rejection of new measures revivalism.

39. See B. H. Pershing, "Paul Henkel: Frontier Missionary, Organizer, and Author," *Concordia Historical Institute Quarterly* 7 (January 1935): 97-119; on the Tennessee Synod, see Edmund J. Wolf, *The Lutherans in America: A Story of Struggle, Progress, Influence, and Marvelous Growth* (New York: J. A. Hill, 1890), 372-86. The Indiana Synod organized in 1835 and was also opposed to popular evangelical Protestant Bible, mission, and tract societies. See Rudolph F. Rehmer, "Indiana Lutherans at the Nineteenth-Century Crossroads," in *American Lutheranism: Crisis in Historical Consciousness? The Lutheran Historical Conference, Essays, and Reports, 1988* (St. Louis: Lutheran Historical Conference, 1990), 76-78.

40. Henry Harbaugh, *Fathers of the German Reformed Church*, 3:44-46. Bollinger County, Missouri, took its name from pioneer G. Frederick Bollinger, son of Heinrich Bollinger, a colonial-era deacon of the Long Swamp German Reformed Church in Berks County, Pa. See Louis Houck, *A History of Missouri from the Earliest Explorations* ... (Chicago: R. R. Donnelley and Sons, 1908), 2:188.

41. Timothy Flint, *Recollections of the Last Ten Years* (New York: Alfred A. Knopf, 1932), 225. Much of Flint's description must be considered with care. A onetime Mississippi Valley representative of the Connecticut Presbyterian (Union) Mission Society, he had broken ranks with that group in 1816 when the Society's members considered his "ultraist" attitudes about alcohol and Sunday amusements too severe. Flint's fascination with the "naturally phlegmatic" character of the Pennsylvania Germans and his extensive description of their use of alcohol—as well as his favorable comparisons of himself with their minister—should be read in light of his particular views. Nevertheless, as an educated Yankee evangelical, his general sense that the community did not fit the cultural and religious norms he espoused is significant.

42. Of course, some German settlers may have also joined the English-speaking Methodists or Baptists directly. Likewise, some British Americans joined the German churches. For example, the German Reformed Church welcomed the Presbyterians John W. Nevin (1803-86), Daniel Young (1795-1831), and a Long Islander, William C. Bennett (1804-70), who joined after moving to Pennsylvania as an adult. Beginning in the late 1830s, the Methodist Episcopal Church itself began to proselytize among German immigrants. However, its work was largely among post-1830s arrivals in the Mississippi Valley, not among the descendants of colonial-stock Pennsylvania Germans. In any event, according to its own sympathetic history, "numerically, German-speaking Methodism was never very strong." See Paul F. Douglass, *The Story of German Methodism: Biography of an Immigrant Soul* (New York: The Methodist Book Concern, 1939), xiii. For criticism of this effort, see William Nast, "Dr. Schaff and Methodism," *Methodist Quarterly Review* 39 (July 1857): 431.

43. Because of their sometimes questionable reliability and two-dimensional character, historical statistics are often a delicate basis on which to ground historical contentions. Given the role that shifts in denominational allegiance play in the historiography of Christianity in the Early Republic, however, Pennsylvania German church affiliation is an important factor in considering the Pennsylvania German community's evolving relationship to larger society. The rapidly growing ranks of the Methodists and other purveyors of popular religion—and their relative and absolute outpacing of competing churches—is at the center of the era's religious historiography, and near the center of its social history more broadly. See Finke and Stark, "How the Upstart Sects Won America." For a specific argument regarding the Methodists, see Wigger, "Taking Heaven by Storm," 167–69. For early American Methodist statistics, see Charles C. Goss, ed., *Statistical History of the First Century of American Methodism, with a Summary of the Origins and Present Operations of Other Denominations* (New York: Carlton and Porter, 1866), 51, 103, and 109. It is interesting to note various denominations' different approaches to church statistics. Methodists, Presbyterians, and Dutch Reformed collected systematic and complete statistical records through nationally centralized church structures, publishing them in detail in annual minutes that were uniform and produced to standard specifications. Lutheran and German Reformed synodic minutes appear in various formats and were issued by several different printers, apparently at the discretion of the synod's local host community. The statistics that these minutes report are very often incomplete and not systematically gathered; individual congregations, in many cases, may have had better records. Still, among the Lutheran and German Reformed churches (which generally had a more local orientation), there was apparently no great emphasis placed on collecting or producing minutes or statistics that were systematic, standardized, and national in scope.

44. See Daniel Berger, *History of the Church of the United Brethren in Christ* (Dayton, Ohio: Otterbein Press, 1897), 646; H. M. J. Klein, *The History of the Eastern Synod of the Reformed Church in the United States* (Lancaster, Pa.: Eastern Synod of the Reformed Church in the United States, 1943), 373, which reports that 21,304 members communed in 1820; and Breyfogel, ed., *Landmarks of the Evangelical Association*, 414. On the Lutheran figures, see Willard D. Allbeck, *A Century of Lutherans in Ohio* (Yellow Springs, Ohio: Antioch Press, 1966), 60. Allbeck cites the 1833 minutes of the Ohio Synod (37) and notes that the 1833 Ohio Lutheran statistics showing 13,252 communicants are quite incomplete.

45. Abram P. Funkhouser, *History of the Church of the United Brethren in Christ, Virginia Conference* (Dayton, Va.: Ruebush-Kieffer, 1921), 92. In this case, Funkhouser was writing and citing statistics for the denomination as a whole, not specifically for Virginia. In 1843, the Evangelical Association authorized the organization of English-language conferences (for the benefit of non-German neighbors); four years later, it also authorized an English-language paper. In the end, however, no English-language conferences were established. Rather, anglicization proceeded so swiftly that separate German-speaking conferences were established for those few who still wished to retain their mother tongue. See Breyfogel, ed., *Landmarks of the Evangelical Association*, 107 and 118, and Edward F. Ohms, "The Language Problem in the Evangelical Association," *Methodist History* 24 (July 1987): 228–29.

46. John C. Guldin, *Directions and Advice in Reference to Revivals of Religion, and Prayer Meetings* (Chambersburg, Pa.: Publication Office of the German Reformed Church, 1841). This twelve-page booklet provided effective tactics for encouraging religious revival and drew on new measures ideas, but also was careful to warn against excessive emotionalism (see 9, for instance).

47. John B. Frantz, "John C. Guldin, Pennsylvania German Revivalist," *Pennsylvania Magazine of History and Biography* 87 (April 1963): 123–38; Heisler and Harbaugh, *Fathers of the German Reformed Church*, 4:159–61. In 1842, Guldin moved to New York City and joined the Dutch Reformed Church.

48. For a time, the Reformed paper was edited by Daniel Young, a pastor of New York Presbyterian background who heartily supported new measures revivalism. *Lutheran Observer* editor Benjamin Kurtz was also a revivalist enthusiast. But the papers sometimes printed letters or articles from opponents of new measures revivalism, such as the essay by esteemed Easton pastor Thomas Pomp in *Weekly Messenger of the German Reformed Church*, 6 January 1841.

49. Frantz, "John C. Guldin," 132–33. The Philadelphia Classis—more open to revivalism—supported Guldin. A number of leading synod members opposed Guldin's style of revivalism. See Theodore Appel, *Recollections of College Life at Marshall College, Mercersburg, Pa., from 1839 to 1845: A Narrative with Reflections* (Reading, Pa.: Daniel Miller, 1886), 323–24.

50. "Notices of the Life and Labours of Martin Boehm and William Otterbein ... ," *The Methodist Magazine* 6 (July 1823): 253.

51. F. Ernest Stoeffler, *German Pietism During the Eighteenth Century* (Leiden: E. J. Brill, 1973); W. Reginald Ward, *The Protestant Evangelical Awakening* (Cambridge: Cambridge University Press, 1992); F. Ernest Stoeffler, ed., *Continental Pietism and Early American Christianity* (Grand Rapids, Mich.: William B. Eerdmans, 1976); and Brecht and Deppermann, eds., *Pietismus im achtzehnten Jahrhundert*, 198–357. Roeber, *Palatines, Liberty, and Property*, 62–75, supplies an overview of the differences between the Pietism of the southwestern German immigrant communities and the variety circulating in Halle, along with a good bibliography.

52. See, e.g., the collection of twenty-one sermons by the noted Germantown, Pa., German Reformed pastor, J. C. Albertus Helfenstein (1748–90). In Helfenstein's sermons, conversion was the "application" of every biblical text. Appeals for holy living and the proper preparation for receiving the sacraments were also common themes (see Helfenstein, *Collection of Choice Sermons*). See also the text, pictures, and editor's introduction to the work of a rather independent-minded Pietist of the period, Ludwig Denig (1755–1830), in *The Picture Bible of Ludwig Denig: A Pennsylvania German Emblem Book*, trans. and ed. Don Yoder (New York: Hudson Hills Press, 1990). J. Steven O'Malley provides eighteenth-century Pietist sources that fed—via Otterbein and other German Reformed pastors—into the German evangelical movement in America. See O'Malley, trans. and ed., *Early German-American Evangelicalism: Pietist Sources on Discipleship and Sanctification* (Lanham, Md.: Scarecrow Press, 1995).

53. Spaeth et al., eds., *Documentary History*, 187.

54. *Der Kleine Catechismus des sel. D. Martin Luthers; Nebst den gewöhnlichen Morgen- Tisch- und Abend-Gebeten ...* [2d ed.] (Germantown, Pa.: Leibert und Billmeyer, 1786), 109. This was the so-called Pennsylvania Ministerium Catechism, with the first edition dating from 1785; the second edition was used from 1786 onward. The quotation—an answer to question number 15 in the section "Ordnung des Heils um Freylinghausen" (see 106–10)—did not appear in the 1785 printing, but was added beginning with the catechism's second edition. (The original question 15 became 16, and so forth; cf. pp. 106–10 in the 1785 edition, especially p. 108.) In other words, it was a Pennsylvania Lutheran addition to the Freylinghausen text that appeared as part of the catechism.

55. Henry Harbaugh, *Fathers of the German Reformed Church*, 2:190.

56. Lewis Mayer, *History of the German Reformed Church, Volume 1* (Philadelphia: Lippincott and Grambo, 1851), 1. Only one volume ever appeared; it includes a posthumous biographical sketch of Mayer, from which the quotation comes.

57. Appel, *Recollections of College Life*, 30–31. John G. Morris (1803–95), a Lutheran student and native of York, Pa., likewise found traditional Presbyterianism both attractive and troubling while he was a student at Princeton. Strict Sabbatarianism was particularly problematic. See John G. Morris, *Life Reminiscences of an Old Lutheran Minister* (Philadelphia: Lutheran Publication Society, 1896), 77.

58. Don Yoder, "The Bench Versus the Catechism: Revivalism and Pennsylvania's Lutheran and Reformed Churches," *Pennsylvania Folklife* 10 (Fall 1959): 14–23. J. C. Albertus

Helfenstein associated preparation for eucharistic communion with religious revival: see Helfenstein, *Collection of Choice Sermons*, 5, 71–80, 144–54, and 198–248. For Lutheran eucharistic piety and the importance of the sacrament (despite a less-than-exact Lutheran formulation of the matter), see Elizabethtown, Pa., pastor Johann H. Bernheim's *Das Abendmahl des Herrn* (Elizabethtaun, Pa.: W. M. Barter, 1834).

59. David H. Focht, *Churches Between the Mountains: A History of the Lutheran Congregations in Perry County, Pennsylvania* (Baltimore: T. Newton Kurtz, 1862), 28–29. See p. 357 for a description of an early-nineteenth-century catechetical session.

60. "The Catechism," *Evangelical Lutheran Intelligencer*, October 1828, 175–76.

61. Arthur C. Repp Jr., *Luther's Catechism Comes to America: Theological Effects on the Issues of the Small Catechism Prepared in or for America prior to 1850* (Metuchen, N.J.: Scarecrow Press, 1982), 214–15, 275–93. In many ways, the catechism served as a confessional standard among American Lutherans: the Lutheran Ministerium continued to endorse its use after 1792, while being vague on the place of other confessional documents. Repp also notes the importance of Lutheran "Orders of Salvation" during this period. Such documents were often used as theological teaching devices alongside the catechism. See also J. Michael Reu, *Dr. Martin Luther's Small Catechism: A History of Its Origin, Its Distribution, and Its Use* (Chicago: Wartburg Publishing, 1929).

62. This is the thesis of O'Malley, *Pilgrimage of Faith*. The Heidelberg Catechism was the most irenic confession to come out of the sixteenth century, developed as part of an unsuccessful effort to unite Rhine Valley Reformed and Lutheran churches. See John Hesselink, "The Dramatic Story of the Heidelberg Catechism," in *Later Calvinism: International Perspectives*, ed. W. Fred Graham (Kirksville, Mo.: Sixteenth Century Journal Publishers, 1994), 273–88.

63. Don Yoder, trans., "Father Pomp's Life Story," *The Pennsylvania Dutchman* 1 (23 June 1949): 5.

64. Joseph F. Berg, *The Ancient Land-Mark, Being the Substance of a Discourse Preached Sept. 29, 1839, by Joseph F. Berg . . .* (Philadelphia: Christian Observer, 1840), 25.

65. Henry Harbaugh, *Fathers of the German Reformed Church*, 2:340; Heisler and Harbaugh, *Fathers of the German Reformed Church*, 4:178–79.

66. Reber journal (no longer extant), quoted in Henry Harbaugh, *Fathers of the German Reformed Church*, 3:433–35.

67. "The Catechism," 174–75.

68. One of several examples reproduced in Focht, *Churches Between the Mountains*, 37–41, comes from the Lebanon Union Church: "In this church it shall never be permitted that any other doctrine be preached or set forth than our Evangelical Lutheran and German Reformed as contained in the Bible, the Augsburg Confession, and the Heidelberg Catechism in our German vernacular language." (An exception was made for the building's use by other clergy conducting community funerals.)

69. Reed and Matheson, *Narrative of the Visit*, 2:302.

70. Focht, *Churches Between the Mountains*, 342–61; quotation from 359.

71. Henry Harbaugh, *Fathers of the German Reformed Church*, 2:307–8.

72. Yoder, *Pennsylvania Spirituals*, 70, quoting [John George Schmucker], *Der Schwärmer-Geist unserer Tage; entlarvt Zur Warnung Erweckter Seelen* (Orwigsburg, Pa.: Grim und Thoma, [1826]), 29. A copy of this pamphlet housed in the Rare Book Room of the Abel Ross Wentz Library, Lutheran Theological Seminary at Gettysburg, Gettysburg, Pa., does not indicate Schmucker's authorship or the 1826 publication date.

73. *Lutheran Observer*, 30 March 1838, [3].

74. David Henkel, *Answer to Mr. Joseph Moore, the Methodist; with a few Fragments on the Doctrine of Justification* (New Market, Va.: S. G. Henkel, 1825), 101–5.

75. Don Yoder, "*Der Fröhliche Botschafter:* An Early American Universalist Magazine," *The American-German Review* 10 (June 1944): 13–16. The paper was published until 1838.

76. George Rogers, *Memoranda of the Experience, Labors, and Travels of a Universalist Preacher, Written by Himself* (Cincinnati: John A. Gurley, 1845), 144–45. German Reformed pastor J. Nicholas Pomp had written against Universalism in his *Kurtzgefasste Pruefungen der Lehre des ewigen Evangeliums . . .* (Philadelphia: Heinrich Miller, 1774).

77. Charles C. Sellers, *Theophilus the Battle-axe: A History of the Lives and Adventures of Theophilus Ransom Gates and the Battle-axes* (Philadelphia: Patterson and White, 1930), 49. The group was established several miles south of Pottstown, Pa., in what became known as "Free-love Vallay."

78. Jon Butler, *Awash in a Sea of Faith,* 225.

79. John B. Frantz, "The Return to Tradition: An Analysis of the New Measure Movement in the German Reformed Church," *Pennsylvania History* 31 (July 1964): 321–26. Nevin's and Schaff's public frustration with democratized Christianity and their criticism of its influence among German Americans, while important and insightful, should not be taken as indirect evidence of mass defection to German evangelical groups or wholesale adoption of popular evangelical styles and orientation within the Reformed and Lutheran communions. Some of these developments occurred, to be sure. But one of the reasons Nevin, Schaff, and others were successful in arguing for a "return to tradition" in the later 1840s and 1850s was that most of the leaders and laity had never completely warmed to revivalism in its Anglo-American idiom. For an example of Schaff's commentary, see Philip Schaf[f], *America: A Sketch of the Political, Social, and Religious Character of the United States of North America* (New York: Scribner, 1855), 193.

80. Francis Asbury, *The Journal and Letters of Francis Asbury,* ed. Elmer T. Clark et al. (Nashville: Abingdon Press, 1958), 2:550 (22 July 1807). But cf. 1:603 (10 July 1789), in which he had pleasant meetings in Lancaster with the "very kind" J. William Hendel Sr. and the "childlike, simple-hearted" pastor and botanist, G. Henry Ernst Muhlenberg.

81. Robert Adair, *Memoir of Rev. James Patterson, Late Pastor of the First Presbyterian Church, N. L., Phila.* (Philadelphia: Henry Perkins, 1840), 199–200.

CHAPTER 4

1. Each spring, on a date tied to Pentecost, pastors and elders met for three days at a host church in Pennsylvania or Maryland. In 1816, the synod switched to a September meeting date. The 1821 synod was held in Reading, Pa. For a complete listing of coetus and synod dates, locations, and officers, see H. M. J. Klein, *History of the Eastern Synod of the Reformed Church,* 370–76.

2. Lewis Mayer to Bernard C. Wolff, 16 October 1821, reproduced in Theodore Appel, *The Beginnings of the Theological Seminary of the Reformed Church in the United States, from 1817 to 1832* (Philadelphia: Reformed Church Publication Board, 1886), 26–30.

3. Franklin P. Watts, "The Free Synod Movement of the German Reformed Church, 1822–1837" (S.T.D. diss., Temple University, 1954); George W. Richards, *History of the Theological Seminary of the Reformed Church in the United States, 1825–1934 [and] Evangelical and Reformed Church, 1934–1952* (Lancaster, Pa.: Theological Seminary of the Evangelical and Reformed Church, 1952), 117.

4. The colonial-era German Reformed Coetus had been under the jurisdiction of the Synod of Amsterdam. In 1793, the coetus became a self-governing synod. See *Minutes and Letters of the Coetus,* 431, and *Acts and Proceedings,* 8–9 (1793).

5. Hierarchical authority was rarely arbitrary or capricious, which was also part of the

delicate balance. For example, congregational election of pastors needed to be ratified by the synod, but such approval was nearly always forthcoming. (See a close approval vote, however, in *Acts and Proceedings*, 33 [1802].)

6. Appel, *Recollections of College Life*, 67. See also the only visual representation of the synod, a contemporary watercolor by Lewis Miller (1796–1882) of York, Pa. His painting of the 1828 synod held at York is in [Lewis Miller], *Lewis Miller, Sketches and Chronicles. The Reflections of a Nineteenth-Century Pennsylvania German Folk Artist* (York, Pa.: Historical Society of York County, 1966), 109.

7. The classes were Philadelphia, Northampton, Lebanon, Zion (i.e., York area), Susquehanna (i.e., north-central Pennsylvania), Western Pennsylvania, Maryland (which also included Virginia, North Carolina, and a few Pennsylvania congregations), and Ohio. (In 1824, the Ohio Classis became an independent synod.)

8. *Verhandlungen der Synode der Hochdeutschen Reformirten Kirche ... 1819* (Hagerstown, Md.: Johann Gruber and Daniel May, 1819), 8–14. They had initially considered such reorganization in 1817; see *Verhandlungen der Synode der Hoch-Deutschen Reformirten Kirche ... 1817* (Philadelphia: Conrad Zentler, 1818), 6. Several years later, in 1847, the penchant for rationalizing denominational structures affected Pennsylvania German Mennonites in Montgomery, Lehigh, Bucks, Berks, and Northampton Counties, producing a schism that bears similarities to the Reformed story detailed here. See Beulah Stauffer Hostetler, *American Mennonites and Protestant Movements: A Community Paradigm* (Scottdale, Pa.: Herald Press, 1987), 125–40, though Hostetler works with a model that simply equates assimilation and Americanization.

9. *Verhandlungen der Synode der Hochdeutschen Reformirten Kirche ... 1819*, 8–14.

10. *Acts and Proceedings*, 36 (1803). See Livingston's entry in *Dictionary of American Biography* (New York: Charles Scribner's Sons, 1928–37), 11:314–15. Livingston received his theological education from Connecticut Congregationalist Nathaniel Taylor and in the Netherlands at the University of Utrecht. Between 1784 and 1810, the Dutch Reformed seminary was located in New York City. In 1810, the school relocated to New Brunswick and shared the Queen's College campus.

11. *Acts and Proceedings*, 60 (1813). See also *Proceedings of the Reformed Dutch Church ...* [1812] (Albany, N.Y.: Farrand and Grear, 1812), 62, and *Proceedings of the General Synod of the Reformed Dutch Church ...* [1813] (Albany, N.Y.: E. E. Hosford, 1813), 19–20. When Dutch delegates appeared again in 1814, the German body resolved to "receive the delegates of the Sister Church in a brotherly and becoming cordial manner," and provide them with suitable lodging during the sessions of synod. See *Acts and Proceedings*, 67–68 (1814).

12. *Verhandlungen der General-Synode der Hochdeutschen Reformirten Kirche ... 1820* (Hagerstown, Md.: Johann Gruber and Daniel May, 1820), 13.

13. Glatfelter, *Pastors and People*, 2:161–70. It is perhaps also worth noting that in the colonial period, a significant number of the coetus's members came from the theological school at Herborn, known for its irenic approach to Lutheranism—a situation that may have contributed to the subsequent prejudice of Pennsylvania German Reformed. On Herborn, see O'Malley, *Pilgrimage of Faith*, 54–60, 98–109.

14. For background, see Balmer, *Perfect Babel*, especially 155–56. Dutch ethnicity remained more securely joined to the Reformed Church in the rural areas around Albany, though even here, by 1800, there had been a great deal of Dutch-Puritan melding (see Hackett, *Rude Hand*).

15. In 1815, the German Reformed congregation in Rockaway, N.J., joined the "Dutch Connection." The German Synod also registered concern about other anglicizing New Jersey Germans who asked for Presbyterian oversight; see *Acts and Proceedings*, 41, 44 (1805–6; Philadelphia incident) and 70, 73 (1815). In 1831 and 1832, Maryland Classis German Reformed churches complained that Presbyterian pastors were wooing their members and

making unwelcome attempts to "Presbyterianize" their congregations. See Guy P. Bready, *History of the Maryland Classis of the Reformed Church in the United States* ... (Taneytown, Md.: Carroll Record Printers, 1938), 39, 41. German Reformed pastor Johannes Braun (1771–1850) had the same complaints in Virginia; see Wust, *Virginia Germans*, 142.

16. *Berrichtungen des Synodes der hoch-Deutschen Reformirten Kirche ... 1818* (Hagerstown, Md.: Johann Gruber and Daniel May, 1819), 14–17, and Klaus G. Wust, *Zion in Baltimore, 1755–1955: The Bicentennial History of the Earliest German-American Church in Baltimore, Maryland* (Baltimore: Zion Church, 1955), 50–52.

17. *Berrichtungen des Synodes der hoch-Deutschen Reformirten Kirche ... 1818*, 9, 12–13.

18. This style of training had, of course, not been unique. For a description of this method in Congregational New England, traced over several generations, see David W. Kling, *A Field of Divine Wonders: The New Divinity and Village Revivals in Northwestern Connecticut, 1792–1822* (University Park: The Pennsylvania State University Press, 1993), 29–42.

19. Good, *History of the Reformed Church in the U.S.*, 12–20, and H. M. J. Klein, *History of the Eastern Synod of the Reformed Church*, 126. An example of student work is "A Catechism on Church Government," the notebook of Daniel Hertz, who studied under Samuel Helfenstein.

20. Students transcribed Herman's lectures, which were drawn from an old manuscript copy of European theological notes. Although fluent in English, Herman insisted on German in the classroom; see "The Late Rev. Joseph S. Dubbs," *Reformed Church Messenger*, 25 April 1877, 4. Other well-known instructors were Christian L. Becker (1756–1818), who trained nineteen candidates while serving as pastor in Lancaster and Baltimore, and Samuel A. Helfenstein (1775–1866) of Philadelphia, who had no fewer than twenty-seven students under his tutelage at one time or another. Helfenstein later published his lectures in English as *The Doctrines of Divine Revelation, as Taught in the Holy Scripture ... for Young Men Preparing for the Gospel Ministry in Particular* (Philadelphia: James Kay Jr. and Bro., 1842). They reveal an irenic and moderate approach reliant on the Heidelberg Catechism.

21. The synod had commissioned pastor William Hendel Jr. to compose a historical account of the German Reformed Church in America; it was appended to the 1817 synodic minutes. In his brief essay, Hendel praised the Dutch seminary and suggested its format for his own church's New World needs. See "Bericht der Committee die bestimmt war eine Untersuchung oder historische Nachricht von dem Ursprung und Fortgang unserer Synode zu geben," *Verhandlungen der Synode der Hoch-Deutschen Reformirten Kirche ... 1817*, 14–20; comments on the Dutch Reformed Church and their seminary appear on 19.

22. The financially endowed but academically impoverished Franklin College was supported by both Lutheran and German Reformed; see Dubbs, *History of Franklin and Marshall College*, 112. See also *Berrichtungen des Synodes des hoch-Deutschen Reformirten Kirche ... 1818*, 5–6 (on the seminary) and 9, 12–13 (on correspondence with the Dutch).

23. John H. Livingston, *An Address to the Reformed German Churches in the United States* (New Brunswick, N.J.: William Myer, 1819), 8, 20, 23–30.

24. In contrast, thirty-seven ministers, thirteen ministerial candidates, and forty-six elders had attended the 1819 synod.

25. *Verhandlungen der General-Synode der Hochdeutschen Reformirten Kirche ... 1820*, 19–21.

26. Milledoler was actually present at this meeting, being the Dutch Reformed fraternal observer sent from New York that year. Born in Rhinebeck, N.Y., to Swiss parents, Milledoler had studied theology under German Reformed pastor John D. Gros (1738–1812). Milledoler was even ordained by the German Reformed Synod in 1794, but had spent most of the next quarter-century as pastor in Presbyterian and Dutch Reformed congregations (serving as moderator of the Presbyterian General Assembly in 1808) and promoting various religious associations, such as the American Bible Society and United Foreign Mission Society. See his entry in the *Dictionary of American Biography*, 12:618–19, and Milledoler's appeal for a broadly

Reformed coalition of public-minded American churches, presented in a July Fourth sermon: *A Discourse Delivered by Appointment of the General Synod of the Reformed Dutch Church . . . at Hackensack, N.J. . . . July 6, 1824* (New York: G. F. Hopkins, 1824), especially 11.

27. *Verhandlungen der General-Synode der Hochdeutschen Reformirten Kirche . . . 1820*, 21–24, records the discussion on the seminary and its proposed role in the synod. Livingston had suggested supporting the school through subscription-paying voluntary societies established for that purpose; see Livingston, *Address to the Reformed German Churches*, 33–34. Apparently exceptions were made to the prohibition of pastoral apprenticeships. It is likely that the last ordination of an apprenticed pastor was in 1862, when the Lancaster Classis ordained George Kurtzman (1819–86), a German immigrant of 1839 and cordwainer by trade. Married to Susanna Salade, a Pennsylvania German woman from Lebanon, Kurtzman was licensed in 1861 and ordained the next year after the Lancaster Classis petitioned to have the formal requirements for ordination reduced. There is no record of Kurtzman's having been enrolled in a formal educational program before that time. He served churches in Pennsylvania, Wisconsin, and Minnesota. Correspondence from Ralph Kurtzman, Berkeley, Calif., May 2001.

28. Much of the negative reaction was centered in the denomination's eastern Pennsylvania strongholds, though opposition also surfaced in the western part of Pennsylvania and in Ohio: pastors there complained about the provision forbidding private ministerial training and said that the seminary was too far from their fields of labor.

29. On the charges and complaints against the seminary, see the articles by Lewis ("Ludwig") Mayer and Ferdinand Bergenmeyer that appeared in the *Reading (Pa.) Adler*, even as the schism was unfolding. Mayer's essays appeared on the following dates: 26 March 1822, [2–3]; 2 April 1822, [1–2]; 9 April 1822, [1–2]; 14 May 1822, [2]; 4 June 1822, [2]; and 18 June 1822, [2]. Bergenmeyer's pieces appeared on 23 April 1822, [1–2]; 30 April 1822, [2]; 7 May 1822, [2]; 11 June 1822, [1–2]; 25 June 1822, [2]; and 16 July 1822, [1]. One of the curious side-debates in this exchange was Bergenmeyer's insistence that Milledoler was not of German extraction—as Mayer maintained—but Danish.

30. Isaiah N. Rapp, comp., "Minutes of the Philadelphia Classis, 1820–25," bound volume dated 1938, Evangelical and Reformed Historical Society, Lancaster, Pa., minutes for 20–22 May 1821, 6–8. Casper Wack (1752–1839), J. William Dechant (1784–1832), and Frederick W. Van der Sloot (1773–1831) constituted the committee. Van der Sloot was the pastor who, in 1818, had led dissident members of the Philadelphia congregation in forming a German-language-only congregation.

31. Lewis Mayer to Bernard C. Wolff, 25 June 1821, reprinted in Appel, *Beginnings of the Theological Seminary*, 24–26. The book contains an entire run of transcribed Mayer correspondence that, according to Appel, was found among Wolff's papers. However, the original letters are no longer extant. In several cases, Appel replaced key proper names with blank spaces to protect the anonymity of individuals about whom Mayer wrote especially critically. To seminary supporters, the Dutch connection via Milledoler was apparently also important because Frederick-area seminary boosters had pledged money on the promise that a professor of national standing could be obtained.

32. In Mayer's opinion, "[t]he object of [Helfenstein's] call appeared to me to be to effect the withdrawal of Dr. Milledoler, a change in the location of the Seminary, and an alteration of its Plan. The call was made at so late a period, and so unexpectedly, that many of the brethren who reside at great distances could not attend; and it was manifestly so irregular and unconstitutional that some who attended brought no lay deputies with them" (Mayer to Wolff, 16 October 1821, in ibid., 26–30). See also Rapp, comp., "Minutes of the Philadelphia Classis," 20–22 May 1821, 7–8.

33. Lewis Mayer reported that the "party in opposition [to establishing a seminary] were an overwhelming majority;" moreover, "[s]ome of our friends had abandoned us, and gone

over to the other side" (ibid.). While the body elected seminary-supporter Lebrecht L. Hinch (1769–1864) as president, the votes did seem to support Mayer's sense of the synod.

34. See the comments and arguments of Ferdinand Bergenmeyer, *Reading Adler,* 23 April 1822, [1–2].

35. Mayer to Wolff, 16 October 1821, in Appel, *Beginnings of the Theological Seminary,* 26–30. See also *Verhandlungen einer Allegemeinen Synode der hochdeutschen Reformirten Kirche ... 1821* (Philadelphia: Conrad Zentler, 1821), 11–16; see 18 on incorporation. The Dutch delegates were Cornelius Westbrook and Thomas DeWitt.

36. Mayer to Wolff, 16 October 1821, in Appel, *Beginnings of the Theological Seminary,* 26–30. This was also the assessment of the committee that prepared the "state of religion" report at the close of the Synod: see *Verhandlungen einer Allegemeinen Synode der hochdeutschen Reformirten Kirche ... 1821,* 21–22.

37. "... zu kostspielig für unsere Gemeinden in diesen drückenden Zeiten werden."

38. *Reading Adler,* 12 February 1822, [3]; the article was reprinted on the first page of the 19 February 1822 issue. Although a secular paper, the *Adler* was a forum for church news. It carried notices of German Reformed classis meetings, for example; see 17 April 1821, [1], and 31 March 1829, [2]. On the *Adler*'s influence, see Karl J. R. Arndt and May E. Olson, eds., *German-American Newspapers and Periodicals, 1732–1955: History and Bibliography* (Heidelberg: Quelle and Meyer, 1961), 587–88.

39. The *Reading Adler* reported the withdrawal of East Vincent, Coventry, and St. Peter's Churches in Chester County, the Center Church in Lancaster County, and the Allegheny congregation in Berks County (see 12 February 1822, [3]).

40. *Reading Adler,* 26 February 1822, [3].

41. On 23 February 1822, Zion Church (Berks County) and the Montgomery County Trappe congregations withdrew. See the *Reading Adler,* 5 March 1822, [3], and 2 April 1822, [2]. On 28 February 1822, the Pottsgrove [Pottstown] church announced its independence as well: *Reading Adler,* 2 April 1822, [2]. On 2 March 1822, the Pike Township (Berks County) congregation withdrew, as did the Colebrook Township (Berks County) Reformed Church; on 20 March 1822, the Bensalem, Zion, Corner, and Jacob's Churches, all in Lehigh County, followed suit. See the *Reading Adler,* 19 March 1822, [3], and 2 April 1822, [2]. The quotation is from the Pike Church declaration, but they all cited similar concerns.

42. See Charles G. Herman, "Private Records of Rev. Chas. G. Herman. Corrected copy," transcribed by C. E. Keiser, Historical Society of Berks County, Reading, Pa. His records illustrate the extensive ministry he performed from 1810 to 1861, listing baptisms, marriages, and funerals. The single-spaced index of his baptismal registry alone—in double columns—runs to 105 pages!

43. The constitution and subsequent minutes of the Free Synod's annual gatherings are transcribed as William J. Hinke, ed., "Synodical Ordnung und Protocoll der Verhandlungen der Synode der Hochdeutschen Freyen Reformirten Gemeinden in Pennsylvanien Angefangen den 24sten Tag April, Anno Domini, 1822," bound volume dated 1934, Evangelical and Reformed Historical Society, Lancaster, Pa. The constitution appears on 2–4; the minutes follow. All are in German except those of 1832, which are in English. An English translation of the minutes appears as a 247-page appendix to Franklin Watts, "Free Synod Movement." The constitution dealt mostly with synod logistics and the duties and powers of Free Synod officers.

44. Berks County's Salem congregation withdrew on 30 March 1822; the White Reformed Church of Berks County withdrew on 26 May 1822; Lebanon County's Mühlbach Church withdrew on 24 March 1822. See the reports in the *Reading Adler,* 9 April 1822, [2]; 11 June 1822, [2]; and 18 June 1822, [2].

45. *Verhandlungen der General Synode der Hochdeutschen Reformirten Kirche ... 1822* (Philadelphia: Conrad Zentler, 1823), 27–28. In contrast, pastor John C. Guldin sent a sharply

worded reply to a similar Philadelphia Classis inquiry, signaling his contempt for the old church (ibid., 28).

46. "Kirchen-Angelegenheiten," *Reading Adler,* 25 June 1822, [3]. Hendel was to have given the charge at the planned June 1822 inauguration of Milledoler. See Mayer to Wolff, 21 February 1822, in Appel, *Beginnings of the Theological Seminary,* 31–32 and 45.

47. Hinke, ed., "Synodical Ordnung und Protocoll," 87–88. In 1832, the old church listed 329 congregations. The last two pages of the appendix in Franklin Watts, "Free Synod Movement," present a listing of all the ministers licensed and ordained by the Free Synod.

48. Mayer to Wolff, 21 May 1822, in Appel, *Beginnings of the Theological Seminary,* 32–34. Milledoler's two letters of resignation (dated 20 February 1822 and 18 March 1822) are reprinted in Clement Z. Weiser, "The External History of the Theological Seminary of the Reformed Church in the United States, Lancaster, Pa.," *Mercersburg Review* 23 (January 1876): 34–36. Milledoler said that he had read copies of the synod minutes and sensed resistance to the school.

49. George Richards, *History of the Theological Seminary,* 129–37.

50. *Verhandlungen der allegemeinen Synode der Hochdeutschen Reformirten Kirche ... 1824* (Baltimore: J. I. Hanzsche, 1824), 13–14. The entire discussion recorded in the minutes is filled with appeals to ethnic pride and "German patriotism." Perhaps this explicit pro-German sentiment emerged after the "English" school provoked such a strong reaction from so many members and clergy. The discussion resulted in the synod's decision to relocate the seminary from its initial home at Dickinson College (a Presbyterian school at the time) to an independent location in York, Pa.

51. Bready, *History of the Maryland Classis,* 36–42. In 1825, one of the classis meeting sermons (delivered by Samuel Helfenstein Jr.) was in English, but through 1849, the annual gatherings of the Maryland Classis also featured German sermons. The congregation in Frederick, where the seminary was to have been, did not begin English worship until 1829; had the seminary been there, it may not have changed even then, because there was still enough German-language sentiment in 1829 to divide the congregation. See Edmund R. Eschbach, *Historic Sketch of the Evangelical Reformed Church of Frederick, Maryland* (Frederick, Md.: Great Southern Printing, 1894), 30.

52. Clearly, the accompanying debates helped sharpen the differences that, by 1824, separated the two sides. As late as 1863, an interpretation of the division could still be presented in stark, if not angry, terms: see [Henry Harbaugh], *Ueber Spaltungen und Unabhängigkeit in der Kirche Christi, mit besonderer Rücksicht auf neuliche Erregungen des schismatischen Geistes in Theilen der Reformirten Kirche in Pennsylvanien. Schriftlich, historisch, und praktisch dargestellt. Rom. 16:17* (Harrisburg, Pa.: Kuhn und Haas, 1863), 25–30.

53. Gock published a mathematics book in addition to plunging into religious polemics: Carl Gock, *Carl Gock's Neuestes selbstlehrendes rechen-buch. Verfasst nach den grundregeln der deutschen hebkunst, wie solche durch prof. Rees in Deutschland eingeführt worden. Nebst einem anhange ueber das ausmessen. Besonders dem werthen bauernstande gewidmet ...* (Reading, Pa.: Heinrich B. Sage, 1823). The book appeared in later editions in 1826 and 1828. Yet even the preface to this text provided Gock a polemical stage from which to attack Johann C. Gossler (see below) and Johann Georg Homan, the author of a popular book of Pennsylvania German folk medicine and magic. Gock accused both men of misrepresenting his opinions.

54. [Henry Harbaugh], "Carl Gock: Sketch of a Character," *The Guardian* 14 (August 1863): 256–60. The piece gives some biographical information, along with a brief description of the pamphlet controversy. One should use the piece with real care, however: its tone is virulent, and some of the names and facts concerning the pamphlet controversy are incorrect. Harbaugh presented Gock as a political swindler and quack doctor, and he described a meeting with Gock in his old age in the Reading poorhouse. Nevertheless, Harbaugh thought

Gock's writings influential: "Notwithstanding the shallowness of the performance, this book exerted a powerful influence upon the ignorant of that day, the effects of which have been felt down to the present time.... Copies of this mischievous book are still extant; and wherever any disposition toward ecclesiastical insubordination manifests itself in any congregation in that region of the country, the book of Carl Gock is still sought and re-read" (285). With regard to politics, Gock reported that he was "a Washington, Federal, Independent Democrat," and in religion, "a Lutheran—an old Lutheran" (259).

55. Carl Gock, *Die Vertheidigung der Freyen Kirche von Nord-Amerika. In sechs Abschnitten abgefaßt ... besonders dem werthen Bauernstande gewidmet* (Reading, Pa.: Carl Gock, 1822), 7.

56. Gudehus, "Journey to America," 262–64.

57. Gock, *Die Vertheidigung der Freyen Kirche*, 11, 12.

58. The Constitution of the Commonwealth of Pennsylvania, art. 3, sec. 1, in *Pennsylvania Archives*, 1st ser., 12:17.

59. Gock, *Die Vertheidigung der Freyen Kirche*, 13–14.

60. On the ecclesiastical oppressors of Europe, see ibid., 14–15. The entire second chapter of the book (39–48) is a harangue against the European clergy, while the fifth section is a brief history of the world as the conflict between tyrannical clergy and liberty-loving people of true faith (73–99). At another place, he suggests that European-style religious persecution has surfaced on American shores in New England (33–34).

61. Ibid., 19–22, 101–3, 111–12.

62. Gock claimed that apprentice-style ministerial training was the "apostolic tradition" (ibid., 32). Gock's penchant for biblical quotations suggesting the foolishness of higher education (compared to the simple faith of children) gives portions of his essay a highly anti-intellectual feel. Yet he also argued for establishing more primary schools for rural Pennsylvania Germans—a project that suffered for funds, he felt, while the seminary would consume an ever-larger budget. See ibid., 49–53, 60; see also 16 for "animals in human form."

63. Ibid., 100, 104, 106, 112, and 107–11 (which includes the story of a seminary graduate in Jena who lacked the spiritual common sense of his uneducated uncle). Some of Gock's anticlerical language sounds similar to that described in Hatch, *Democratization of American Christianity*.

64. Such a body would only "test candidates to see if they have enough knowledge and fortitude to be a preacher and take counsel of the teaching of Jesus." Indeed, he hoped that some day, Lutherans might even join the group and establish a church organized on Pennsylvania German principles. See Gock, *Die Vertheidigung der Freyen Kirche*, 22–24, 28, 114, 118.

65. Ibid., 114, 116, and 19–22.

66. Theodor Eylert, *Die Finsterniß in der freyen Kirche von America. Eine Abhandlung, veranlaßt durch die in Reading erschienene Schrift, betitelt: "die Vertheidigung der freyen Kirche" von Carl Gock* (Reading, Pa.: n.p., 1823), 3; 13, 18, 20, 30; and 5, 8.

67. Ibid., 10. See also the comments on order, society, and church (17).

68. Ibid., 11, 25–26. See Bushman, *Refinement of America*, for a scholarly treatment of this paradox in antebellum American culture. Eylert's comments here parallel the sentiments of Gudehus in his "Journey to America," 264, 278, and 292–94.

69. Eylert, *Die Finsterniß in der freyen Kirche*, 32.

70. J[ohann] C. Gossler, *Carl Gock's Verläumdungen, oder die Rechtfertigung der hochdeutschen Lutherischen und Reformirten Synoden von Nord-America. In 3 Abschnitten ...* (Reading, Pa.: C. A. Bruckman, 1823).

71. J[ohann] C. Gossler, *Lebensgeschichte Napoleon Bonaparte's, des Ersten Kaisers der Franzosen, mit besonderer Rücksicht auf dessen zehnjährige Regierung, Verbannung und Tod. Vier Theile in einem Band, mit Kupfern ...* (Reading, Pa.: C. A. Bruckman, 1822). Gossler was apparently involved in a variety of publishing enterprises; see his obituary in the *Reading Adler*, 12 April 1831, [3].

72. Gossler, *Carl Gock's Verläumdungen*, 23, 65, 74, 96, and 12–13.

73. Gossler charged Gock with an anticlericalism that unconstitutionally abrogated the clergy's legal rights (see ibid., 97–98).

74. Ibid., 33, 35–36, 40–41, 95–96. He was also sure that the synodic form of church government was republican (123–24).

75. Ibid., 35. Gossler similarly asserted that America, by law, cannot have an aristocracy; therefore, there is no danger of social stratification (124–25).

76. Ibid., 37 and 92; 95; and 144–45. In fact, Gossler insisted that "the reverends of the 'Free Synod' already some time ago completely discarded the old symbolical book, namely the Heidelberg school catechism, after which the members of the German Reformed Church in North America and their parents and grandparents were confirmed," and introduced "a whole new teaching book" (154). The charge was incorrect, however, as it referred to the group's republishing L. F. Herman's text to accompany the catechism—a type of book several Reformed pastors had issued in America to assist in teaching (not replacing) the Heidelberg document. See Lebrecht F. Hermann [*sic*], *Catechismus der Glaubenslehren und Lebenspflichten der Christlichen Religion* ... (Reading, Pa.: J. Ritter, 1813 [and various later reprintings and editions]).

77. Gossler, *Carl Gock's Verläumdungen*, 155. L. F. Herman's son, Charles, hosted the Free Synod organizational meeting. Son-in-law John C. Guldin pastored three Chester County churches that were among the first to leave the old church.

78. There was no provision in Reformed polity for such a sweeping exclusion of Frederick Herman, and he was later reinstated, in fact, by the Lebanon Classis. Later, another of L. F. Herman's sons, Augustus L. Herman (1804–72), was also suspended by the old church. See Heisler and Harbaugh, *Fathers of the German Reformed Church*, 5:36–37, and *Verhandlungen einer Allgemeinen Synode der hochdeutschen Reformirten Kirche* ... *1821*, 21.

79. Gossler, *Carl Gock's Verläumdungen*, 18–21, 138. The forgery charge involved a 9 February 1822 meeting at the New Hanover congregation.

80. "Kirchen-Angelegenheiten," *Reading Adler*, 24 June 1823, [2]. The resolutions quoted from and refuted the Gossler book, particularly on the charges of forgery, financial mismanagement of contributions, and disregard for the Heidelberg Catechism. The protesting group also cited the Tennessee Lutheran Synod as another body of Pennsylvania German church folk who had refused to accept distant, centralizing authority—in their case, that of the Lutheran General Synod.

81. Appel, *Beginnings of the Theological Seminary*, 35–36.

82. By the 1850s, the American evangelical coalition was becoming more critical of the United States, but even that criticism was not set against the glories of the Old World. See Mark Y. Hanley, *Beyond a Christian Commonwealth: The Protestant Quarrel with the American Republic, 1830–1860* (Chapel Hill: The University of North Carolina Press, 1994).

83. Appel, *Beginnings of the Theological Seminary*, 34. Of course, Appel's commitment to a version of late-nineteenth-century Protestant ecumenicity likely colored his interpretation of any sort of schism.

CHAPTER 5

1. Reed and Matheson, *Narrative of the Visit*, 2:302, 315. It is not entirely clear which central-Pennsylvanian "valley" is meant here. See Charles I. Foster, *An Errand of Mercy: The Evangelical United Front, 1790–1837* (Chapel Hill: The University of North Carolina Press, 1960), 148–55, for a secondary discussion of the Matheson and Reed trip and their interest in British and American evangelical reformism. On the transatlantic element within evangelicalism, see Noll et al., *Evangelicalism*, especially 113–36.

2. Despite many common commitments, antebellum English-speaking evangelical Protestantism was not entirely united in its social outlook, though the activist, reformist wing mentioned here attained notable public prominence and influence. Curtis D. Johnson, *Redeeming America: Evangelicals and the Road to Civil War* (Chicago: I. R. Dee, 1993), 5–9, provides a concise survey and differentiation of antebellum anglophone evangelicals.

3. *New York Observer,* quoted in *Magazine of the German Reformed Church* 2 (September 1829): 281–82.

4. Randolph A. Roth, *The Democratic Dilemma: Religion, Reform, and the Social Order in the Connecticut River Valley of Vermont, 1791–1850* (New York: Cambridge University Press, 1987), 299–300.

5. Fred J. Hood, *Reformed America: The Middle and Southern States, 1783–1837* (Tuscaloosa: University of Alabama Press, 1980), 26, 198–99.

6. Gardiner Spring, *Memoirs of the Rev. Samuel J. Mills, late Missionary to the South Western Section of the United States and Agent of the American Colonization Society, deputed to Explore the Coast of Africa* (New York: New York Evangelical Missionary Society, 1820), 106–7.

7. Hood, *Reformed America,* 26. See also Feller, *Jacksonian Promise,* 95–117. On the Reformed tradition's influence as cultural custodian, see Paul K. Conkin, *The Uneasy Center: Reformed Christianity in Antebellum America* (Chapel Hill: The University of North Carolina Press, 1995). Categorizing support for evangelical united front ideas is far from exact. For example, Old School Presbyterians were often cool toward such efforts, yet the *New York Observer* (cited above), which generally opposed New School ideas, found Pennsylvania German reluctance to join in the spirit of national reformation alarming.

8. Foster, *Errand of Mercy,* 275–79, lists some 159 voluntary societies formed in the United States during the period 1790–1837; the list is not exhaustive. Lefferts A. Loetscher used the term "evangelical empire" to describe the same mainstream evangelical movement in "The Problem of Christian Unity in Early Nineteenth-Century America," *Church History* 32 (March 1963): 9. For an example of this movement's influence beyond its original Reformed constituency, see Diana Hochstedt Butler, *Standing Against the Whirlwind: Evangelical Episcopalians in Nineteenth-Century America* (New York: Oxford University Press, 1995). Jon Butler connected this evangelical institution-building impulse to the Revolution in his essay "Coercion, Miracle, Reason: Rethinking the American Religious Experience in the Revolutionary Age," in *Religion in a Revolutionary Age,* ed. Ronald Hoffman and Peter J. Albert (Charlottesville: The University Press of Virginia, 1994), 25–26.

9. George Potts, *An Address Delivered in Philadelphia, July 4, 1826, by George Potts, Pastor of the First Presbyterian Church . . .* (Philadelphia: Clark and Raser, 1826), 3, 12, 31–32. For an expression of these ideas in action, see the commentary in the 1815 Presbyterian General Assembly's discussion of the role of religion in the United States (as well as the issue of Sunday mail delivery): *Minutes of the General Assembly of the Presbyterian Church of the United States of America . . . 1789 to 1820, Inclusive* (Philadelphia: Presbyterian Board of Publication, [1847]), 592–94, 597–98. Johnson, *Redeeming America,* 7–8, uses the categories "formalist" and "antiformalist" to point to differences among antebellum English-speaking white evangelicals on the question of reform and national redemption. On some Baptists' distrust of the evangelical united front, see Foster, *Errand of Mercy,* 249–54. For an example of the relationship between rhetoric and reality, see William Breitenbach, "Sons of the Fathers: Temperance Reformers and the Legacy of the American Revolution," *Journal of the Early Republic* 3 (Spring 1983): 69–82.

10. For their part, some members of the evangelical united front saw in the historical figure of Martin Luther a symbol for their efforts; they even published biographies of the German reformer. See Lehmann, *Martin Luther,* 41–55.

11. See Robisheaux, *Rural Society;* Walker, *German Home Towns;* Gagliardo, *Reich and Nation;*

and Sabean, *Power in the Blood*. See also Roth, *Democratic Dilemma*, 304–5, for a brief comparison of New England, Wales, and Württemberg. Foster, *Errand of Mercy*, stresses the British origin of evangelical revivalism, stating in fact that his "book is a case study in … the transmission of British ideas to the United States and their adaptation to American purposes" ([vii]). His study makes no direct references to German Americans.

12. Rosalind Remer, *Printers and Men of Capital: Philadelphia Book Publishers in the New Republic* (Philadelphia: University of Pennsylvania Press, 1996), 125–48; Good, *History of the Reformed Church in the U.S.*, 50. The *Magazine*, begun in the fall of 1827, carried some original articles on German church history as well as synod and classis news, but in the early years, most of its material was reprinted from other religious papers of the day and so conveyed the activities of the evangelical united front. The same situation prevailed in the *Evangelical Lutheran Intelligencer* (1826–31) and the early *Lutheran Observer* (begun in 1831).

13. A broader context is available in Bertram Wyatt-Brown, "Prelude to Abolitionism: Sabbatarian Politics and the Rise of the Second Party System," *Journal of American History* 58 (September 1971): 316–41, and "Notes: The Rev. Dr. Ezra Stiles Ely," *Journal of the Presbyterian Historical Society* 2 (September 1904): 321–24.

14. Ezra Stiles Ely, *The Duty of Christian Freemen to Elect Christian Rulers; a Discourse Delivered on the Fourth of July, 1827, in the Seventh Presbyterian Church, in Philadelphia* (Philadelphia: W. F. Geddes, 1828), 5–6, 8, 11, 13. The next year, when the association sought a charter from the Pennsylvania Senate, senators found on each of their desks an anti–Sunday School Union broadside quoting portions of Ely's sermon and copies of Sunday School Union correspondence that spoke of "becoming dictators to the consciences of thousands." After sharp debate, the Senate denied granting the charter. Ely and fellow evangelicals then took their battle to the public, reprinting the pastor's controversial July Fourth sermon along with a seventeen-page appendix on "the liberty of Christians and of the American Sunday School Union"; portions of the Senate debate and a defense of Presbyterian-backed reform efforts appear on 15–32. As the text and the notes below illustrate, Ely's comments were known and quoted among Pennsylvania Germans. Negative reaction to Ely was not confined to Pennsylvania Germans, however. For a larger context and interpretation, see John G. West Jr., *The Politics of Revolution and Reason: Religion and Civic Life in the New Nation* (Lawrence: University Press of Kansas, 1996).

15. Richard R. John, *Spreading the News: The American Postal System from Franklin to Morse* (Cambridge: Harvard University Press, 1995), 169–205.

16. William P. Vaughn, *The Antimasonic Party in the United States, 1826–1843* (Lexington: The University Press of Kentucky, 1983), 89–90; on later Pennsylvania anti-Masonic activity, see 99–114. For a broader cultural study, see Steven C. Bullock, *Revolutionary Brotherhood: Freemasonry and the Transformation of the American Social Order, 1730–1840* (Chapel Hill: The University of North Carolina Press, 1996), 277–307. During 1829, a significant number of articles on Freemasonry and its threat to the country appeared in the *Reading Adler*, even though that paper continued to support Jacksonian Democrats rather than Anti-Masonic Party candidates. See, e.g., "Freymaurerey," *Reading Adler*, 31 March 1829, [3], which included an account of the William Morgan affair; "Freymaurerey," *Reading Adler*, 23 June 1829, [1–2]; "Freymaurerey," *Reading Adler*, 30 June 1829, [2–3]. See also Baglyos, "In This Land of Liberty," 126 n. 93, on Lutheran fear of Masonry.

17. Charles E. Hambrick-Stowe, *Charles G. Finney and the Spirit of American Evangelicalism* (Grand Rapids, Mich.: William B. Eerdmans, 1996), 83, 86; David Van Horne, *A History of the Reformed Church in Philadelphia* (Philadelphia: Reformed Church Publication Board, 1876), 64–73. Debates over revivalism in the Philadelphia German Reformed community eventually resulted in the defection of two ministers and an entire congregation from the denomination. Pastors Jacob Helfenstein (1802–84) and Joseph F. Berg (1812–71) favored new measures

revivalism and evangelical reformism. Race Street's pro-revivalist pastor, Berg, left the German Reformed Church for the Dutch Reformed in 1845; Germantown pastor Helfenstein and his congregation joined the Presbyterians, though not without a lengthy battle over church property that only concluded in 1856. See Charles E. Schaeffer, "The Helfenstein Family," *Bulletin: Theological Seminary of the Evangelical and Reformed Church* 26 (July 1955): 35–37. See also Jacob Helfenstein, "Revivals of Religion the Hope of the Church and the World," *Christian Observer,* 28 April 1855, 65–66. For his part, Finney's primary concern in Philadelphia was not the Germans but the city's Old School Presbyterians, who rebuffed his new measures techniques.

18. Finney, *Memoirs,* 260–69. The *Memoirs* point to a January 1830 arrival in Reading, but in a 19 September 1872 letter to Louis Richards (later president of the Berks County Historical Society), Finney drew on his wife's diary to document his stay in Reading as lasting from 9 January to 7 May 1829. This letter and two others to Richards are published as Milton W. Hamilton, ed., "Religious Revival in Reading, 1829," *Historical Review of Berks County* 15 (October 1949): 148–50. The letters reveal further details about the Reading revival than are recorded in Finney's *Memoirs.*

19. Charles Yrigoyen Jr., "The Second Great Awakening and Finney's Revival in Reading," *Historical Review of Berks County* 38 (Spring 1973): 65–73. See also Samuel E. Bertolet, "The Presbyterian Church in Reading," *Historical Review of Berks County* 7 (January 1943): 34–37, for information on the host congregation. The Reading Presbyterian Church was a relatively young congregation, formed in 1814, and was only the second English-speaking church in the community (after the Friends Meeting).

20. Finney to Louis Richards, 6 September 1872, in Hamilton, ed., "Religious Revival," 149; Finney, *Memoirs,* 267–68.

21. William Bell et al., letter dated 31 March 1829, in *Berks and Schuylkill Journal,* 4 April 1829, [3]; "To the elders . . . ," *Berks and Schuylkill Journal,* 18 April 1829, [3]. By way of comparison, see the description of Pietistic—but quiet and highly ordered—household spirituality promoted by Reformed layman Johannes Bausman (1782–1861). The Bausman children did not participate in Sunday schools, as the German Reformed church in their part of Lancaster County did not have such programs and discouraged participation in "Union" schools, fearing that they would draw children into English churches. See Henry H. Ranck, *The Life of the Reverend Benjamin Bausman, D.D., LL.D.* (Philadelphia: The Publication and Sunday School Board of the Reformed Church in the United States, 1912), 18–19, 30–32. In contrast, the Race Street Reformed Church—one of the denomination's few urban churches—had one of the earliest Sunday school programs in that city.

22. "Versammlungen in Cocalico Taunschip, Lancaster County," *Reading Adler,* 7 April 1829, [1–2]. The resolutions were signed by 130 men with German surnames. They also resolved to form committees of correspondence to communicate with residents of other counties.

23. "Meeting of Freemen," *Berks and Schuylkill Journal,* 30 May 1829, [3]. Those assembled were mostly said to be residents of Berks and Lebanon Counties. The ideas expressed by this gathering were essentially the same as those of the Cocalico group and the other subsequent gatherings (see below), but the Heidelberg meeting receives focused attention here because it was the gathering that seems to have drawn the most direct response in the denominational press. A German account of this meeting appeared as "Versammlung von Freyleuten in Heidelberg Taunschip," *Reading Adler,* 26 May 1829, [2], with the names of 171 signatories. This is the only list from any of the meetings that included pastors' names. Two Free Synod ministers—Joseph S. Dubbs of Lehigh County and Thomas H. Leinbach, who served a Lebanon and western Berks Counties charge—participated.

24. "Meeting of Freemen," [3].

25. Ibid.

26. Ibid.

27. Ibid.; their italics. Other resolutions included formally stating solidarity with the earlier Cocalico Township meeting and ordering the printing of the proceedings.

28. "Meeting of Freemen in Exeter Township," *Berks and Schuylkill Journal,* 11 July 1829, [3]. Again, the group noted its support of Bible reading and the promotion of Christian knowledge while rejecting the manner in which such things were currently promoted. They promised "respect and due deference" to ministers who stood by traditional understandings. A report of this meeting also appeared as "Versammlung der Freyleute von Exeter Taunschip," *Reading Adler,* 7 July 1829, [1–2], with 74 signatories.

29. "Freyleuten Versammlungen in Bern Taunschip," *Reading Adler,* 4 August 1829, [2]. The 24 July 1829 meeting attracted 166 signatories.

30. "Sunday Mails," *Berks and Schuylkill Journal,* 30 January 1830, [3]. The *Reading Adler* of 28 July 1829 had carried a critique of Presbyterian ministers and the anti–Sunday mail campaign under the title "Wahre und richtige Ansicht einer Sache" (see [1–2]).

31. Compare their rhetoric to that of antimissionary Baptists or restorationists in Hatch, *Democratization of American Christianity.*

32. "Meeting of Freemen," [3].

33. *The Lutheran Magazine* 3 (July 1829): 145–47. *The Lutheran Magazine* was a publication of the Western Conference of Lutheran Ministers in the state of New York. The editor was responding to an article in the *Western Recorder,* 28 July 1829, that was highly critical of Lutheran and German Reformed "meetings which were held in different parts of Pennsylvania, in opposition to the Bible, Tract, Missionary and Sabbath School Societies, Theological Seminaries, etc.," and which were "going the rounds of the public journals" and "doing an injury to the cause of benevolence" (1). Soon after these events, some upstate New York Lutherans formed the Hartwick Synod, which took a sympathetic stance toward the program of the evangelical united front. A strong antislavery, pro-revivalism faction within the synod later split away to form the Franckian Synod. See Paul P. Kuenning, *The Rise and Fall of American Lutheran Pietism: The Rejection of an Activist Heritage* (Macon: Mercer University Press, 1988).

34. "Meeting at Heidelberg, Berks County, Pa.," *Magazine of the German Reformed Church* 2 (August 1829): 229. The author was "A Christian Freeman."

35. Ibid., 230–31, 233.

36. Cf. Johnson, *Redeeming America,* who treats the "anti-formalist" English-speaking evangelicals' reasons for rejecting the activist political agenda of the "formalist" evangelicals.

37. *Minutes of the German Evangelical Lutheran Synod of Pennsylvania ... 1829* (Philadelphia: Conrad Zentler, 1829), 14–16.

38. Ibid.

39. "Review: Address to the Classis of East Pennsylvania," *Magazine of the German Reformed Church* 2 (September 1829): 279. Presenting news of the meeting, editor Daniel Young reported that "[t]he preceding article will be new to few of our readers, as it has been before the public several months and extensively circulated, especially by the German papers. We have translated it from the *Hanover* [Pa.] *Gazette,* the Editor of which states that he 'as well as *all other German Editors* had been requested to publish it,' but we know not that it has before made its appearance in an English dress" (280). The statement also appears in the "Minutes of the East Pennsylvania Classis, 1829," 67–73, Evangelical and Reformed Historical Society, Lancaster, Pa., and the *Reading Adler,* 9 July 1829, [2].

40. "Review," 279–80. The *New York Observer* reported that many Pennsylvania Germans feared "the object of the American Sunday School Union is to draw away young people from the German churches" (quoted in *Magazine of the German Reformed Church* 2 [September 1829]: 281).

41. "Review," 279. Hood, *Reformed America*, set out to discuss a variety of Reformed groups, but ultimately drew examples almost exclusively from Presbyterians. The British evangelical visitors reported that the Presbyterians were the most influential denomination in Pennsylvania. See Reed and Matheson, *Narrative of the Visit*, 2:315. The Presbyterians, divided along Old School and New School lines, were not as united as the Pennsylvania Germans believed them to be.

42. "Meeting at Heidelberg," 234.

43. Henry Harbaugh, *Fathers of the German Reformed Church*, 2:315–20; *Proceedings of the Synod of the German Reformed Church . . . 1829* (York, Pa.: Samuel Wagner, 1829), 19–20. A graduate of Union College, Young also attended Princeton Theological Seminary.

44. [Daniel Young], "Introduction," *Magazine of the German Reformed Church* 2 (January 1829): 1–2. See also Young's 27 September 1829 sermon, "The Influence of the Church," published in *Magazine of the German Reformed Church* 2 (November 1829): 321–28.

45. "Review," 280.

46. Ibid., 281. The *Evangelical Lutheran Intelligencer* of March 1830 reported that some Lutheran parents suspicious of the interdenominational designs of Sunday school programs were withdrawing their children in protest (9).

47. "Classis of East Pennsylvania," *Magazine of the German Reformed Church* 2 (October 1829): 320. Young had promised to address "the peculiar state of society, the history of the recent general and unhappy excitement and its special bearing on the pastors of those churches," but later complained that "[o]nly one individual of the few contributors to the magazine possesses the requisite local knowledge" to investigate such a piece, "and circumstances beyond our control have necessarily prevented him from writing." James I. Good believed that pastors warned Young that he would lose all credibility if he continued his argument: see Good, *History of the German Reformed Church in the U.S.*, 52. Good incorrectly identified Lewis Mayer as the author. On Young's editorship, see *Magazine of the German Reformed Church* 1 (October 1828): 383, and [Young], "Introduction," 1.

48. "Union of Church and State," *Magazine of the German Reformed Church* 2 (September 1829): 268–69. The author was "No Presbyterian."

49. Ibid., 269, and 270–71. The *Reading Adler*, 9 July 1829, [1–2], had carried an article on the "union of church and state" that was far less generous to "Presbyterian" and "New England clergy." It also quoted Ely's widely reported remarks.

50. Carl Gock, *Meine religiöse und darauf Bezug habende politische Ansicht von Nord-Amerika und Fortsetzung der "Vertheidigung der freyen Kirche." Verfaßt in drey Theilen . . .* (Reading, Pa.: Carl Gock, 1830), 5–8. Much of the introduction and some portions of the text itself (e.g., 20–23) repeat Gock's earlier arguments and illustrations from 1822. Gock-style views against the seminary were still very much in circulation. See "Der Geistliche Stand u. Seminarium," *Reading Adler*, 2 June 1829, [2].

51. Gock, *Meine religiöse und darauf Bezug habende politische Ansicht*, 55, 62–63.

52. Ibid., 71–72. He also criticized Methodists, Episcopalians, and Catholics (73–75), though his comments here and elsewhere on Presbyterians were the most extensive.

53. Ibid., 87–88. In the eighteenth century, Lutheran patriarch Heinrich M. Muhlenberg had occasionally complained about Presbyterians' political power in Pennsylvania. See his comments in Muhlenberg, *Journals*, 3:551 (8 July 1783) and 3:625 (23 October 1784). The Lutheran seminary professor, Samuel S. Schmucker, had attended Princeton Theological Seminary. The German Reformed seminary professor, Lewis Mayer, had no seminary training himself, but assistant professor Daniel Young had studied at Princeton. Since both groups' seminaries were quite new and very small, few students had actually graduated at this time. Gock's fears were more forward-looking than present-minded.

54. Gock, *Meine religiöse und darauf Bezug habende politische Ansicht*, 89–113.

55. Ibid., 93–94, 108 [Matt. 11:25–26], 112 [John 18:36], 109, 113.

56. *Proceedings of the Synod of the German Reformed Church in the United States ... 1829*, 17. Of course, this observation did not include the many Free Synod German Reformed who generally were decidedly "prejudiced" against such institutions.

57. *Magazine of the German Reformed Church* 2 (November 1829): 349. Founded in 1827, the "American Missionary Society for the German Reformed Church" was to provide preachers for far-flung German frontier settlers, and its interests remained rather sectarian, charged with ensuring the church's "soundness of ... doctrines and its chaste and rational mode of worship." See *Proceedings of the Synod of the German Reformed Church in North America ... 1827* (Hagerstown, Md.: Gruber and May, 1828), 35; the organization's constitution appears on 29–32.

58. "State of religion" report in "Proceedings of the Synod of the German Reformed Church in the U. States of N. America, held at Hagerstown, Md., September 26, 1830," *Magazine of the German Reformed Church* 4 (January 1831): 19.

59. *Minutes of the German Evangelical Lutheran Synod of Pennsylvania ... 1830* (Easton, Pa.: Christian J. Hutter, 1830), 6.

60. Good, *History of the Reformed Church*, 37 n. See the biographical sketch of Ritner in *Dictionary of American Biography*, 15:629–30. The Indiana Lutheran Synod, organized in 1835, went on record as opposing "the falsely so-called benevolent societies of today, such as the Tract, Temperance, Mission, Bible, and a host of other such fanatical societies": see the quotation in Rehmer, "Indiana Lutherans at the Nineteenth-Century Crossroads," 76–78.

CHAPTER 6

1. David F. Schaeffer, *Historical Address Commemorative of the Blessed Reformation, Commenced by Dr. Martin Luther, ... Delivered in the Lutheran Church at Frederick Town, Md., October 31, A.D. 1817* (Frederick, Md.: William B. Burke, 1818), opening quotation, [5]; hymn, 22–23.

2. Samuel S. Schmucker, *Elements of Popular Theology, with Special Reference to the Doctrines of the Reformation as Avowed Before the Diet at Augsburg, in MDXXX*, 2d and corrected ed. (New York: Leavitt, Lord, 1834), 37.

3. Spaeth et al., eds., *Documentary History*, 468, 476. Samuel Schmucker gave the dollar amount in "Retrospect of Lutheranism in the United States," in *The American Lutheran Church, Historically, Doctrinally, and Practically Delineated, in Several Occasional Discourses*, 2d ed. (Springfield, Ohio: David Harbaugh, 1851), 28. The Francke Foundation operated the famed Halle orphanage and other projects. The sources cited here suggest that the Americans thought they were sending funds to prop up the orphanage and the University of Halle, which had been closed by Napoleon.

4. Vergilius Ferm, *The Crisis in American Lutheran Theology: A Study of the Issue Between American Lutheranism and Old Lutheranism* (New York: Century, 1927), 32–33.

5. This sort of ahistorical orientation among Pietists also surfaced in their approach to biblical interpretation, which favored subjective, allegorical renderings in place of the more historical readings that had been recovered during the Reformation. See Hans W. Frei, *The Eclipse of Biblical Narrative: A Study in Eighteenth and Nineteenth Century Hermeneutics* (New Haven: Yale University Press, 1974), 1–50.

6. Leaders such as the Henkel family and (after 1820) the Tennessee Synod were key exceptions; see Pershing, "Paul Henkel," 97–119; on the Tennessee Synod, see Edmund Wolf, *Lutherans in America*, 372–86.

7. From his perspective in 1898, historian and denominational leader Henry E. Jacobs thought that the Reformation anniversary marked a turning point in discussions of Lutheran identity. See his "Confessional History of the Ministerium of Pennsylvania," *Lutheran Church*

Review 17 (April 1898): 367. From a confessional Missouri Synod perspective, the Reformation anniversary was also significant, though the assessment was much less sanguine than that of Jacobs. See Augustus L. Gräbner, *Geschichte der Lutherischen Kirche in America* (St. Louis: Concordia Publishing, 1892), 1:647–50, 664–66, 671, 679–83. In 1832, the Maryland Lutheran Synod resolved that "the 31st of October, the anniversary of the Reformation, be annually celebrated by holding public worship—or if it be not convenient, it is recommended to be celebrated on the Lord's day nearest the 31st of October each year": see *Lutheran Observer,* 15 December 1832, 74.

8. Spaeth et al., eds., *Documentary History,* 503. In 1833, the Lutheran General Synod would recommend that 31 October be celebrated annually in commemoration of the Reformation. See *Verhandlungen der General Synode der Evangelisch-Lutherischen Kirche ... 1833* (Gettysburg, Pa.: Heinrich C. Neinstedt, 1834), 48.

9. Spaeth et al., eds., *Documentary History,* 506, 513. The original letters from Bishop Carl Gottlieb Reichel (Bethlehem, Pa., 17 July 1817) and Bishop William White (Philadelphia, 14 October 1817) are located in the collection of Synodical Correspondence, Evangelical Lutheran Ministerium of Pennsylvania and Adjacent States, 1813–18, Lutheran Archives Center at Philadelphia, Lutheran Theological Seminary at Philadelphia, Philadelphia, Pa. (For events in New York City, see also Abdel Ross Wentz, *A Basic History of Lutheranism in America,* rev. ed. [Philadelphia: Fortress Press, 1964], 91.)

10. *Verhandlungen der Synode der Hoch-Deutschen Reformirten Kirche ... 1817,* 11. The letter from the Lutheran Ministerium appears on 7; it left promotion of the event up to each congregation, and it is not exactly clear what activities resulted.

11. Johann A. Probst, "Predigt am Reformations Fest," 11, manuscript, Lutheran Archives Center at Philadelphia, Lutheran Theological Seminary at Philadelphia, Philadelphia, Pa., quoted in Baglyos, "In This Land of Liberty," 208–9.

12. [John George Schmucker], *Die Augsburgische Confession der Evangelisch Lutherischen Kirche, nebst eine kurzen Reformations-Geschichte ...* (York, Pa.: C. T. Melsheimer, 1817), 1, 11, and 14–27 [history pagination]; the hymns appear on 28–32 (quotation from 30).

13. The relatively small number of Catholics within the Pennsylvania German pale may have also assuaged temporarily dormant Protestant fears. Statistics are difficult to obtain; in *Has the Immigrant Kept the Faith? A Study of Immigration and Catholic Growth in the United States, 1790–1920* (New York: Macmillan, 1925), Gerald Shaughnessy estimated that there were only 8,000 German Catholics in the United States in 1790, and 10,800 in 1800 (see 48, 238). They were concentrated in eastern cities such as Baltimore, Philadelphia, and New York. On the image of Luther in American anti-Catholicism, see Lehmann, *Martin Luther,* 47–55.

14. Fecher, *Movement for German National Parishes,* 93–96. In 1787, the Lutheran and Reformed clergy who operated Franklin College had included on the board of trustees the local priest, Father J. B. Causse, who served Lancaster's largely German-speaking parish. See Dubbs, *History of Franklin and Marshall College,* 26.

15. Joseph P. Chinnici, "American Catholics and Religious Pluralism, 1775–1820," *Journal of Ecumenical Studies* 16 (Fall 1979): 727–28. The essay deals with Catholic tolerance of Protestants, not with the emergence of Protestant anti-Catholicism. Beschter, later president of Georgetown College, was a traveling mission preacher between 1807 and 1813. The dedication was for Lebanon's St. Mary of the Assumption.

16. Light, *Rome and the New Republic,* 3–93. The eventual establishment of national parishes turned ethnic Catholic struggles inward and away from the attention and ideas attractive to previously sympathetic Pennsylvania German Protestants. Enough German Catholics were willing to accept episcopal authority, end agitation for lay trustees, and give up separate ethnic cemeteries in exchange for national parishes that their primary public identity became religious rather than linguistic or national. German Catholics in Pennsylvania saw their

influence dwindle as Irish immigrants increasingly assumed a dominant and public role in the church—a trend that also affected Pennsylvania German Protestant perceptions of Catholics. See Jay P. Dolan, "Philadelphia and the German Catholic Community," in *Immigrants and Religion in Urban America*, ed. Randall M. Miller and Thomas D. Marzik (Philadelphia: Temple University Press, 1977), 69–83, and Fecher, *Movement for German National Parishes*, 85, 97–107.

17. See Gottlieb Schober, *A Comprehensive Account of the Rise and Progress of the Blessed Reformation of the Christian Church by Dr. Martin Luther* . . . (Baltimore: Schaeffer und Maund, 1818), 128–31, on Britain's unacknowledged debt to Luther and negative characterization of Puritans and John Knox; ecumenical quotation from 211.

18. Gottlieb Schober to Pennsylvania Ministerium, 11 May 1814, translated letter in Synodical Correspondence, Evangelical Lutheran Ministerium of Pennsylvania and Adjacent States, 1813–18, Lutheran Archives Center at Philadelphia, Lutheran Theological Seminary at Philadelphia, Philadelphia, Pa. Little information on Luther and Lutheranism was available in early American textbooks or to the general public. See Lehmann, *Martin Luther*, 55–65.

19. E.g., Schober, *Comprehensive Account*, 208.

20. Lochman, *History, Doctrine, and Discipline of the Evangelical Lutheran Church*, 161.

21. Benjamin Kurtz, *Why Are You a Lutheran? Or a Series of Dissertations . . . of the Evangelical Lutheran Church in the United States* (Baltimore: Publication Rooms of the Evangelical Lutheran Church, 1843), 145.

22. Schmucker, *Elements of Popular Theology*, 38.

23. Don Yoder, "Lutheran-Reformed Union Proposals, 1800–1850: An American Experiment in Ecumenics," *Bulletin: Theological Seminary of the Evangelical and Reformed Church* 17 (January 1946): 39–77, engages many of the figures in this debate. However, the article's theme of ecumenism tends to conflate ethnically linked schemes with more theologically oriented programs, such as those of Samuel Schmucker and Philip Schaff (whose ecumenical notions were of a much different order). Likewise, Baglyos, "In This Land of Liberty," provides details on Lutherans' efforts to come to terms with American life, but draws heavily on the Samuel Schmucker circle of leaders especially engaged with popular American evangelicalism and thus obscures other ways in which Pennsylvania German Lutherans appropriated and worked with American ideals apart from such alliances.

24. On the Prussian union, see the brief treatment in Conser, *Church and Confession*, 13–27, or the more thorough J. F. Gerhard Goeters and Joachim Mau, eds., *Die Geschichte der Evangelische Kirche der Union*, vol. 1, *Die Anfänge der Union unter landesherrlichem Kirchenregiment (1817–1850)* (Leipzig: Evangelische Verlagsanstalt, 1992), 83–174. The Prussian union was only the best known of several Lutheran-Reformed church unions undertaken in German lands between 1817 and 1823.

25. *Minutes of the Proceedings of the General Synod of the Evangelical Lutheran Church . . . 1825*, 4, 13–15. The full text of the letter was published in translation in the first volume of *The Evangelical Lutheran Intelligencer*: see the issues for March 1826 (5–8) and April 1826 (25–28). On Gottlieb J. Planck (1751–1833), see Goeters and Mau, eds., *Geschichte der Evangelische Kirche*, 97, 105, 106, 333, 431.

26. Quoted in Adolph Spaeth, *Charles Porterfield Krauth, D.D., LL.D.* . . . (New York: Christian Literature, 1898), 1:323.

27. Mark O. Heller, "The Union Church Problem in Eastern Pennsylvania," *The Lutheran Church Quarterly* 14 (April 1941): 177; Abdel Ross Wentz, "Relations Between the Lutheran and Reformed Churches in the Eighteenth and Nineteenth Centuries," *Lutheran Church Quarterly* 6 (July 1933): 303, 308–13; and Glatfelter, *Pastors and People*, 2:161–70.

28. *Das Gemeinschaftliche Gesangbuch, zum gottesdienstlichen Gebrauch der Lutherischen und Reformirten Gemeinden in Nord-America* (Baltimore: Schaeffer und Maund, 1817). Its popularity was such that it was reprinted in 1817 (again), 1818, 1827, 1828, 1834, 1836, 1838, 1845,

and 1848. See Carl F. Schalk, *God's Song in a New Land: Lutheran Hymnals in America* (St. Louis: Concordia Publishing, 1995), 75–80, 90, and 200 n. 39. (Schalk acknowledges the hymnal's broad popularity despite the fact that his own confessional criteria produce a harsh evaluation of the book from his Lutheran theological standpoint.)

No other official German Reformed hymnal appeared between 1797 and 1843, and no Pennsylvania Lutheran Ministerium-issued book came out between 1786 and 1849. The Lutheran General Synod issued an English hymnal in 1828 and a German hymnal in 1833; the English one did not really penetrate the Pennsylvania Ministerium congregations in this period, however, and the German book drew heavily on *Das Gemeinschaftliche Gesangbuch* (Schalk, *God's Song*, 82, 91). For the endorsements of *Das Gemeinschaftliche Gesangbuch* by the ministerium and synod, see Spaeth et al., eds., *Documentary History*, 491–92, and *Acts and Proceedings*, 79 (1816). Because the book drew especially on eighteenth-century hymns, it was disliked by later-arriving immigrants (and contemporary scholars such as Schalk: see *God's Song*, 80, 227, 232). Yet that composition provided another mark of symbolic separation between Pennsylvania Germans and later German arrivals. See Yoder, "Lutheran-Reformed Union Proposals," 56 n. 41.

29. John W. Richards, "Diary," vol. 1, 21 September 1824–31 December 1830, Lutheran Archives Center at Philadelphia, Lutheran Theological Seminary at Philadelphia, Philadelphia, Pa. Richards was in Womelsdorf from 23 September to 11 October 1824, preaching for three Sundays: 26 September, 3 October, and 10 October. Other examples of interdenominational assistance include the aged and ailing Lutheran pastor, Benjamin German of Lehigh County, receiving assistance from both a Lutheran associate and a Reformed theology student. See Laury, *History of the Allentown Conference*, 111.

30. *Lutheran Observer*, 2 April 1832, 261–62. See also the description in Ernst L. Hazelius, *History of the American Lutheran Church from Its Commencement in the Year of Our Lord 1685 to the Year 1842* (Zanesville, Ohio: Edwin C. Church, 1846), 105–6, that minimized differences between the two groups.

31. Lutheran eucharistic piety was significant and the sacrament vitally important to faith, yet eucharistic theology was not highly developed or precisely Lutheran in dogmatic formulation and presentation (see Bernheim, *Das Abendmahl des Herrn*).

32. Spaeth et al., eds., *Documentary History*, 437.

33. See Samuel S. Schmucker, *Discourse in Commemoration of the Glorious Reformation of the Sixteenth Century*, 4th ed. (New York: Gould and Newman, 1838), 25–99, on links to civil and religious liberty. Schmucker did aver that most American Catholics were patriotic citizens, innocent of wrongdoing, and unacquainted with their history (1). In his *Portraiture of Lutheranism: A Discourse* (Baltimore: Publication Rooms [of the Evangelical Lutheran Church], 1840), Schmucker said that Catholicism, "[t]hough lamentably corrupt" in Luther's day, was in fact "a part of the true church of Christ." Only the Council of Trent had pushed it beyond the pale (15–16). Perhaps the most extended Lutheran-produced piece of anti-Catholicism was John G. Morris's translation of Carl G. Bretschneider, *Henry and Antonio, or the Proselytes of the Romish and Evangelical Churches . . . annotated by a Minister in the Lutheran Church* (Baltimore: Lucas and Deaver, 1834).

34. Samuel S. Schmucker, "Vocation of the Lutheran Church in America," in *American Lutheran Church*, 252. The standard biography of Schmucker is Abdel Ross Wentz, *Pioneer of Christian Unity: Samuel Simon Schmucker* (Philadelphia: Fortress Press, 1967).

35. Schmucker, *Discourse in Commemoration*, 24.

36. Spaeth et al., eds., *Documentary History*, 517, 522 (1818); 528, 538 (1819); 556–57 (1820).

37. *Plan-Entwurf zu einer Central Verbindung der Evangelisch-Lutherischen Kirche in den Vereinigten Staaten von Nord-Amerika* (Baltimore: Schaeffer und Maund, 1819), and *Constitution of the*

Evangelical Lutheran General Synod in the United States of North America; Together with the Proceedings of the Convention in which it was Formed. Translated from the German (Lancaster, Pa.: John Baer, [1820]), 8–9. See also John W. Early, "The Ministerium of Pennsylvania and the Organization of the General Synod," *Lutheran Church Review* 11 (January 1892): 61–70.

38. *Verrichtungen der Vierten General-Conferenz der Evangelisch-Lutherischen Prediger in Ohio ... [1821]* (n.p., [1821]), 5. The Ohio Synod sent observing delegates in 1823, but never joined. The New York Synod later joined in 1837.

39. *Verrichtungen der Evangelisch Lutherischen Synode von Maryland, Virginia, u.s.w. ... 1820* (Baltimore: Friedrich G. Schaeffer, [1820]), [3], 5.

40. Provision for a seminary was section six of the third article of the General Synod's constitution. Schmucker later raised money for the seminary with just such a public platform, speaking in June 1836 at Boston's Old South Church along with Presbyterian leaders from Philadelphia and New York and professors from Princeton and Andover Theological Seminaries. See "In Behalf of the Germans and the Seminary," 27 June 1836, unidentified newspaper article in Microfilm Corpus of American Lutheranism, reel 34.

41. *Verhandlungen der Deutsch-Evangelisch Lutherischen Synode von Pennsylvanien ... 1823* (Reading, Pa.: Johann Ritter, [1823]), 14–17 (14: "widerrufen und zur alten Ordnung der Dinge zurückkehren möchte"). The vote was seventy-two in favor and nine opposed, with three abstentions and three absentees. Years later, Schmucker recounted this event in very uncomplimentary terms to his seminary students. See the manuscript student notebook of J. W. Schwartz, 86–89, Archives, Abdel Ross Wentz Library, Lutheran Theological Seminary at Gettysburg, Gettysburg, Pa. See also *Minutes of the Proceedings of the General Synod of the Evang. Luth. Church ... 1823* (York, Pa.: Henry C. Neinstedt, 1823), 4; with sadness, the General Synod acknowledged the news of the Pennsylvania Ministerium's withdrawal (5–6).

42. Adam Stump and Henry Anstadt, eds., *History of the Evangelical Lutheran Synod of West Pennsylvania ... 1825–1925* (Chambersburg, Pa.: J. R. Kerr, 1925), 73–83.

43. Ibid., 84–90.

44. In 1829, the West Pennsylvania Synod reported 8,339 communicants (compared with at least 18,500 reported communicants in the Pennsylvania Ministerium). See *Minutes of the Proceedings of the Fifth General Synod of the Ev. Luth. Church ... 1829* (Gettysburg, Pa.: H. C. Neinstedt, 1829), 20–23.

45. The school was "to provide our churches with pastors who sincerely believe and cordially approve of the doctrines of the Holy Scriptures as they are fundamentally taught in the Augsburg Confession." Such wording would later raise the hackles of strict confessionalists, but at the time, it positioned the new school as a clearly Lutheran institution. Even later confessional opponents of the General Synod, such as David Henkel, initially objected to the General Synod on the basis of its perceived threat to local synodic rights as much as on doctrinal grounds. See Henkel's *Carolinian Herald of Liberty, Religious and Political; or a Testimony against attempted Measures, which in their Nature are Calculated to lead to the Establishment of Popery among Protestants* (Salisbury, N.C.: Krider and Bingham, 1821), especially 8–10, where he charges that the plan will allow "for Pennsylvania to sway her regal scepter over her sister states."

46. Schmucker's formulations eventually received the appellation "American Lutheranism." The term was first used in 1840, according to Ferm, *Crisis in American Lutheran Theology*, 131. As discussed elsewhere in this text, "American Lutheranism" is rather misleading from an analytical historical perspective, because Lutheran confessionalists and members of the Pennsylvania Ministerium (discussed below) also represented Americanizing propositions—though of a different sort. See also Wentz, *Pioneer of Christian Unity*, 46–49, on Schmucker's critique of Presbyterianism and affirmation of Lutheranism after his time at Princeton.

47. Schmucker, *Portraiture of Lutheranism*, 6. On Schmucker's and other U.S. Lutherans' use of Martin Luther in such arguments, see Lehmann, *Martin Luther*, 75–88.

48. Ibid., 9, 14–15. See also Schmucker, *Elements of Popular Theology*, 38, where Luther's Reformation produced the freedom for which "we [are] also indebted for the liberty, civil and religious, which distinguish this favoured land."

49. Schmucker, *Elements of Popular Theology*, 273. See also Baglyos, "In This Land of Liberty," 79–91, on Luther as America's forefather. Baglyos's most potent example, however, is Frederick H. Quitman, a non–Pennsylvania German whose influence on the people discussed here was marginal.

50. From an 1826 West Pennsylvania Synod circular quoted in Stump and Anstadt, eds., *History of the Evangelical Lutheran Synod of West Pennsylvania*, 89.

51. Schmucker, *Elements of Popular Theology*, 41–43. An example of this sort of argument with regard to traditional Lutheran doctrines is Samuel S. Schmucker and J. Oswald, "The Baptism of Children Whose Parents Are Not Connected with the Church," pamphlet collection, Abdel Ross Wentz Library, Lutheran Theological Seminary at Gettysburg, Gettysburg, Pa. However, one should note that even Charles Philip Krauth (1797–1867), a confessional conservative, also appealed to "scripture alone" sorts of argumentation on subjects such as the sacraments. See Spaeth, *Charles Porterfield Krauth*, 1:18–19.

52. Samuel S. Schmucker diary, 9 February 1820 and 19 May 1824, reproduced in Peter Anstadt, *Life and Times of Rev. S. S. Schmucker, D.D., first Professor of Theology in the Lutheran Theological Seminary at Gettysburg, Pa.* (York, Pa.: P. Anstadt and Sons, 1896), 71, 109.

53. See Hay, *Memoirs of Rev. Jacob Goering . . .* , 107–211. Eventually Kurtz became frustrated with the pace of evangelical activism among Lutherans, even in the Gettysburg circle. In 1858, he founded the Missionary Institute of the Evangelical Lutheran Church in Selinsgrove, Pa.—now Susquehanna University—as a revivalist-oriented, broadly evangelical Lutheran school. See Charles H. Glatfelter, *A Salutary Influence: Gettysburg College, 1832–1985* (Gettysburg: Gettysburg College, 1987), 1:178.

54. Kurtz, *Why Are You a Lutheran?* 21, 152–54.

55. See, for example, *Minutes of the Proceedings of the Fifth General Synod of the Ev. Luth. Church . . . 1829*, 7–8.

56. Wentz, *Pioneer of Christian Unity*, 243–315; John R. Bodo, *The Protestant Clergy and Public Issues, 1812–1848* (Princeton: Princeton University Press, 1954), 82 n. 69.

57. Samuel S. Schmucker, *The Christian Pulpit, the Rightful Guardian of Morals in Political no less than in Private Life. A Discourse . . .* (Gettysburg, Pa.: H. C. Neinstedt, 1846), 8–10 and 30–32. In the pamphlet Schmucker disclosed his strong opposition to the Mexican War, which he termed a moral rather than political issue. See also Schmucker's homiletics lecture notes in the manuscript notebook of D. Swope [1853?], 19, 29–30, Archives, Abdel Ross Wentz Library, Lutheran Theological Seminary at Gettysburg, Gettysburg, Pa.

58. For instance, Schmucker noted that while a rising chorus of Christian philanthropy called for the abolition of the death penalty, he could not support such measures, owing to traditional Lutheran two-kingdom theology and positivist understandings of the state. See Samuel S. Schmucker, "Capital Punishment," *American Biblical Repository* 10 (1837): 67–88. On his American Bible Society choice, see Samuel S. Schmucker diary, 9 October 1823, reproduced in Anstadt, *Life and Times of Rev. S. S. Schmucker*, 107.

59. Schmucker, "The Doctrinal Basis and Ecclesiastical Position of the American Lutheran Church," in *American Lutheran Church*, 204, quoting Ernst L. Hazelius (1777–1853), a Lutheran theology teacher in New York, Pennsylvania, and South Carolina.

60. Schmucker contended that Lutheranism was the world's largest Protestant communion; see his *Elements of Popular Theology*, 40–41.

61. Samuel S. Schmucker, *Fraternal Appeal to the American Churches; with a Plan for Catholic Union on Apostolic Principles* (New York: Gould and Newman, 1838). A more widely circulated and expanded second edition appeared in 1839 from the same press and from the New York

publisher Taylor and Dodd. The *Fraternal Appeal* had originally appeared as a two-part article in *American Biblical Repository* 29 (January 1838): 86–101 and 30 (April 1838): 363–415. In 1833, Baltimore pastor David F. Schaeffer had proposed a similar model, arguing that those who called for a union of Lutheran and German Reformed churches had too narrow a vision. All orthodox Protestant groups, he insisted, should see themselves as cooperating cohorts in "an invincible phalanx" against Catholicism. See *Minutes of the Proceedings of the Evangelical Lutheran Synod of Maryland ... 1833* (Baltimore: Cloud and Pouder, 1833), 8–9.

62. Schmucker, *Fraternal Appeal*, e.g., 50–51. Cf. his comments on Lutheranism as the leading voice of the Reformation tradition (48); on the creeds giving structure to the group, see 92–99.

63. *Proceedings of the Tenth Convention of the General Synod of the Evangelical Lutheran Church in the United States ... 1839* (Gettysburg, Pa.: H. C. Neinstedt, 1839), 19.

64. Samuel S. Schmucker, "Overture for Christian Union, Submitted for the Consideration of the Evangelical Denominations in the United States," *Protestant Quarterly* 3 (April 1846): 148–53.

65. None, however, were members of the Pennsylvania Ministerium; all were members of synods (West Pennsylvania, Hartwick, Maryland, and South Carolina) that were part of the General Synod. The largest group of signatories (sixteen) was Presbyterian.

66. Philip D. Jordan, *The Evangelical Alliance for the United States of America, 1847–1900: Ecumenism, Identity, and the Religion of the Republic* (New York: Edwin Mellen Press, 1982), 20–21, 33–67. Schmucker issued a third edition of his *Appeal* just before the major 1873 Evangelical Alliance convention.

67. Abdel Ross Wentz, *History of the Gettysburg Theological Seminary ... 1826–1926* (Philadelphia: United Lutheran Publication House, [1926]), 158–59; and Wentz, *Pioneer of Christian Unity*, 181–89. Carl Gock had criticized the Lutheran and Reformed theological seminaries with similar sarcastic terminology: "zwey aristokratische Manufakturen, Deutsch-Eyrisch zugeschnitten," in his *Meine religiöse und darauf Bezug habende politische Ansicht*, 86. In his synodic correspondence, Lutheran pastor Schweizerbath of Zanesville, Ohio—who disliked the seminary at Gettysburg—is reported to have labeled it an "Irish Seminary." See Sheatsley, *History of the Evangelical Lutheran Joint Synod of Ohio and Other States*, 67–69.

68. Wentz, *History of the Gettysburg Theological Seminary*, 158–59. In 1813, the Pennsylvania Ministerium had licensed Brauns as a candidate, but then censured him in 1818; he moved to Europe, embittered. See Spaeth et al., eds., *Documentary History*, 453, 459, 527.

69. Longenecker, *Piety and Tolerance*. In contrast to the shared Pietistic heritage of Pennsylvania Germans, New York Germans eventually tended toward a version of Halle-inspired rationalism as epitomized by New York's Frederick H. Quitman. See his *Evangelical Catechism; or Short Exposition of the Principal Doctrines and Precepts of the Christian Religion, for the Use of the Churches Belonging to the Evangelical Lutheran Synod of New York* (Hudson, N.Y.: William E. Norman, 1814).

70. *Acts and Proceedings*, 57 (1812). A later jointly endorsed paper was the short-lived *Die Evangelische Zeitung der Lutherischen, Reformirten, unter anderer Protestantischen Kirchen in den Vereinigten Staaten* (1833–34), of York, Pa. See Arndt and Olson, eds., *German-American Newspapers and Periodicals*, 604.

71. "Gestalt des Reichs Gottes unter den Deutschen in Amerika," *Evangelisches Magazin* 3 (January–March 1814): 68.

72. Richard E. Wentz, ed., *Pennsylvania Dutch Folk Spirituality* (New York: Paulist Press, 1993). See, e.g., *Vollständiges Gebät-Buch auf alle Zeiten, in allen Ständen, und bey allen Angelegenheiten nützlich zu gebrauchen ...* (Reading, Pa.: Heinrich B. Sage, 1813), iv, which carries a foreword endorsed by both Reading Lutheran pastor Henry A. Muhlenberg and the borough's German Reformed pastor, Philip R. Pauli (1742–1815).

73. *Verhandlungen der Deutsch-Evangelisch-Lutherischen Synode von Pennsylvanien ... 1822* (Reading, Pa.: Johann Ritter, [1822]), 16.

74. *Verhandlungen der Deutsch-Evangelisch Lutherischen Synode von Pennsylvanien ... 1823*, 8, 16.

75. *Proceedings of the Evangelical Lutheran Synod of Maryland and Virginia ... 1822* (Baltimore: Frederick G. Schaeffer, 1822), 10; *Minutes of the Session of the Evangelical Lutheran Synod of Maryland and Virginia ... 1823* (Philadelphia: Conrad Zentler, 1824), 14. The polity differences between the denominations included differences in organizational structure. The Reformed Synod encompassed clergy and laity; the Lutheran organization, in contrast, comprised both a clergy-only ministerium and a clergy/lay-elder synod, the latter body having less authority than the former. For example, the Lutheran Ministerium had sole control over the licensing and ordination of pastors, which in the Reformed system was a synodic concern.

76. As late as 1839, these congregations rejected General Synod membership, insisting that they wished for future union only with the German Reformed; see *Verhandlungen der Deutschen Evangelischen Synode von Pennsylvanien ... 1839* (Easton, Pa.: Lafayette College Printer, 1839), 14, 16 (accompanying resolution no. 3).

77. For biographical information on Probst, see Laury, *History of the Allentown Conference,* 88–89, 258–60, as well as Spaeth et al., eds., *Documentary History,* 459–60, 478.

78. Johann August Probst, *Die Wiedervereinigung der Lutheraner und Reformirten; Ein fassliches Lesebuch für nachdenkende Glieder beider Konfessionen welche über diesen wichtigen Gegenstand gründlichern Unterricht und Aufschluss zu haben wünschen. Begleitet mit einer Abhandlung über das Abendmahl und die Grundsätze der Reformation* (Allentown, Pa.: H. Ebner, 1826).

79. On Jaeger, see Laury, *History of the Allentown Conference,* 86–87, 239–40. Probst and Jaeger were among the ministers who had voted against the General Synod in 1821 (two years before the ministerium as a whole voted to withdraw). See Spaeth et al., eds., *Documentary History,* 581–82.

80. Probst, *Wiedervereinigung der Lutheraner und Reformirten,* xvii, xv, xviii.

81. Ibid., Part 1, 7–29, details the story of the eucharistic split between Luther and Zwingli—a split that Probst claims was partly a personality conflict—and the resulting division between the Lutheran and Reformed Churches. Part 2, 29–47, discusses the "unbelievable damage which this separation caused," e.g., the political battle between Protestants in the Palatinate. Part 3, 47–66, concerns various meetings for dialogue and disputation between Protestants (including the moderating work of George Calixtus, 57–58). For his vision of a German church union in America, see 3–4; on the Prussian union, see 66–67. In a historical section, Probst points out that Switzerland was and is a republic like the United States (15).

82. Ibid., 73–74, 76. See 68–69 on the historical problem of the eucharist, with the notion of sacrifice cast as a remnant of Catholicism that continues to agitate Protestants.

83. Ibid., 79–81 (quotation from 80). See similar sentiments in *Evangelisches Magazin* 3 (1814): 204–6.

84. Probst, *Wiedervereinigung der Lutheraner und Reformirten,* 108–9.

85. Ibid., 128–29, 132–33.

86. Ibid., 92–94, 145. Probst was sure to explain that the liberty that he praised was true liberty in Christ, in contrast to human-promised liberty bought with blood. The book's last pages (147–72) are an appendix suggesting a common catechism on the Lord's Supper and a longer excursus on matters mentioned earlier in the book.

87. *Messenger of the German Reformed Church,* May 1833, 38–39. The editorial introduction presented the correspondent's plea in a favorable light. However, another anonymous Reformed writer ("Alter") soon countered with essays on the importance of doctrinal tradition. See *Messenger of the German Reformed Church,* July 1833, 49–50; August 1833, 57–58; and September 1833, 66–69.

88. *Minutes of the German Evangelical Lutheran Synod of Pennsylvania ... 1836* (Allentown, Pa.: A. and W. Blumer, 1836), 21.

89. *Acts and Proceedings of the Synod of the German Reformed Church of North America ... 1837* (Chambersburg, Pa.: H. Ruby, 1837), 14–15.

90. The 1839 gathering charged each pastor with discussing the question with his congregation and then reporting the results the next year. Based on those discussions, the 1840 ministerium rejected General Synod membership. *Verhandlungen der Deutschen Evangelisch-Lutherischen Synode von Pennsylvanien ... 1839*, 9; *Minutes of the German Evangelical Lutheran Synod of Pennsylvania ... 1840* (Baltimore: Publication Rooms of the Evangelical Lutheran Church, 1840), 10–11.

91. "Thoughts on the Formation of a New Synod in the Eastern District of Pennsylvania, Addressed to Ministers and Churches now in Connection with the Synod of Pennsylvania," broadside attached to the inside flyleaf of the copy of *Proceedings of the Evangelical Lutheran Synod of East Pennsylvania, 1842* (Gettysburg, Pa.: H. C. Neinstedt, 1842), housed in the Abdel Ross Wentz Library, Lutheran Theological Seminary at Gettysburg, Gettysburg, Pa.

92. Ibid.

93. Ibid.

94. The text of this memorial appears in *Proceedings of the Evangelical Lutheran Synod of East Pennsylvania, 1842* (Gettysburg, Pa.: H. C. Neinstedt, 1842), 4–5.

95. The East Pennsylvania Synod remained rather small. In 1845, it had 5,207 communicants—compared with the Pennsylvania Ministerium's more than 32,000. See *Proceedings of the Thirteenth Convention of the General Synod of the Evangelical Lutheran Church ... 1845* (Baltimore: Publication Rooms of the Evangelical Lutheran Church, 1845), 83.

96. *History of the Evangelical Lutheran Synod of East Pennsylvania, with Brief Sketches of its Congregations ... 1842–1892* (Philadelphia: Lutheran Publication Society, [1892]), 20–21, 26–27. Yeager was the son of J. C. Jaeger, author of the preface to Probst's book, described above.

97. Ferm, *Crisis in American Lutheran Theology.* See also David A. Gustafson, *Lutherans in Crisis: The Question of Identity in the American Republic* (Minneapolis: Fortress Press, 1993), 121–64, and Jacobs, *History of the Evangelical Lutheran Church*, 415–42.

98. Gock, *Meine religiöse und darauf Bezug habende politische Ansicht*, 21–22.

99. [Benjamin S. Schneck], "Letter from the Senior Editor" [dated 2 September 1843], *Weekly Messenger of the German Reformed Church*, 1 November 1843, 1695. Seven years earlier, an essay in the same periodical had spoken in optimistic terms of the Prussian union and its potential for good: see *Weekly Messenger of the German Reformed Church*, 24 February 1836, 103.

CHAPTER 7

1. Bernard C. Wolff, *The Work Before Us and the Motives to its Performance: A Sermon Delivered at the Opening of the Synod of the German Reformed Church, at Reading, Pa., October 21, 1841* (Chambersburg, Pa.: German Reformed Church, 1841), 6, 12. At the time, celebrants believed that 1841 marked the centennial of German Reformed church life in North America, though the group's actual origins dated before 1741.

2. For a summary of the background and composition of the 1840s–1850s German immigration, see Nadel, *Little Germany*, 13–28.

3. Wolff, *The Work Before Us*, 9.

4. Nor did all newcomers want to be associated with Pennsylvania German culture: see Schaf[f], *Anglo-Germanism*, 10. One Pennsylvania German minister who saw work with German immigrants as a personal ministry was former Free Synod pastor John C. Guldin, who moved to New York City to undertake such labor. For this period of his life, see Isaac Ferris,

Discourse Commemorative of the Services and Character of Rev. John C. Guldin, D.D. (New York: Board of Publication of the Reformed Dutch Church, [1863]).

Of course, some of the immigrants identified with the Prussian union church that had no direct American counterpart. Neither Lutheran nor Reformed, they created their own Mississippi Valley-based denomination. See Carl E. Schneider, *The German Church on the American Frontier: A Study in the Rise of Religion Among the Germans of the West, based on the History of the Evangelischer Kirchenverein des Westens, 1840–1866* (St. Louis: Eden Publishing House, 1939).

5. Friedrich Bente, *American Lutheranism: Early History of American Lutheranism and the Tennessee Synod* (St. Louis: Concordia Publishing, 1919), 1:220–27, which includes reprinted sections of the Tennessee Synod constitutions for the 1820s, 1830s, and 1850s. The arguments it contained (e.g., against ecclesiastical incorporation) are all but identical to those used by remonstrants in Berks County, Pennsylvania, in the 1820s (see Chap. 4). The Tennessee Synod also opposed synodic mission treasuries.

6. Higham, "Integrating America."

7. *Weekly Messenger of the German Reformed Church,* 19 September 1838, 628.

8. John W. Nevin, "The Year 1848," *Mercersburg Review* 1 (January 1849): 31. While Nevin expressed some anxiety over the popularity of "Manifest Destiny," he saw the unsettled nature of American identity as an unfolding promise rather than a stifling problem.

9. Gleason, "American Identity and Americanization," 31–58; Knobel, *Paddy and the Republic.*

10. *Reformed Church Messenger,* 11 July 1866, 1. The Free Synod itself had made fraternal overtures to the conservative Lutheran Synod of Tennessee and the Lutheran Pennsylvania Ministerium. See Hinke, ed., "Synodical Ordnung und Protocoll," 1828:5 and 1829:43–44 [pagination is not entirely uniform], bound volume dated 1934, Evangelical and Reformed Historical Society, Lancaster, Pa. On this theme, see also Appel, *Recollections of College Life,* 41, 50–52, 64–65, 180. The *Weekly Messenger of the German Reformed Church* began a series on "The Germans in this Country" (see 8 April 1840, 942).

11. Samuel S. Schmucker, "Retrospect of Lutheranism in the United States. A Discourse Delivered before the General Synod at Baltimore, 1841," 39, in Schmucker, *American Lutheran Church.*

12. Quotation from Emanuel V. Gerhart (1817–1904) in Linn Harbaugh, *Life of the Rev. Henry Harbaugh, D.D.* (Philadelphia: Reformed Church Publication Board, 1900), 34. Gerhart also contended that Harbaugh "was a genuine Pennsylvania German; the best type, taken all in all, of German life, of German geniality, and German modes of thought, that has come to view in our day" (51).

13. Harbaugh's description of his upbringing, quoted in Elizabeth Clarke Kieffer, *Henry Harbaugh: Pennsylvania Dutchman, 1817–1867* (Norristown, Pa.: Pennsylvania German Society, 1945), 13. Harbaugh grew up in Franklin County, Pa. His mother, Anna Snyder Harbaugh (1787–1837), was of Mennonite background. A younger brother, David (1823–1911), became a Lutheran pastor. His father, George (1774–1853), was a grandson of Jost Harbaugh (d. 1762), a German Reformed immigrant to Berks County in 1736 who later moved to the Kreutz Creek settlement in York County, Pa. See Linn Harbaugh, *Life of the Rev. Henry Harbaugh,* 73–75.

14. Writers from nineteenth-century contemporary Emanuel Gerhart to twentieth-century scholar Don Yoder have tied Harbaugh to the Mercersburg movement. In 1853, Harbaugh did publicly defend Mercersburg advocates against attacks from his publishing associate and fellow Lancaster, Pa., pastor, Elias Heiner (1810–63). But Harbaugh was less a Mercersburg advocate than a promoter of a broadly Pennsylvania German religious idiom. He accepted some Mercersburg notions, such as the objective value of liturgy and the importance of doctrinal tradition (ideas not necessarily foreign to the Pennsylvania German mind), but he

was not pleased with the manifesto of Philip Schaff, *The Principle of Protestantism as Related to the Present State of the Church* (Chambersburg, Pa.: Publication Office of the German Reformed Church, 1845), and he opposed Mercersburg-style ecumenism. See Elizabeth Kieffer, *Henry Harbaugh*, 115, and Henry Harbaugh, "Christian Union," *The Guardian* 17 (June 1866): 165–67. And while from a distance some critics charged that the subject of Harbaugh's book, *The True Glory of Woman as Portrayed in the Beautiful Life of the Virgin Mary, Mother of Our Lord and Saviour, Jesus Christ* (Philadelphia: Lindsay and Blakiston, 1858), signaled crypto-Catholicism, at least one student who heard Harbaugh's oral presentation of the material thought that the pastor was quite anti-Catholic. See Henry Kyd Douglas, *The Douglas Diary: Student Days at Franklin and Marshall College, 1856–1858, by Henry Kyd Douglas*, ed. Frederic S. Klein and John H. Carrill (Lancaster: Franklin and Marshall College, 1973), 101.

15. Harbaugh was "in many ways the quintessential Pennsylvania Dutchman," described in Wentz, ed., *Pennsylvania Dutch Folk Spirituality*, 54. For broader context and a description of Pennsylvania German popular religion, see 7–32 of that work.

16. For example, Henry Harbaugh, *The Drunkard Maker taken from his Bar to the Bar of God, Tried, Found Guilty, and Condemned for Murder*, 2d ed. (Chambersburg, Pa.: Office of the German Reformed Messenger, 1849). See also Harbaugh's sentimental and rather theologically generic *The Heavenly Home; or the Employments and Enjoyments of the Saints in Heaven*, 3d ed. (Philadelphia: Lindsay and Blakiston, 1853) for an example of writing that could have appealed to a broad nineteenth-century audience.

17. Linn Harbaugh, *Life of the Rev. Henry Harbaugh*, 73.

18. Henry Harbaugh, "Strange," *The Guardian* 1 (June 1850): 140.

19. A champion of the dialect, Harbaugh had struggled to learn English grammar when he lived among Yankees in Ohio. Yet he found standard High German even more difficult to master. As a Pennsylvania pastor, he was always at home in the dialect, but "[a]fter ten years of pulpit experience and no small amount of translating of the German language, he still found it something of an effort to preach in German." See ibid., 63 and 102; see also Linn Harbaugh, *Life of the Rev. Henry Harbaugh*, 165. Although initially published in church magazines during his lifetime, several of his dialect poems were posthumously collected as Henry Harbaugh, *Harbaugh's Harfe: Gedichte in Pennsylvanisch-deutscher Mundart, von H. Harbaugh*, ed. Benjamin Bausman (Philadelphia: Reformed Church Publication Board, 1870). Many dealt with rural Pennsylvania German life. See also Linn Harbaugh, *Life of the Rev. Henry Harbaugh*, 232–35, and Elizabeth Kieffer, *Henry Harbaugh*, 225, 281–365, on his dialect poetry. Into the twentieth century, Harbaugh's dialect poems were known and cherished among Pennsylvania Germans in the Midwest; see Paul Hoover, *My Memories in Poetry and Prose: Life at Five Points, Goshen, Indiana* (Nappanee, Ind.: Evangel Press, 1996), 171. Harbaugh also wrote some English poems, collected as Henry Harbaugh, *Poems by Henry Harbaugh* (Philadelphia: Lindsay and Blakiston, 1860), a work that contained the especially popular "The Mystic Weaver" (13–20), which appeared in Pennsylvania school textbooks as late as 1910.

20. In his dialect endeavors, Harbaugh may have drawn inspiration from the work of C. Friedrich Hebbel (1813–63), the creator of modern Alemannic dialect literature in Germany. See David S. Schaff, *The Life of Philip Schaff, in part Autobiographical* (New York: Charles Scribner's Sons, 1897), 243, for Philip Schaff's contention that this was the case.

21. Gerhart in Linn Harbaugh, *Life of the Rev. Henry Harbaugh*, 46 (and comments in 47–49 and 52); see also Henry Harbaugh's *Fathers of the German Reformed Church* and his *Life of Rev. Michael Schlatter; with a Full Account of His Travels and Labors among the Germans in Pennsylvania … to 1790* (Philadelphia: Lindsay and Blakiston, 1857). Harbaugh was also the major promoter of the 1863 tercentary of the Heidelberg Catechism and edited a special anniversary edition of the text that appeared as *Heidelberg Catechism in German, Latin, and English, with an Historical Introduction. Prepared and Published by the Direction of the German Reformed Church in the United States of America* (New York: Charles Scribner, 1863).

22. Linn Harbaugh, *Life of the Rev. Henry Harbaugh,* 6.

23. Cf. the comments of Nathan C. Schaeffer (1849–1919) in ibid., 5. The magazine was aimed at youth aged 15–25.

24. "Our Object," *The Guardian* 1 (January 1850): 5–7.

25. See, e.g., "History of First German Reformed Church, Baltimore," *The Guardian* 3 (January 1852): 25–29, Rev. J. P. Lesley, "A Flying Visit to Germany," *The Guardian* 3 (December 1852): 376–80, and Henry Harbaugh, "The Ancient Germans," *The Guardian* 3 (September 1852): 257. See also a story on Johann Gottfried von Herder (1744–1803) in *The Guardian* 4 (June 1853): 174–76, and a translation of Herder in *The Guardian* 5 (February 1854): 51–52.

26. "Our Forefathers," *The Guardian* 6 (November 1855): 336–40.

27. E.g., Henry Harbaugh, "Christmas," *The Guardian* 5 (January 1854): 18–20; idem, "Grandfather's Christmas-Tree," *The Guardian* 7 (January 1856): 10; I. Daniel Rupp, "Baptismal Names of Germans, with their Significance," *The Guardian* 6 (December 1855): 369–72; Henry Harbaugh, "A Public Profession of Religion, by Connecting with the Church," *The Guardian* 2 (June 1851): 178–92; translation of J. J. Hottinger's "Life and Times of Zwingli," *The Guardian* 7 (September 1856): 275–83; and a biography of William Hendel Sr., *The Guardian* 7 (June 1856): 161–64. The March 1856 issue of *The Guardian* (p. 96) included the advertisement for Rupp's book, *A Collection of Thirty Thousand Names of German, Swiss ... and other Immigrants in Pennsylvania ...* (Harrisburg, Pa.: T. F. Schaeffer, 1856). Mayer's *History of the German Reformed Church* was commended in *The Guardian* 2 (August 1851): 256.

28. Henry Harbaugh, "New England Superstition," *The Guardian* 5 (July 1854): 194. However, in its October 1854 issue, *The Guardian* did publish an extract from a forthcoming book by I. Daniel Rupp on Pennsylvania German history that explored amulets, charms, talismans, and unlucky days in Pennsylvania German folklore (312–15).

29. "Our Forefathers," 336–40. See also *The Guardian* 6 (April 1855) for comments from Harbaugh on older parochial school traditions that combined religion and ethnic community values (108).

30. Henry Harbaugh, "New England Superstition," 193–94.

31. Ibid., 196. Cf. the earlier essay in the *Weekly Messenger of the German Reformed Church,* 30 September 1835, 22, that opined, "The besetting sin of the present day is the spirit of *ultraism* on every subject and topic which has apparently taken hold of the people."

32. See S. A. H. [Samuel A. Helfenstein], "Listen to the Storm," *The Guardian* 1 (April 1850): 89–90, that warned of the way in which the rhetoric of radical liberty had been co-opted by violent, unchristian political characters.

33. [Henry Harbaugh], "Playing on the Surface," *The Guardian* 2 (August 1851): 243.

34. J. E. G., "Complaining of Hard Times," *The Guardian* 1 (October 1850): 228–29. See also a bitter piece entitled "A Chapter on Politics," *The Guardian* 3 (October 1852): 290–93.

35. J. E. G., "Complaining of Hard Times," 228. See also the ambivalence in Frederick A. Muhlenberg's sermon reprinted in Charles F. Schaeffer and Frederick A. Muhlenberg, *Memorial Volume of the Evangelical Lutheran Church of the Holy Trinity, Lancaster, Pa. Discourses Delivered on the Occasion of the Centenary Jubilee* (Lancaster, Pa.: John Baer's Sons, 1861), 27, that contrasted the popular faith placed in the strength of the Northern Union Army with traditional Pietist devotional concerns, concluding that German parishioners view "all these things in a different light" than their neighbors. Similar sentiments would later emerge in ethnic communities beset by pressures to assimilate to Anglo-American public culture. The early Pennsylvania German arguments that republican liberty implied the freedom to pursue cultural particularism would find echoes in German-American efforts to institute German-language education in Buffalo, N.Y., for example. In the Midwest, meanwhile, German church folk who were Free-Soilers and no friends of slavery would nonetheless reject the new Republican Party, except where its leaders specifically distanced themselves from eastern evangelical Protestant reformers and causes. See Gerber, *Making of an American Pluralism,* 218–22, and Frederick C.

Luebke, ed., *Ethnic Voters and the Election of Lincoln* (Lincoln: University of Nebraska Press, 1971).

36. See Conser, *Church and Confession*. On Mercersburg, see James H. Nichols, *Romanticism in American Theology: Nevin and Schaff at Mercersburg* (Chicago: The University of Chicago Press, 1961), and Frantz, "Return to Tradition." On Lutheran controversy, see Gustafson, *Lutherans in Crisis;* Kuenning, *Rise and Fall of American Lutheran Pietism;* and Ferm, *Crisis in American Lutheran Theology.*

37. E.g., Gustafson, *Lutherans in Crisis;* Kuenning, *Rise and Fall of American Lutheran Pietism.* An exception is Richard E. Wentz, *John Williamson Nevin, American Theologian* (New York: Oxford University Press, 1997), which treats Americanization in a complex way.

38. Don Yoder, "The Reformed Church and Pennsylvania German Identity," *Yearbook of German-American Studies* 18 (1983): 63–82.

39. See his biographical sketch in J. C. Jensson, *American Lutheran Biographies; or Historical Notices of over Three Hundred and Fifty Leading Men of the American Lutheran Church from its Establishment to the Year 1890* (Milwaukee: A. Houtkamp and Son, 1890), 111–13. There were other German publications for later immigrants, such as the *Deutsche Kirchenfreund: Organ für die Gemeinsamen Interessen der Amerikanisch-Deutschen Kirchen,* edited by Philip Schaff and later by William Julius Mann (1819–93), a Lutheran immigrant of 1845 who joined the German Reformed Church in America, but later returned to Lutheranism.

40. Samuel K. Brobst, "English and German in the People's Schools; an Address by Rev. S. K. Brobst before the Pennsylvania State Teachers' Association, Philadelphia, August 21, 1872," pamphlet collection, Abdel Ross Wentz Library, Lutheran Theological Seminary at Gettysburg, Gettysburg, Pa. Reprinted from *Pennsylvania School Journal,* September 1872. Keystone Normal School became Kutztown State Normal School, and today it is Kutztown University.

41. For example, from 1866 to 1903, Benjamin Bausman (1824–1909) edited *Der Reformirte Hausfreund,* a Pennsylvania German publication that competed with German church periodicals of later arrivals. On Bausman, see Ranck, *Life of the Reverend Benjamin Bausman.* On the subject of Pennsylvania German and later immigrant interaction more generally, see Yoder, "The 'Dutchman' and the '*Deitschlenner,*'" 1–17. For one contemporary appraisal, see Herman J. Ruetenik, "The Pennsylvanians and the Foreign Germans," *Reformed Church Messenger,* 26 September 1895, 3, which claimed that although members of both groups possessed similar work ethics and intelligence, "[t]he Pennsylvanians have lived and have formed their characters under the influence of a republican polity, [and] they have been educated to [*sic*] habits of self government."

42. Homer T. Rosenberger, *The Pennsylvania Germans, 1891–1965 (Frequently Known as the "Pennsylvania Dutch"): Seventy-fifth Anniversary Volume of the Pennsylvania German Society* (Lancaster, Pa.: Pennsylvania German Society, 1966), 73–90.

43. *The Guardian* 6 (November 1855): 339.

44. Niebuhr's classic heuristic, however, is largely theological, not historical or contextual, and contains a number of assumptions about "culture." For example, many sectarians accept the term if one takes "culture" to mean language, basic civil law, foodways, and the like. Similarly, groups are said to represent "Christ the transformer of culture" or "Christ and culture in paradox" when they function as social and cultural leaders, but they can seem defensively reactionary or even withdrawn when placed in the position of cultural minority. See H. Richard Niebuhr, *Christ and Culture* (New York: Harper and Row, 1951). This is not to say that Niebuhr's grid is useless, but that the contingencies of history are very important in making sense of specific cases, a point Niebuhr himself made in *The Social Sources of Denominationalism* (New York: Henry Holt, 1929).

45. Conzen, "Paradox of German-American Assimilation," 156–57.

BIBLIOGRAPHY

PRIMARY SOURCES: UNPUBLISHED

Appel, Theodore. "Biography of Rev. Thomas Pomp (1773–1852)." Manuscript. Evangelical and Reformed Historical Society, Lancaster, Pa.

Butler, John George. "Diary of Journey to Knoxville, Tenn., 27 July–27 September 1805." [Composed 1806.] Lutheran Archives Center at Philadelphia, Lutheran Theological Seminary at Philadelphia, Philadelphia, Pa.

Evangelical Lutheran Ministerium of Pennsylvania and Adjacent States. Synodical Correspondence, 1813–1818. Lutheran Archives Center at Philadelphia, Lutheran Theological Seminary at Philadelphia, Philadelphia, Pa.

Herman, Charles G. "Private Records of Rev. Chas. G. Herman. Corrected copy." Transcribed by C. E. Keiser. Historical Society of Berks County, Reading, Pa.

Hertz, Daniel. "A Catechism on Church Government." Manuscript book of notes [last page with text dated 18 February 1823, Philadelphia]. Evangelical and Reformed Historical Society, Lancaster, Pa.

Morris, James L. "Diary, or Daily Notes of the Weather together with the Events of the Neighborhood, etc., etc." 3 vols. [vols. 1–2, microfilm roll 74; vol. 3, original manuscript only]. Historical Society of Berks County, Reading, Pa.

Reily, James Ross. "Diary of Trip to Europe, 1825–1826." Evangelical and Reformed Historical Society, Lancaster, Pa.

Richards, John W. "Diary." Vol. 1, 21 September 1824–31, December 1830. Lutheran Archives Center at Philadelphia, Lutheran Theological Seminary at Philadelphia, Philadelphia, Pa.

Schwartz, J. W. Manuscript student notebook. 1853. Archives, Abdel Ross Wentz Library, Lutheran Theological Seminary at Gettysburg, Gettysburg, Pa.

Swope, D. Manuscript student notebook. [1853?] Archives, Abdel Ross Wentz Library, Lutheran Theological Seminary at Gettysburg, Gettysburg, Pa.

PRIMARY SOURCES: PROCEEDINGS

Acts and Proceedings of the Coetus and Synod of the German Reformed Church in the United States from 1791 to 1816, Inclusive. Chambersburg, Pa.: M. Kieffer, 1854; reprint, Allentown: Zion's Reformed Church, 1930.

Breyfogel, Sylvanus C., ed. *Landmarks of the Evangelical Association, Containing all the Official Records of the Annual and General Conferences . . . to the Year 1840; and the Proceedings of the East Pennsylvania Conference together with Important Extracts from . . . the General Conference from 1840 to the Present Time.* Reading, Pa.: Eagle Book Printers, 1888.

Constitution of the Evangelical Lutheran General Synod in the United States of North America; Together with the Proceedings of the Convention in which it was Formed. Translated from the German. Lancaster, Pa.: John Baer, [1820].

Drury, Augustus W., trans. *Minutes of the Annual and General Conferences of the Church of the United Brethren in Christ, 1800–1818.* Dayton, Ohio: United Brethren Publishing House, 1897.

Hinke, William J., ed. "Synodical Ordnung und Protocoll der Verhandlungen der Synode der Hochdeutschen Freyen Reformirten Gemeinden in Pennsylvanien Angefangen den 24sten Tag April, Anno Domini, 1822." Bound volume dated 1934. Evangelical and Reformed Historical Society, Lancaster, Pa.

Minutes and Letters of the Coetus of the German Reformed Congregations in Pennsylvania, 1747–1792. Together with Three Preliminary Reports by Rev. John Philip Boehm, 1734–1744. Philadelphia: Reformed Church Publication Board, 1903.

Minutes of the General Assembly of the Presbyterian Church of the United States of America . . . 1789 to 1820, Inclusive. Philadelphia: Presbyterian Board of Publication, [1847].

Minutes of the Proceedings of the Evangelical Lutheran Synod of Maryland. 1830–. Various publishers.

Minutes of the Proceedings of the Evangelical Lutheran Synod of Maryland and Virginia. 1820–29. Various publishers.

Printed Synodical Minutes of the Evangelical Lutheran General Synod. 1820–50. Various titles and publishers.

Printed Synodical Minutes (*Verhandlungen*, etc.) of the German Reformed Church. 1817–63. Various titles and publishers.

Printed Synodical Minutes (*Verhandlungen*, etc.) of the Lutheran Ministerium/Synod of Pennsylvania. 1822–55. English and German. Various titles and publishers.

Printed Synodical Minutes (*Verrichtungen*, etc.) of the Lutheran Synod of Ohio. 1818–. Various titles and publishers.

Proceedings of the Evangelical Lutheran Church of West Pennsylvania. Gettysburg, Pa.: H. C. Neinstedt, 1825–.

Proceedings of the Evangelical Lutheran Synod of East Pennsylvania. Gettysburg, Pa.: H. C. Neinstedt, 1842–.

Proceedings of the General Synod of the Reformed Dutch Church. 1801–. Various publishers.

Rapp, Isaiah N., comp. "Minutes of the Philadelphia Classis [of the German Reformed Church], 1820–1825." Bound volume dated 1938. Evangelical and Reformed Historical Society, Lancaster, Pa.

Spaeth, Adolph, Henry E. Jacobs, and George F. Spieker, eds. *Documentary History of the Evangelical Lutheran Ministerium of Pennsylvania and Adjacent States. Proceedings of the Annual Conventions from 1748 to 1821.* Philadelphia: Board of Publication of the General Council of the Evangelical Lutheran Church in North America, 1898.

PRIMARY SOURCES: PUBLISHED

Adair, Robert. *Memoir of Rev. James Patterson, Late Pastor of the First Presbyterian Church, N.L., Phila.* Philadelphia: Henry Perkins, 1840.

Appel, Theodore. *Recollections of College Life at Marshall College, Mercersburg, Pa., from 1839 to 1845: A Narrative with Reflections.* Reading, Pa.: Daniel Miller, 1886.

Asbury, Francis. *The Journal and Letters of Francis Asbury.* 3 vols. Edited by Elmer T. Clark et al. Nashville: Abingdon Press, 1958.

Berg, Joseph F. *The Ancient Land-Mark, Being the Substance of a Discourse Preached Sept. 29, 1839, by Joseph F. Berg. . . .* Philadelphia: Christian Observer, 1840.

Bernheim, Johann H. *Das Abendmahl des Herrn.* Elizabethtaun, Pa.: W. M. Barter, 1834.

Bretschneider, Carl G. *Henry and Antonio, or the Proselytes of the Romish and Evangelical Churches . . . annotated by a Minister in the Lutheran Church.* Baltimore: Lucas and Deaver, 1834.

Brobst, Samuel K. "English and German in the People's Schools; an Address by Rev. S. K. Brobst before the Pennsylvania State Teachers' Association, Philadelphia, August 21, 1872." Pamphlet collection, Abdel Ross Wentz Library, Lutheran Theological Seminary at Gettysburg, Gettysburg, Pa.

Butterfield, Lyman H., ed. *Adams Family Correspondence.* 6 vols. Cambridge: Harvard University Press, 1963–93.

Colonial Records, or Minutes of the Provincial Council of Pennsylvania. 16 vols. Harrisburg, Pa.: Theodore Fenner, 1851–53.

Cooke, Jacob E., ed. *The Federalist.* 2 vols. Middletown: Wesleyan University Press, 1961.

Denig, Ludwig. *The Picture Bible of Ludwig Denig: A Pennsylvania German Emblem Book.* Translated and edited by Don Yoder. 2 vols. New York: Hudson Hills Press, 1990.

Douglas, Henry Kyd. *The Douglas Diary: Student Days at Franklin and Marshall College, 1856–1858, by Henry Kyd Douglas.* Edited by Frederic S. Klein and John H. Carrill. Lancaster: Franklin and Marshall College, 1973.

Ely, Ezra Stiles. *The Duty of Christian Freemen to Elect Christian Rulers; a Discourse Delivered on the Fourth of July, 1827, in the Seventh Presbyterian Church, in Philadelphia.* Philadelphia: W. F. Geddes, 1828.

Eylert, Theodor. *Die Finsterniß in der freyen Kirche von America. Eine Abhandlung, veranlaßt durch die in Reading erschienene Schrift, betitelt: "die Vertheidigung der freyen Kirche" von Carl Gock.* Reading, Pa.: n.p., 1823.

Ferris, Isaac. *Discourse Commemorative of the Services and Character of Rev. John C. Guldin, D.D.* New York: Board of Publication of the Reformed Dutch Church, [1863].

Finney, Charles G. *Memoirs of Rev. Charles G. Finney, Written by Himself.* New York: A. S. Barnes, 1876.

Flint, Timothy. *Recollections of the Last Ten Years.* New York: Alfred A. Knopf, 1932.

Franklin, Benjamin. *The Papers of Benjamin Franklin.* 33 vols. Edited by Leonard W. Labaree. New Haven: Yale University Press, 1959–.

Fries, Yost H. *Die Wahre Liebe eines republicanischen Helden, in einer Ermahnung, zu seinem Volk. Eine Predigt gehalten den 10ten September 1812, bey Zusammenkunft der*

Freywilligen zu Jungmanstaun in der Elias-Kirche. New Bern, Pa.: G. N. H. Peters, 1845.

Gallatin, Albert. *The Writings of Albert Gallatin.* 3 vols. Edited by Henry Adams. Philadelphia: J. B. Lippincott, 1879.

Galloway, Joseph. *Historical and Political Reflections on the Rise and Progress of the American Revolution....* London: G. Wilkie, [1780].

Das Gemeinschaftliche Gesangbuch, zum gottesdienstlichen Gebrauch der Lutherischen und Reformirten Gemeinden in Nord-America. Baltimore: Schaeffer und Maund, 1817.

Gilbert, Russell W., ed. "The Unpublished Autobiography of Ernst Max Adam, M.D. [1801–1880], Settler in Dunker Blooming Grove." *Susquehanna University Studies* 5 (May 1953): 17–49.

Gock, Carl. *Carl Gock's Neuestes selbstlehrendes rechen-buch. Verfasst nach den grundregeln der deutschen hebkunst, wie solche durch prof. Rees in Deutschland eingeführt worden. Nebst einem anhange ueber das ausmessen. Besonders dem werthen bauernstande gewidmet....* Reading, Pa.: Heinrich B. Sage, 1823.

———. *Meine religiöse und darauf Bezug habende politische Ansicht von Nord-Amerika und Fortsetzung der "Vertheidigung der freyen Kirche." Verfaßt in drey Theilen....* Reading, Pa.: Carl Gock, 1830.

———. *Die Vertheidigung der Freyen Kirche von Nord-Amerika. In sechs Abschnitten abgefaßt ... besonders dem werthen Bauernstande gewidmet.* Reading, Pa.: Carl Gock, 1822.

Gossler, J[ohann] C. *Carl Gock's Verläumdungen, oder die Rechtfertigung der hochdeutschen Lutherischen und Reformirten Synoden von Nord-America. In 3 Abschnitten....* Reading, Pa.: C. A. Bruckman, 1823.

———. *Lebensgeschichte Napoleon Bonaparte's, des Ersten Kaisers der Franzosen, mit besonderer Rücksicht auf dessen zehnjährige Regierung, Verbannung und Tod. Vier Theile in einem Band, mit Kupfern....* Reading, Pa.: C. A. Bruckman, 1822.

Gudehus, Jonas Heinrich. "Journey to America." Translated by Larry M. Neff. In *Ebbes fer Alle—Ebber Ebbes fer Dich: Something for Everyone—Something for You,* ed. Albert F. Buffington, 173–329. Breinigsville, Pa.: Pennsylvania German Society, 1980.

Guldin, John C. *Directions and Advice in Reference to Revivals of Religion, and Prayer Meetings.* Chambersburg, Pa.: Publication Office of the German Reformed Church, 1841.

Harbaugh, Henry. *The Drunkard Maker taken from his Bar to the Bar of God, Tried, Found Guilty, and Condemned for Murder.* 2d ed. Chambersburg, Pa.: Office of the German Reformed Messenger, 1849.

———. *The Fathers of the German Reformed Church in Europe and America.* 2d ed. 3 vols. Lancaster, Pa.: J. M. Westhaeffer, 1872.

———. *Harbaugh's Harfe: Gedichte in Pennsylvanisch-deutscher Mundart, von H. Harbaugh.* Edited by Benjamin Bausman. Philadelphia: Reformed Church Publication Board, 1870.

———. *The Heavenly Home; or the Employments and Enjoyments of the Saints in Heaven.* 3d ed. Philadelphia: Lindsay and Blakiston, 1853.

———. *The Life of Rev. Michael Schlatter; with a Full Account of His Travels and Labors among the Germans in Pennsylvania ... to 1790.* Philadelphia: Lindsay and Blakiston, 1857.

———. *Poems by Henry Harbaugh.* Philadelphia: Lindsay and Blakiston, 1860.

———. *The True Glory of Woman as Portrayed in the Beautiful Life of the Virgin Mary, Mother of Our Lord and Saviour, Jesus Christ.* Philadelphia: Lindsay and Blakiston, 1858.

[———]. *Ueber Spaltungen und Unabhängigkeit in der Kirche Christi, mit besonderer Rücksicht auf neuliche Erregungen des schismatischen Geistes in Theilen der Reformirten Kirche in Pennsylvanien. Schriftlich, historisch, und praktisch dargestellt. Rom. 16:17.* Harrisburg, Pa.: Kuhn und Haas, 1863.

Hazelius, Ernst L. *History of the American Lutheran Church from Its Commencement in the Year of Our Lord 1685 to the Year 1842.* Zanesville, Ohio: Edwin C. Church, 1846.

Heidelberg Catechism in German, Latin, and English, with an Historical Introduction. Prepared and Published by the Direction of the German Reformed Church in the United States of America. New York: Charles Scribner, 1863.

Heisler, Daniel Y., and Henry Harbaugh. *The Fathers of the German Reformed Church in Europe and America, continued by D. Y. Heisler.* Vol. 4, Lancaster, Pa.: J. M. Westhaeffer, 1872; vols. 5–6, Reading, Pa.: Daniel Miller, 1881–88.

Helfenstein, J. C. Albertus. *A Collection of Choice Sermons by the Rev. J. C. Albertus Helfenstein ... translated from the German by I. Daniel Rupp.* Carlisle, Pa.: George Fleming, 1832.

Helfenstein, Samuel A. *The Doctrines of Divine Revelation, as Taught in the Holy Scripture ... for Young Men Preparing for the Gospel Ministry in Particular.* Philadelphia: James Kay Jr. and Bro., 1842.

Henkel, David. *Answer to Mr. Joseph Moore, the Methodist; with a few Fragments on the Doctrine of Justification.* New Market, Va.: S. G. Henkel, 1825.

———. *Carolinian Herald of Liberty, Religious and Political; or a Testimony against attempted Measures, which in their Nature are Calculated to lead to the Establishment of Popery among Protestants.* Salisbury, N.C.: Krider and Bingham, 1821.

Hermann, Lebrecht F. *Catechismus der Glaubenslehren und Lebenspflichten der Christlichen Religion....* Reading, Pa.: J. Ritter, 1813.

Hoover, Paul. *My Memories in Poetry and Prose: Life at Five Points, Goshen, Indiana.* Nappanee, Ind.: Evangel Press, 1996.

Jackson, Andrew. *Correspondence of Andrew Jackson.* 7 vols. Edited by John S. Bassett. Washington, D.C.: Carnegie Institution, 1926–35.

Jaeger, Gottlieb F. J. *Leben des Generals-Majors Andreas Jackson, enthaltend eine Geschichte des Kriegs in Süden....* Reading, Pa.: Johann Ritter, 1831.

Kieffer, Henry M., trans. *Some of the First Settlers of "The Forks of the Delaware" and their Descendants; Being a Translation from the German of the Recordbook of the First Reformed Church of Easton, Penna., from 1760 to 1852.* Easton, Pa.: [First Reformed Church of Easton], 1902.

Der Kleine Catechismus des sel. D. Martin Luthers; Nebst den gewöhnlichen Morgen- Tisch- und Abend-Gebeten. [2d ed.] Germantown, Pa.: Leibert und Billmeyer, 1786.

Koch, Carl G. *Lebenserfahrungen von Carl Koch, Prediger der Evangeliums.* Cleveland: Verlagshaus der Evangelischen Gemeinschaft, 1871.

Kohl, Johann G. *Reisen in Canada und durch die Staaten New York und Pennsylvanien, von J. G. Kohl.* Stuttgart: J. G. Cotta, 1856.

Kurtz, Benjamin. *Why Are You a Lutheran? Or a Series of Dissertations ... of the Evangelical Lutheran Church in the United States.* Baltimore: Publication Rooms of the Evangelical Lutheran Church, 1843.

Livingston, John H. *An Address to the Reformed German Churches in the United States.* New Brunswick, N.J.: William Myer, 1819.

Lochman, Johann Georg. *The History, Doctrine, and Discipline of the Evangelical Lutheran Church.* Harrisburg, Pa.: John Wyeth, 1818.

Mahnenschmidt, John Peter. *Der kleine Heidelbergische Catechismus, oder: kurzen Unterricht Christlicher Lehre, für die Jugend, in der Reformirten Kirche....* Canton, Ohio: Peter Kaufmann, 1834.

Marshall, Christopher. *Extracts from the Diary of Christopher Marshall, kept in Philadelphia and Lancaster during the American Revolution, 1774–1781.* Edited by William Duane. Albany, N.Y.: Joel Munsell, 1877.

Mayer, Lewis. *History of the German Reformed Church, Volume 1.* Philadelphia: Lippincott and Grambo, 1851.

Milledoler, Philip. *A Discourse Delivered by Appointment of the General Synod of the Reformed Dutch Church ... at Hackensack, N.J.... July 6, 1824.* New York: G. F. Hopkins, 1824.

Miller, George. *Jacob Albrecht.* Reading, Pa.: Johannes Ritter, 1811.

[Miller, Lewis]. *Lewis Miller: Sketches and Chronicles. The Reflections of a Nineteenth-Century Pennsylvania German Folk Artist.* York, Pa.: Historical Society of York County, 1966.

Mittelberger, Gottlieb. *Gottlieb Mittleberger's Journey to Pennsylvania in the Year 1750 and Return to Germany in the Year 1754.* Translated by Oscar Handlin and John Clive. Cambridge: Harvard University Press, 1960.

Morris, John G. *Fifty Years in the Lutheran Ministry.* Baltimore: James Young, 1878.

———. *Life Reminiscences of an Old Lutheran Minister.* Philadelphia: Lutheran Publication Society, 1896.

Muhlenberg, Heinrich A. *Busstags-Predigt....* Reading, Pa.: Johann Ritter, 1812.

Muhlenberg, Heinrich M. *The Journals of Henry Melchior Muhlenberg.* Translated by Theodore G. Tappert and John W. Doberstein. Philadelphia: Evangelical Lutheran Ministerium of Pennsylvania and Adjacent States, 1942.

Nevin, John W. "The Year 1848." *Mercersburg Review* 1 (January 1849): 10–44.

Newcomer, Christian. *The Life and Journal of the Rev'd Christian Newcomer, Late Bishop of the Church of the United Brethren in Christ. Written by Himself.* Hagerstown, Md.: F. G. W. Kapp, 1834.

Niemcewicz, Julian U. *Under Their Own Vine and Fig Tree: Travels through America in 1797–1799 and 1805, with Some Further Account of Life in New Jersey.* Translated and edited by Metchie J. E. Budka. Elizabeth, N.J.: Grassmann Publishing, 1965.

O'Malley, J. Steven, trans. and ed. *Early German-American Evangelicalism: Pietist Sources on Discipleship and Sanctification.* Lanham, Md.: Scarecrow Press, 1995.

Pennsylvania Archives. 1st ser. 12 vols. Philadelphia: Joseph Severns, 1852–56.

Plan-Entwurf zu einer Central Verbindung der Evangelisch-Lutherischen Kirche in den Vereinigten Staaten von Nord-Amerika. Baltimore: Schaeffer und Maund, 1819.

Pomp, J. Nicholas. *Kurtzgefasste Pruefungen der Lehre des ewigen Evangeliums....* Philadelphia: Heinrich Miller, 1774.

Potts, George. *An Address Delivered in Philadelphia, July 4, 1826, by George Potts, Pastor of the First Presbyterian Church....* Philadelphia: Clark and Raser, 1826.

Probst, Johann August. *Die Wiedervereinigung der Lutheraner und Reformirten; Ein fassliches Lesebuch für nachdenkende Glieder beider Konfessionen welche über diesen wichtigen Gegenstand gründlichern Unterricht und Aufschluss zu haben wünschen. Begleitet mit einer Abhandlung über das Abendmahl und die Grundsätze der Reformation.* Allentown, Pa.: H. Ebner, 1826.

Quitman, Frederick H. *Evangelical Catechism; or Short Exposition of the Principal Doctrines and Precepts of the Christian Religion, for the Use of the Churches Belonging to the Evangelical Lutheran Synod of New York.* Hudson, N.Y.: William E. Norman, 1814.

Reber, Joel L. *Ein Ernsthaftes Wort über den Secten-Geist und das Sect-Wesen.* Chambersburg, Pa.: Moses Kieffer, 1850.

Reed, Andrew, and James Matheson. *A Narrative of the Visit to the American Churches by Deputation from the Congregational Union of England and Wales.* 2 vols. New York: Harper and Brothers, 1835.

Rogers, George. *Memoranda of the Experience, Labors, and Travels of a Universalist Preacher, Written by Himself.* Cincinnati: John A. Gurley, 1845.

Royall, Anne Newport. *Mrs. Royall's Pennsylvania, or Travels Continued in the United States.* Washington, D.C.: by the author, 1829.

Rupp, I. Daniel. *A Collection of Thirty Thousand Names of German, Swiss ... and other Immigrants in Pennsylvania....* Harrisburg, Pa.: T. F. Schaeffer, 1856.

Rush, Benjamin. *An Account of the Manners of the German Inhabitants of Pennsylvania by Benjamin Rush.* Edited by Theodore E. Schmauk. Lancaster, Pa.: Pennsylvania German Society, 1910.

———. *A Letter by Dr. Benjamin Rush Describing the Consecration of the German College at Lancaster, in June, 1787.* Edited by Lyman H. Butterfield. Lancaster: Franklin and Marshall College, 1945.

———. *The Selected Writings of Benjamin Rush.* Edited by Dagobert D. Runes. New York: Philosophical Library, 1947.

Sargent, Nathan. *Public Men and Events: From the Commencement of Mr. Monroe's Administration, in 1817, to the Close of Mr. Fillmore's Administration, in 1853.* 2 vols. Philadelphia: J. B. Lippincott, 1875.

Schaeffer, Charles F., and Frederick A. Muhlenberg. *Memorial Volume of the Evangelical Lutheran Church of the Holy Trinity, Lancaster, Pa. Discourses Delivered on the Occasion of the Centenary Jubilee.* Lancaster, Pa.: John Baer's Sons, 1861.

Schaeffer, David F. *Historical Address Commemorative of the Blessed Reformation, Commenced by Dr. Martin Luther, ... Delivered in the Lutheran Church at Frederick Town, Md., October 31, A.D. 1817.* Frederick, Md.: William B. Burke, 1818.

Schaf[f], Philip. *America: A Sketch of the Political, Social, and Religious Character of the United States of North America.* New York: Scribner, 1855.

————. *Anglo-Germanism, or the Significance of the German Nationality in the United States. . . .* Chambersburg, Pa.: Publication Office of the German Reformed Church, 1846.

————. *The Principle of Protestantism as Related to the Present State of the Church.* Chambersburg, Pa.: Publication Office of the German Reformed Church, 1845.

[Schmucker, John George]. *Die Augsburgische Confession der Evangelisch Lutherischen Kirche, nebst eine kurzen Reformations-Geschichte. . . .* York, Pa.: C. T. Melsheimer, 1817.

[————]. *Der Schwärmer-Geist unserer Tage; entlarvt Zur Warnung Erweckter Seelen.* Orwigsburg, Pa.: Grim und Thoma, [1826].

Schmucker, Samuel S. *The American Lutheran Church, Historically, Doctrinally, and Practically Delineated, in Several Occasional Discourses.* 2d ed. Springfield, Ohio: David Harbaugh, 1851.

————. "Capital Punishment." *American Biblical Repository* 10 (1837): 67–88.

————. *The Christian Pulpit, the Rightful Guardian of Morals in Political no less than in Private Life. A Discourse. . . .* Gettysburg, Pa.: H. C. Neinstedt, 1846.

————. *Discourse in Commemoration of the Glorious Reformation of the Sixteenth Century.* 4th ed. New York: Gould and Newman, 1838.

————. *Elements of Popular Theology, with Special Reference to the Doctrines of the Reformation as Avowed Before the Diet at Augsburg, in MDXXX.* 2d and corrected ed. New York: Leavitt, Lord, 1834.

————. *Fraternal Appeal to the American Churches; with a Plan for Catholic Union on Apostolic Principles.* New York: Gould and Newman, 1838.

————. "Overture for Christian Union, Submitted for the Consideration of the Evangelical Denominations in the United States." *Protestant Quarterly* 3 (April 1846): 148–53.

————. *Portraiture of Lutheranism: A Discourse.* Baltimore: Publication Rooms [of the Evangelical Lutheran Church], 1840.

Schmucker, Samuel S., and J. Oswald. "The Baptism of Children Whose Parents Are Not Connected with the Church." Pamphlet collection, Abdel Ross Wentz Library, Lutheran Theological Seminary at Gettysburg, Gettysburg, Pa.

Schober, Gottlieb. *A Comprehensive Account of the Rise and Progress of the Blessed Reformation of the Christian Church by Dr. Martin Luther. . . .* Baltimore: Schaeffer und Maund, 1818.

Schoepf, Johann David. *Travels in the Confederation* [1783–84]. Translated by Alfred J. Morrison. New York: Bergman, 1911.

Sneider, John. *The Two Trials of John Fries on an Indictment for Treason. . . .* Philadelphia: William W. Woodward, 1800.

Sprague, William B. *Annals of the American Lutheran Pulpit; or Commemorative Notices of Distinguished Clergymen of the Lutheran Denomination. . . .* New York: Robert Carter and Bros., 1869.

Spring, Gardiner. *Memoirs of the Rev. Samuel J. Mills, late Missionary to the South Western Section of the United States and Agent of the American Colonization Society, deputed to Explore the Coast of Africa.* New York: New York Evangelical Missionary Society, 1820.

Stowe, Harriet Beecher. *Oldtown Folks*. Edited by Dorothy Berkson. New Brunswick: Rutgers University Press, 1987.

Strassburger, Ralph B., and William J. Hinke. *Pennsylvania German Pioneers: A Publication of the Original Lists of Arrivals in the Port of Philadelphia from 1727 to 1808*. 3 vols. Norristown, Pa.: Pennsylvania German Society, 1934.

Tappert, Theodore G., trans. and ed. "Helmuth and the Fries Rebellion in 1799." *Lutheran Quarterly* 17 (August 1965): 265–69.

Vollständiges Gebät-Buch auf alle Zeiten, in allen Ständen, und bey allen Angelegenheiten nützlich zu gebrauchen. . . . Reading, Pa.: Heinrich B. Sage, 1813.

Wentz, Richard E., ed. *Pennsylvania Dutch Folk Spirituality*. New York: Paulist Press, 1993.

Winebrenner, John. *A Brief View of the Formation, Government, and Discipline of the Church of God*. Harrisburg, Pa.: Montgomery and Dexter, 1829.

Wolff, Bernard C. *The Work Before Us and the Motives to its Performance: A Sermon Delivered at the Opening of the Synod of the German Reformed Church, at Reading, Pa., October 21, 1841*. Chambersburg, Pa.: German Reformed Church, 1841.

Yoder, Don, trans. "Father Pomp's Life Story." *The Pennsylvania Dutchman* 1 (23 June 1949): 5.

———, ed. "A Letter to Bishop Asbury." *The Pennsylvania Dutchman* 1 (12 May 1949): 5.

Zahm, Matthias. "Matthias Zahm's Diary." Edited by Robert H. Goodell. *Proceedings of the Lancaster County Historical Society* 47 (1943): 61–92.

Zitzman, Manfred S., trans. and ed. "William Helffrich, Horse and Buggy Preacher." *Historical Review of Berks County* 47 (Summer 1982): 104–6, 118–20; 47 (Fall 1982): 142–45, 148–60.

PRIMARY SOURCES: PERIODICALS

The Berks and Schuylkill Journal, Reading, Pa., 1816–1910.

Christian Observer, Philadelphia and Louisville, Ky., 1821–1910.

Evangelical Lutheran Intelligencer, Frederick, Md., 1826–31.

Evangelisches Magazin, Philadelphia, 1812–17.

The Guardian, Lewisburg, Pa., and Lancaster, Pa., 1850–90.

The Lutheran Magazine, Schoharie, N.Y., 1827–31.

Lutheran Observer, Baltimore, 1831–1915.

Magazine of the German Reformed Church, Carlisle, Pa., and York, Pa., 1827–31.

Messenger of the German Reformed Church, York, Pa., 1832–34.

The Methodist Magazine, New York, 1818–40.

Methodist Quarterly Review, New York, 1841–84.

Niles Weekly Register, Baltimore, 1814–37.

Reading Adler, Reading, Pa., 1797–1913.

Reformed Church Messenger, Philadelphia, Pa., 1867–1936.

Der Volksfreund, Lancaster, Pa., 1808–1910.

Weekly Messenger of the German Reformed Church, Chambersburg, Pa., 1835–48.

The Western Recorder, Utica, N.Y., 1824–33.

SECONDARY SOURCES

Abzug, Robert H. *Cosmos Crumbling: American Reform and the Religious Imagination.* New York: Oxford University Press, 1994.

Adams, Willi Paul. "The Colonial German-Language Press and the American Revolution." In *The Press and the American Revolution,* edited by Bernard Bailyn and John B. Hench, 151–228. Worcester, Mass.: American Antiquarian Society, 1980.

Albanese, Catherine L. *Sons of the Fathers: The Civil Religion of the American Revolution.* Philadelphia: Temple University Press, 1976.

Allbeck, Willard D. *A Century of Lutherans in Ohio.* Yellow Springs, Ohio: Antioch Press, 1966.

American Lutheranism: Crisis in Historical Consciousness? The Lutheran Historical Conference, Essays and Reports, 1988. St. Louis: Lutheran Historical Conference, 1990.

Anstadt, Peter. *Life and Times of Rev. S. S. Schmucker, D.D., first Professor of Theology in the Lutheran Theological Seminary at Gettysburg, Pa.* York, Pa.: P. Anstadt and Sons, 1896.

Appel, Theodore. *The Beginnings of the Theological Seminary of the Reformed Church in the United States, from 1817 to 1832.* Philadelphia: Reformed Church Publication Board, 1886.

Appleby, Joyce. *Capitalism and a New Social Order: The Republican Vision of the 1790s.* New York: New York University Press, 1984.

Archdeacon, Thomas J. *Becoming American: An Ethnic History.* New York: Free Press, 1983.

Arndt, Karl J. R., and May E. Olson, eds. *German-American Newspapers and Periodicals, 1732–1955: History and Bibliography.* Heidelberg: Quelle and Meyer, 1961.

Baglyos, Paul A. "In This Land of Liberty: American Lutherans and the Young Republic, 1787–1837." Ph.D. diss., University of Chicago Divinity School, 1997.

Bailyn, Bernard. *The Ideological Origins of the American Revolution.* Cambridge: Harvard University Press, 1967.

Bailyn, Bernard, and John B. Hench, eds. *The Press and the American Revolution.* Worcester, Mass.: American Antiquarian Society, 1980.

Bailyn, Bernard, and Philip D. Morgan, eds. *Strangers Within the Realm: Cultural Margins of the First British Empire.* Chapel Hill: The University of North Carolina Press, 1991.

Balmer, Randall. *A Perfect Babel of Confusion: Dutch Religion and English Culture in the Middle Colonies.* New York: Oxford University Press, 1989.

Barclay, David E., and Elisabeth Glaser-Schmidt, eds. *Transatlantic Images and Perceptions: Germany and America Since 1776.* New York: Cambridge University Press, 1997.

Barth, Fredrik, ed. *Ethnic Groups and Boundaries: The Social Organization of Cultural Differences.* Boston: Little, Brown, 1969.

Bassler, Gerhard. "German Immigration and Settlement in Canada: English-Canadian Perspectives." In *Emigration and Settlement Patterns of German Communities in North America,* edited by Eberhard Reichmann, LaVern J. Rippley, and

Jörg Nagler, 325–36. Indianapolis: Max Kade German-American Center/ Indiana University–Purdue University at Indianapolis, 1995.

Baur, R. H. "Paul Henkel and the Revivals." *Concordia Historical Institute Quarterly* 63 (Fall 1990): 113–22.

Becker, Laura. "Diversity and Its Significance in an Eighteenth-Century Pennsylvania Town." In *Friends and Neighbors: Group Life in America's First Pluralist Society,* edited by Michael Zuckerman, 196–221. Philadelphia: Temple University Press, 1982.

Beeman, Richard, et al., eds. *Beyond Confederation: Origins of the Constitution and American National Identity.* Chapel Hill: The University of North Carolina Press, 1987.

Behney, Bruce, and Paul H. Eller. *The History of the Evangelical United Brethren Church.* Nashville: Abingdon Press, 1979.

Bell, Whitfield J., Jr. "Benjamin Franklin and the German Charity Schools." *Proceedings of the American Philosophical Society* 99 (December 1955): 381–87.

Bente, Friedrich. *American Lutheranism: Early History of American Lutheranism and the Tennessee Synod.* 2 vols. St. Louis: Concordia Publishing, 1919.

Berger, Daniel. *History of the Church of the United Brethren in Christ.* Dayton, Ohio: Otterbein Press, 1897.

Bernheim, Gotthardt D. *History of the German Settlements and of the Lutheran Church in North and South Carolina . . . to the Close of the First Half of the Present Century.* Philadelphia: Lutheran Book Store, 1872.

Bertolet, Samuel E. "The Presbyterian Church in Reading." *Historical Review of Berks County* 7 (January 1943): 34–37.

Bilhartz, Terry D. *Urban Religion and the Second Great Awakening: Church and Society in Early National Baltimore.* Cranbury, N.J.: Associated University Presses, 1986.

Bockelman, Wayne L., and Owen S. Ireland. "The Internal Revolution in Pennsylvania: An Ethnic Religious Interpretation." *Pennsylvania History* 41 (April 1974): 125–60.

Bodo, John R. *The Protestant Clergy and Public Issues, 1812–1848.* Princeton: Princeton University Press, 1954.

Bouton, Terry. "'No Wonder the Times Were Troublesome': The Origins of the Fries Rebellion, 1783–1799." *Pennsylvania History* 67 (Winter 2000): 21–42.

Bready, Guy P. *History of the Maryland Classis of the Reformed Church in the United States. . . .* Taneytown, Md.: Carroll Record Printers, 1938.

Brecht, Martin, and Klaus Deppermann, eds. *Der Pietismus im achtzehnten Jahrhundert.* Geschichte des Pietismus, vol. 2. Göttingen: Vandenhoeck and Ruprecht, 1995.

Breitenbach, William. "Sons of the Fathers: Temperance Reformers and the Legacy of the American Revolution." *Journal of the Early Republic* 3 (Spring 1983): 69–82.

Bridenbaugh, Carl. *Myths and Realities: Societies of the Colonial South.* Baton Rouge: Louisiana State University Press, 1952.

Buffington, Albert F., ed. *Ebbes fer Alle—Ebber Ebbes fer Dich: Something for Everyone— Something for You.* Breinigsville, Pa.: Pennsylvania German Society, 1980.

Bullock, Steven C. *Revolutionary Brotherhood: Freemasonry and the Transformation of the*

American Social Order, 1730–1840. Chapel Hill: The University of North Carolina Press, 1996.

Burke, Susan M., and Matthew H. Hill, eds. *From Pennsylvania to Waterloo: Pennsylvania-German Folk Culture in Transition*. Kitchener, Ontario: Friends of the Joseph Schneider Haus, 1991.

Bushman, Richard L. *The Refinement of America: Persons, Houses, Cities*. New York: Alfred A. Knopf, 1992.

Butler, Diana Hochstedt. *Standing Against the Whirlwind: Evangelical Episcopalians in Nineteenth-Century America*. New York: Oxford University Press, 1995.

Butler, Jon. *Awash in a Sea of Faith: Christianizing the American People*. Cambridge: Harvard University Press, 1990.

———. "Coercion, Miracle, Reason: Rethinking the American Religious Experience in the Revolutionary Age." In *Religion in a Revolutionary Age*, edited by Ronald Hoffman and Peter J. Albert, 1–30. Charlottesville: The University Press of Virginia, 1994.

Cazden, Robert E. *A Social History of the German Book Trade in America to the Civil War*. Columbia, S.C.: Camden House, 1984.

Chinnici, Joseph P. "American Catholics and Religious Pluralism, 1775–1820." *Journal of Ecumenical Studies* 16 (Fall 1979): 727–46.

Cohn, Henry J. "The Territorial Princes in Germany's Second Reformation, 1559–1622." In *International Calvinism, 1541–1715*, edited by Menna Prestwich, 135–66. Oxford: Clarendon Press, 1985.

Conkin, Paul K. *The Uneasy Center: Reformed Christianity in Antebellum America*. Chapel Hill: The University of North Carolina Press, 1995.

Conser, Walter H., Jr. *Church and Confession: Conservative Theologians in Germany, England, and America, 1815–1866*. Macon: Mercer University Press, 1984.

Conzen, Kathleen Neils. *Immigrant Milwaukee, 1836–1860: Accommodation and Community in a Frontier City*. Cambridge: Harvard University Press, 1976.

———. *Making Their Own America: Assimilation Theory and the German Peasant Pioneer*. New York: Berg Publishing, 1990.

———. "The Paradox of German-American Assimilation." *Yearbook of German-American Studies* 16 (1981): 153–60.

———. "Peasant Pioneers: Generational Succession Among German Farmers in Frontier Minnesota." In *The Countryside in the Age of Capitalist Transformation: Essays in the Social History of Rural America*, edited by Stephen Hahn and Jonathan Prude, 259–92. Chapel Hill: The University of North Carolina Press, 1985.

Conzen, Kathleen Neils, David A. Gerber, Ewa Morawska, George E. Pozzetta, and Rudolph J. Vecoli. "The Invention of Ethnicity: A Perspective from the U.S.A." *Journal of American Ethnic History* 12 (Fall 1992): 3–63.

Cunz, Dieter. *The Maryland Germans: A History*. Princeton: Princeton University Press, 1948.

D'Elia, Donald J. *Benjamin Rush: Philosopher of the American Revolution*. Philadelphia: American Philosophical Society, 1974.

DeVos, George, and Lola Romanucci-Ross, eds. *Ethnic Identity: Cultural Continuities and Change*. Palo Alto, Calif.: Mayfield Publishing, 1975.

Dictionary of American Biography. 22 vols. New York: Charles Scribner's Sons, 1928–37.

Dolan, Jay P. *The Immigrant Church: New York's Irish and German Catholics, 1815–1865.* Baltimore: The Johns Hopkins University Press, 1975.

———. "Philadelphia and the German Catholic Community." In *Immigrants and Religion in Urban America,* edited by Randall M. Miller and Thomas D. Marzik, 69–83. Philadelphia: Temple University Press, 1977.

Douglass, Paul F. *The Story of German Methodism: Biography of an Immigrant Soul.* New York: The Methodist Book Concern, 1939.

Drury, Augustus W. *The Life of Rev. Philip William Otterbein, Founder of the Church of the United Brethren in Christ.* Dayton, Ohio: United Brethren Publishing House, 1884.

Dubbs, Joseph H. *Historic Manual of the Reformed Church in the United States.* Lancaster, Pa.: Inquirer Printing, 1885.

———. *History of Franklin and Marshall College.* Lancaster, Pa.: Franklin and Marshall College Alumni Association, 1903.

Dundore, M. Walter. "A Population Study of the Pennsylvania Germans in Berks and Neighboring Counties." *Historical Review of Berks County* 28 (Autumn 1963): 113–16.

Early, John W. "The Ministerium of Pennsylvania and the Organization of the General Synod." *Lutheran Church Review* 11 (January 1892): 61–70, 172–86.

Eschbach, Edmund R. *Historic Sketch of the Evangelical Reformed Church of Frederick, Maryland.* Frederick, Md.: Great Southern Printing, 1894.

Fecher, Vincent J. *A Study of the Movement for German National Parishes in Philadelphia and Baltimore, 1787–1802.* Rome: Apud Aedes Universitatis Gregorianae, 1955.

Feller, Daniel. *The Jacksonian Promise: America, 1815–1840.* Baltimore: The Johns Hopkins University Press, 1995.

Ferm, Vergilius. *The Crisis in American Lutheran Theology: A Study of the Issue Between American Lutheranism and Old Lutheranism.* New York: Century, 1927.

Finke, Roger, and Rodney Stark. "How the Upstart Sects Won America: 1776–1850." *Journal for the Scientific Study of Religion* 28 (March 1989): 27–44.

Fischer, David Hackett. *Albion's Seed: Four British Folkways in America.* New York: Oxford University Press, 1989.

———. *The Revolution of American Conservatism: The Federalist Party in the Era of Jeffersonian Democracy.* New York: Harper and Row, 1965.

Fishman, Joshua A., ed. *Language Loyalty in the United States: The Maintenance and Perpetuation of Non-English Mother Tongues by American Ethnic and Religious Groups.* The Hague: Mouton, 1966.

Focht, David H. *Churches Between the Mountains: A History of the Lutheran Congregations in Perry County, Pennsylvania.* Baltimore: T. Newton Kurtz, 1862.

Fogleman, Aaron S. "From Slaves, Convicts, and Servants to Free Passengers: The Transformation of Immigration in the Era of the American Revolution." *Journal of American History* 85 (June 1998): 43–76.

———. *Hopeful Journeys: German Immigration, Settlement, and Political Culture in Colonial America, 1717–1775.* Philadelphia: University of Pennsylvania Press, 1996.

———. "Migrations to the Thirteen British North American Colonies, 1700–1775: New Estimates." *Journal of Interdisciplinary History* 22 (Spring 1992): 691–709.

Foner, Eric. *The Story of American Freedom.* New York: Norton, 1998.

Foster, Charles I. *An Errand of Mercy: The Evangelical United Front, 1790–1837.* Chapel Hill: The University of North Carolina Press, 1960.

Frantz, John B. "The Awakening of Religion Among the German Settlers in the Middle Colonies." *William and Mary Quarterly,* 3d ser., 33 (April 1976): 266–88.

———. "Early German Methodism in America." *Yearbook of German-American Studies* (1991): 171–84.

———. "Franklin and the Pennsylvania Germans." *Pennsylvania History* 65 (Winter 1998): 21–34.

———. "John C. Guldin, Pennsylvania German Revivalist." *Pennsylvania Magazine of History and Biography* 87 (April 1963): 123–38.

———. "The Return to Tradition: An Analysis of the New Measure Movement in the German Reformed Church." *Pennsylvania History* 31 (July 1964): 311–26.

Frei, Hans W. *The Eclipse of Biblical Narrative: A Study in Eighteenth and Nineteenth Century Hermeneutics.* New Haven: Yale University Press, 1974.

Funkhouser, Abram P. *History of the Church of the United Brethren in Christ, Virginia Conference.* Dayton, Va.: Ruebush-Kieffer, 1921.

Gagliardo, John G. *Reich and Nation: The Holy Roman Empire as Idea and Reality, 1763–1806.* Bloomington: Indiana University Press, 1980.

Garvan, Beatrice B. *The Pennsylvania German Collection.* Philadelphia: Philadelphia Museum of Art, 1982.

Gehret, Ellen J. *Rural Pennsylvania Clothing, Being a Study of the Wearing Apparel of the German and English Inhabitants . . . [of] Southeastern Pennsylvania in the Late Eighteenth and Early Nineteenth Centuries.* York, Pa.: Liberty Cap, 1976.

Geitz, Henry, Jürgen Heideking, and Jurgen Herbst, eds. *German Influences on Education in the United States to 1917.* New York: Cambridge University Press, 1995.

Gerber, David A. *The Making of an American Pluralism: Buffalo, New York, 1825–1860.* Urbana: University of Illinois Press, 1989.

Gjerde, Jon. *The Minds of the Middle West: Ethnocultural Evolution in the Rural Middle West, 1830–1917.* Chapel Hill: The University of North Carolina Press, 1997.

Glatfelter, Charles H. *Pastors and People: German Lutheran and Reformed Churches in the Pennsylvania Field, 1717–1793.* 2 vols. Breinigsville, Pa.: Pennsylvania German Society, 1980–81.

———. *A Salutary Influence: Gettysburg College, 1832–1985.* 2 vols. Gettysburg: Gettysburg College, 1987.

Gleason, Philip. "American Identity and Americanization." In *Harvard Encyclopedia of American Ethnic Groups,* edited by Stephan Thernstrom, 31–58. Cambridge: Harvard University Press, 1980.

Goeters, J. F. Gerhard, and Rudolf Mau, eds. *Die Geschichte der Evangelische Kirche der Union.* Vol. 1, *Die Anfänge der Union unter landesherrlichem Kirchenregiment (1817–1850).* Leipzig: Evangelische Verlagsanstalt, 1992.

Good, James I. *History of the Reformed Church in the U.S. in the Nineteenth Century.* New York: The Board of Publication of the Reformed Church in America, 1911.

Goodfriend, Joyce D. *Before the Melting Pot: Society and Culture in Colonial New York City, 1664–1730.* Princeton: Princeton University Press, 1992.

Gordon, Milton M. *Assimilation in American Life: The Role of Race, Religion, and National Origins.* New York: Oxford University Press, 1964.

Gorrell, Donald K. "'Ride a Circuit or Let It Alone': Early Practices That Kept the United Brethren, Albright People, and Methodists Apart." *Methodist History* 25 (October 1986): 4–16.

Goss, Charles C., ed. *Statistical History of the First Century of American Methodism, with a Summary of the Origins and Present Operations of Other Denominations.* New York: Carlton and Porter, 1866.

Grabbe, Hans-Jürgen. "Besonderheiten der europäischen Einwanderung in die USA während der frühen nationalen Periode, 1783–1820." *Amerikastudien/American Studies* 33 (1988): 271–90.

Gräbner, Augustus L. *Geschichte der Lutherischen Kirche in America.* St. Louis: Concordia Publishing, 1892.

Graeff, Arthur D. "Pennsylvania, the Colonial Melting Pot." In *The Pennsylvania Germans,* edited by Ralph Wood, 1–26. Princeton: Princeton University Press, 1942.

Graham, W. Fred, ed. *Later Calvinism: International Perspectives.* Kirksville, Mo.: Sixteenth Century Journal Publishers, 1994.

Greene, Jack P. *Pursuits of Happiness: The Social Development of Early Modern British Colonies and the Formation of American Culture.* Chapel Hill: The University of North Carolina Press, 1988.

Greene, Victor. *For God and Country: The Rise of Polish and Lithuanian Ethnic Consciousness in America.* Madison: University of Wisconsin Press, 1975.

Grumbine, Ezra. "Stories of Old Stumpstown." *Papers and Addresses of the Lebanon County Historical Society* 5 (1909–12): 153–276.

Gustafson, David A. *Lutherans in Crisis: The Question of Identity in the American Republic.* Minneapolis: Fortress Press, 1993.

Hackett, David G. *The Rude Hand of Innovation: Religion and the Social Order in Albany, New York, 1652–1836.* New York: Oxford University Press, 1991.

Hahn, Stephen, and Jonathan Prude, eds. *The Countryside in the Age of Capitalist Transformation: Essays in the Social History of Rural America.* Chapel Hill: The University of North Carolina Press, 1985.

Hambrick-Stowe, Charles E. *Charles G. Finney and the Spirit of American Evangelicalism.* Grand Rapids, Mich.: William B. Eerdmans, 1996.

Hamilton, Milton W., ed. "Religious Revival in Reading, 1829." *Historical Review of Berks County* 15 (October 1949): 148–50.

Hanley, Mark Y. *Beyond a Christian Commonwealth: The Protestant Quarrel with the American Republic, 1830–1860.* Chapel Hill: The University of North Carolina Press, 1994.

Harbaugh, Linn. *Life of the Rev. Henry Harbaugh, D.D.* Philadelphia: Reformed Church Publication Board, 1900.

Hatch, Nathan O. *The Democratization of American Christianity.* New Haven: Yale University Press, 1989.

Hay, Charles A. *Memoirs of Rev. Jacob Goering, Rev. George Lochman, D.D., and Rev. Benjamin Kurtz, D.D., LL.D.* Philadelphia: Lutheran Publication Society, 1887.

Heisey, Terry. "*Singet Hallelujah!* Music in the Evangelical Association, 1800–1894." *Methodist History* 28 (July 1990): 237–51.

Heller, Mark O. "The Union Church Problem in Eastern Pennsylvania." *The Lutheran Church Quarterly* 14 (April 1941): 174–90.

Hellmuth, Eckhart, ed. *The Transformation of Political Culture: England and Germany in the Late Eighteenth Century.* New York: Oxford University Press, 1990.

Hersh, Tandy, and Charles Hersh. *Samplers of the Pennsylvania Germans.* Birdsboro, Pa.: Pennsylvania German Society, 1991.

Hesselink, John. "The Dramatic Story of the Heidelberg Catechism." In *Later Calvinism: International Perspectives,* edited by W. Fred Graham, 273–88. Kirksville, Mo.: Sixteenth Century Journal Publishers, 1994.

Higginbotham, Sanford W. *The Keystone in the Democratic Arch: Pennsylvania Politics, 1800–1816.* Harrisburg, Pa.: Pennsylvania Historical and Museum Commission, 1952.

Higham, John. "Integrating America: The Problem of Assimilation in the Nineteenth Century." *Journal of American Ethnic History* 1 (Fall 1981): 7–25.

Hinke, William J. *The Life and Letters of the Rev. John Philip Boehm, Founder of the Reformed Church in Pennsylvania, 1683–1749.* Philadelphia: Publication and Sunday School Board of the Reformed Church in the United States, 1916.

———. *Ministers of the German Reformed Congregations in Pennsylvania and Other Colonies in the Eighteenth Century.* Lancaster, Pa.: Historical Commission of the Evangelical and Reformed Church, 1951.

Historic Sketch of the Reformed Church in North Carolina by a Board of Editors under the Classis of North Carolina. Philadelphia: Publication Board of the Reformed Church in the United States, 1908.

History of the Evangelical Lutheran Synod of East Pennsylvania, with Brief Sketches of its Congregations . . . 1842–1892. Philadelphia: Lutheran Publication Society, [1892].

Hoffman, Ronald, and Peter J. Albert, eds. *Religion in a Revolutionary Age.* Charlottesville: The University Press of Virginia, 1994.

Hood, Fred J. *Reformed America: The Middle and Southern States, 1783–1837.* Tuscaloosa: University of Alabama Press, 1980.

Hostetler, Beulah Stauffer. *American Mennonites and Protestant Movements: A Community Paradigm.* Scottdale, Pa.: Herald Press, 1987.

Houck, Louis. *A History of Missouri from the Earliest Explorations. . . .* 3 vols. Chicago: R. R. Donnelley and Sons, 1908.

Howe, Daniel Walker. *The Political Culture of the American Whigs.* Chicago: The University of Chicago Press, 1979.

Hutson, James H. *Pennsylvania Politics, 1746–1770: The Movement for Royal Government and Its Consequences.* Princeton: Princeton University Press, 1972.

Ignatiev, Noel. *How the Irish Became White.* New York: Routledge, 1995.

Ireland, Owen S. *Religion, Ethnicity, and Politics: Ratifying the Constitution in Pennsylvania.* University Park: The Pennsylvania State University Press, 1995.

Jacobs, Henry E. "The Confessional History of the Ministerium of Pennsylvania." *Lutheran Church Review* 17 (April 1898): 358–69.

———. *A History of the Evangelical Lutheran Church in the United States.* New York: Christian Literature, 1893.

Jensson, J. C. *American Lutheran Biographies; or Historical Notices of over Three Hundred and Fifty Leading Men of the American Lutheran Church from its Establishment to the Year 1890.* Milwaukee: A. Houtkamp and Son, 1890.

John, Richard R. *Spreading the News: The American Postal System from Franklin to Morse.* Cambridge: Harvard University Press, 1995.

Johnson, Curtis D. *Islands of Holiness: Rural Religion in Upstate New York, 1790–1860.* Ithaca: Cornell University Press, 1989.

———. *Redeeming America: Evangelicals and the Road to Civil War.* Chicago: I. R. Dee, 1993.

Jordan, Philip D. *The Evangelical Alliance for the United States of America, 1847–1900: Ecumenism, Identity, and the Religion of the Republic.* New York: Edwin Mellen Press, 1982.

Katz, Michael B. "From Voluntarism to Bureaucracy in American Education." In *Education in American History: Readings on the Social Issues,* edited by Michael B. Katz, 38–50. New York: Praeger, 1973.

———, ed. *Education in American History: Readings on the Social Issues.* New York: Praeger, 1973.

Kazal, Russell A. "Revisiting Assimilation: The Rise, Fall, and Reappraisal of a Concept in American Ethnic History." *American Historical Review* 100 (April 1995): 437–71.

Keller, Kenneth W. "Cultural Conflict in Early Nineteenth-Century Pennsylvania Politics." *Pennsylvania Magazine of History and Biography* 110 (October 1986): 509–30.

———. *Rural Politics and the Collapse of Pennsylvania Federalism.* Philadelphia: American Philosophical Society, 1982.

Kern, Richard. *John Winebrenner: Nineteenth Century Reformer.* Harrisburg, Pa.: Central Publishing, 1974.

Kieffer, Elizabeth Clarke. *Henry Harbaugh: Pennsylvania Dutchman, 1817–1867.* Norristown, Pa.: Pennsylvania German Society, 1945.

Klein, Frederic S. *The Spiritual and Educational Background of Franklin and Marshall College.* Lancaster: Franklin and Marshall College, 1939.

Klein, H. M. J. *The History of the Eastern Synod of the Reformed Church in the United States.* Lancaster, Pa.: Eastern Synod of the Reformed Church in the United States, 1943.

Klein, Philip S. *Pennsylvania Politics, 1817–1832: A Game Without Rules.* Philadelphia: Historical Society of Pennsylvania, 1940.

Klein, Philip S., and Ari Hoogenboom. *A History of Pennsylvania.* 2d ed. University Park: The Pennsylvania State University Press, 1980.

Klepp, Susan. "Five Early Pennsylvania Censuses." *Pennsylvania Magazine of History and Biography* 106 (October 1982): 483–514.

Kleppner, Paul. *The Cross of Culture: A Social Analysis of Midwestern Politics, 1850–1900.* New York: Free Press, 1970.

Kling, David W. *A Field of Divine Wonders: The New Divinity and Village Revivals in Northwestern Connecticut, 1792–1822.* University Park: The Pennsylvania State University Press, 1993.

Klippel, Diethelm. "The True Concept of Liberty: Political Theory in Germany in the Second Half of the Eighteenth Century." In *The Transformation of Political Culture: England and Germany in the Late Eighteenth Century,* edited by Eckhart Hellmuth, 447–66. New York: Oxford University Press, 1990.

Kloos, John M., Jr. *A Sense of Deity: The Republican Spirituality of Dr. Benjamin Rush.* Brooklyn: Carlson Publishing, 1991.

Kloppenberg, James T. "The Virtues of Liberalism: Christianity, Republicanism, and Ethics in Early American Discourse." *Journal of American History* 74 (June 1987): 9–33.

Kloss, Heinz. "Fünf Stationen einer Reise in Pennsylvanien." *Der Auslanddeutsche: Halbmonatsschrift für Auslanddeutschtum und Auslandkunde. Mitteilungen des Deutschen Ausland-Institutes, Stuttgart* 14 (1931): 2–4.

———. "German-American Language Maintenance Efforts." In *Language Loyalty in the United States: The Maintenance and Perpetuation of Non-English Mother Tongues by American Ethnic and Religious Groups,* edited by Joshua A. Fishman, 206–52. The Hague: Mouton, 1966.

Knobel, Dale T. *Paddy and the Republic: Ethnicity and Nationality in Antebellum America.* Middletown: Wesleyan University Press, 1986.

Kohn, Hans. *American Nationalism: An Interpretive Essay.* New York: Macmillan, 1957.

Kroes, Rob. *The Persistence of Ethnicity: Dutch Calvinist Pioneers in Amsterdam, Montana.* Urbana: University of Illinois Press, 1992.

Kuenning, Paul P. *The Rise and Fall of American Lutheran Pietism: The Rejection of an Activist Heritage.* Macon: Mercer University Press, 1988.

Lane, Robert E. *Political Life: Why People Get Involved in Politics.* Glencoe, Ill.: Free Press, 1959.

Laury, Preston A. *The History of the Allentown Conference of the Ministerium of Pennsylvania.* Kutztown, Pa.: Kutztown Publishing, 1926.

Lehmann, Hartmut. *Martin Luther in the American Imagination.* München: Wilhelm Fink Verlag, 1988.

Lemon, James T. *The Best Poor Man's Country: A Geographical Study of Early Southeastern Pennsylvania.* Baltimore: The Johns Hopkins University Press, 1972.

Light, Dale B. *Rome and the New Republic: Conflict and Community in Philadelphia Catholicism Between the Revolution and the Civil War.* Notre Dame: University of Notre Dame Press, 1996.

Livingood, Frederick G. *Eighteenth-Century Reformed Church Schools.* Norristown, Pa.: Pennsylvania German Society, 1930.

Lodge, Martin E. "The Crisis of the Churches in the Middle Colonies." *Pennsylvania Magazine of History and Biography* 95 (April 1971): 195–220.

Loetscher, Lefferts A. "The Problem of Christian Unity in Early Nineteenth-Century America." *Church History* 32 (March 1963): 3–16.

Longenecker, Stephen L. *Piety and Tolerance: Pennsylvania German Religion, 1700–1850.* Metuchen, N.J.: Scarecrow Press, 1994.

Luebke, Frederick C., ed. *Ethnic Voters and the Election of Lincoln*. Lincoln: University of Nebraska Press, 1971.

———. *Germans in the New World: Essays in the History of Immigration*. Urbana: University of Illinois Press, 1990.

Maurer, Charles L. *Early Lutheran Education in Pennsylvania*. Norristown, Pa.: Pennsylvania German Society, 1932.

May, Henry F. "The Recovery of American Religious History." *American Historical Review* 70 (October 1964): 79–92.

McClelland, Peter D., and Richard J. Zeckhauser. *Demographic Dimensions of the New Republic: American Interregional Migration, Vital Statistics, and Manumissions, 1800–1860*. Cambridge: Cambridge University Press, 1982.

McPherson, Donald S. "The Fight Against Free Schools in Pennsylvania: Popular Opposition to the Common School System, 1834–1874." Ph.D. diss., University of Pittsburgh, 1977.

Meynen, Emil, comp. and ed. *Bibliography on German Settlements in Colonial North America, Especially on the Pennsylvania Germans and Their Descendants, 1683–1933*. Leipzig: Otto Harrassowitz, 1937.

Miller, Daniel. *History of the Reformed Church in Reading, Pa*. Reading, Pa.: Daniel Miller, 1905.

Miller, Randall M., ed. *Germans in America: Retrospect and Prospect*. Philadelphia: German Society of Pennsylvania, 1984.

Miller, Randall M., and Thomas D. Marzik, eds. *Immigrants and Religion in Urban America*. Philadelphia: Temple University Press, 1977.

Moore, R. Laurence. *Religious Outsiders and the Making of America*. New York: Oxford University Press, 1986.

Murrin, John M. "A Roof Without Walls: The Dilemma of American National Identity." In *Beyond Confederation: Origins of the Constitution and American National Identity*, edited by Richard Beeman et al., 333–48. Chapel Hill: The University of North Carolina Press, 1987.

Nadel, Stanley. *Little Germany: Ethnicity, Religion, and Class in New York City, 1845–80*. Urbana: University of Illinois Press, 1990.

Nagel, Paul C. *This Sacred Trust: American Nationality, 1798–1898*. New York: Oxford University Press, 1971.

Newman, Paul Douglas. "The Fries Rebellion of 1799." Ph.D. diss., University of Kentucky, 1996.

Newman, Simon P. *Parades and the Politics of the Street: Festive Culture in the Early Republic*. Philadelphia: University of Pennsylvania Press, 1997.

———. "The World Turned Upside Down: Revolutionary Politics, Fries and Gabriel's Rebellions, and the Fears of the Federalists." *Pennsylvania History* 67 (Winter 2000): 5–20.

Nichols, James H. *Romanticism in American Theology: Nevin and Schaff at Mercersburg*. Chicago: The University of Chicago Press, 1961.

Niebuhr, H. Richard. *Christ and Culture*. New York: Harper and Row, 1951.

———. *The Social Sources of Denominationalism*. New York: Henry Holt, 1929.

Nissenbaum, Stephen. *The Battle for Christmas*. New York: Alfred A. Knopf, 1996.

Noll, Mark A., David W. Bebbington, and George A. Rawlyk, eds. *Evangelicalism: Comparative Studies of Popular Protestantism in North America, the British Isles, and Beyond, 1700–1990.* New York: Oxford University Press, 1994.

"Notes: The Rev. Dr. Ezra Stiles Ely." *Journal of the Presbyterian Historical Society* 2 (September 1904): 321–24.

Nugent, Walter. *Structures of American Social History.* Bloomington: Indiana University Press, 1981.

Oboler, Suzanne. *Ethnic Labels, Latino Lives: Identity and the Politics of (Re)Presentation in the United States.* Minneapolis: University of Minnesota Press, 1995.

Ohms, Edward F. "The Language Problem in the Evangelical Association." *Methodist History* 24 (July 1987): 222–38.

O'Malley, J. Steven. "A Distinctive German-American Credo: The United Brethren Confession of Faith." *Asbury Theological Journal* 42 (Spring 1987): 51–64.

———. *Pilgrimage of Faith: The Legacy of the Otterbeins.* Metuchen, N.J.: Scarecrow Press, 1973.

———. *Touched by Godliness: Bishop John Seybert and the Evangelical Heritage.* [Independence, Mo.]: Granite Publications, 1984.

Peck, George. *Early Methodism Within the Bounds of the Old Genesee Conference from 1788 to 1828....* New York: Carlton and Porter, 1860.

Pershing, B. H. "Paul Henkel: Frontier Missionary, Organizer, and Author." *Concordia Historical Institute Quarterly* 7 (January 1935): 97–120.

Petersen, William. "Concepts of Ethnicity." In *Harvard Encyclopedia of American Ethnic Groups,* edited by Stephan Thernstrom, 234–42. Cambridge: Harvard University Press, 1980.

Prestwich, Menna, ed. *International Calvinism, 1541–1715.* Oxford: Clarendon Press, 1985.

Pritzker-Ehrlich, Marthi. "Michael Schlatter (1716–1790): A Man-in-Between." *Yearbook of German-American Studies* 20 (1985): 83–95.

Purvis, Thomas L. "Patterns of Ethnic Settlement in Late Eighteenth-Century Pennsylvania." *Western Pennsylvania Historical Magazine* 70 (April 1987): 107–22.

———. "The Pennsylvania Dutch and the German-American Diaspora in 1790." *Journal of Cultural Geography* 6 (Spring/Summer 1986): 81–99.

Ranck, Henry H. *The Life of the Reverend Benjamin Bausman, D.D., LL.D.* Philadelphia: The Publication and Sunday School Board of the Reformed Church in the United States, 1912.

Rawlyk, George A. *The Canada Fire: Radical Evangelicalism in British North America, 1775–1812.* Montreal: McGill-Queens University Press, 1994.

Rehmer, Rudolph F. "Indiana Lutherans at the Nineteenth-Century Crossroads." In *American Lutheranism: Crisis in Historical Consciousness? The Lutheran Historical Conference, Essays and Reports, 1988,* 70–87. St. Louis: Lutheran Historical Conference, 1990.

Reichmann, Eberhard, LaVern J. Rippley, and Jörg Nagler, eds. *Emigration and Settlement Patterns of German Communities in North America.* Indianapolis: Max Kade German-American Center/Indiana University–Purdue University at Indianapolis, 1995.

Remer, Rosalind. *Printers and Men of Capital: Philadelphia Book Publishers in the New Republic.* Philadelphia: University of Pennsylvania Press, 1996.

Remini, Robert V. *The Election of Andrew Jackson.* Philadelphia: J. B. Lippincott, 1963.

Repp, Arthur C., Jr. *Luther's Catechism Comes to America: Theological Effects on the Issues of the Small Catechism Prepared in or for America prior to 1850.* Metuchen, N.J.: Scarecrow Press, 1982.

Restad, Penne L. *Christmas in America: A History.* New York: Oxford University Press, 1995.

Reu, J. Michael. *Dr. Martin Luther's Small Catechism: A History of Its Origin, Its Distribution, and Its Use.* Chicago: Wartburg Publishing, 1929.

Richards, George W. *History of the Theological Seminary of the Reformed Church in the United States, 1825–1934 [and] Evangelical and Reformed Church, 1934–1952.* Lancaster, Pa.: Theological Seminary of the Evangelical and Reformed Church, 1952.

Riforgiato, Leonard R. *Missionary of Moderation: Henry Melchior Muhlenberg and the Lutheran Church in English America.* Lewisburg: Bucknell University Press, 1980.

Robisheaux, Thomas. *Rural Society and the Search for Order in Early Modern Germany.* New York: Cambridge University Press, 1989.

Rodgers, Daniel T. "Republicanism: The Career of a Concept." *Journal of American History* 79 (June 1992): 11–38.

Roeber, A. G. "Citizens or Subjects? German-Lutherans and the Federal Constitution in Pennsylvania, 1789–1800." *Amerikastudien/American Studies* 34 (1989): 49–68.

———. "In a German Way? Problems and Potentials of Eighteenth-Century German Social and Emigration History." *William and Mary Quarterly,* 3d ser., 44 (October 1987): 750–74.

———. "J. H. C. Helmuth, Evangelical Charity, and the Public Sphere in Pennsylvania, 1793–1800." *Pennsylvania Magazine of History and Biography* 121 (January–April 1997): 77–100.

———. "'The Origin of Whatever is not English Among Us.'" In *Strangers Within the Realm: Cultural Margins of the First British Empire,* edited by Bernard Bailyn and Philip D. Morgan, 220–83. Chapel Hill: The University of North Carolina Press, 1991.

———. *Palatines, Liberty, and Property: German Lutherans in Colonial British America.* Baltimore: The Johns Hopkins University Press, 1993.

———. "'Through a Glass, Darkly': The Changing German Ideas of American Freedom, 1776–1806." In *Transatlantic Images and Perceptions: Germany and America Since 1776,* edited by David E. Barclay and Elisabeth Glaser-Schmidt, 19–40. New York: Cambridge University Press, 1997.

———. "The von Mosheim Society and the Preservation of German Education and Culture in the New Republic, 1789–1813." In *German Influences on Education in the United States to 1917,* edited by Henry Geitz, Jürgen Heideking, and Jurgen Herbst, 157–76. New York: Cambridge University Press, 1995.

Rolland, Susanne M. "From the Rhine to the Catawba: A Study of Eighteenth-Century Germanic Migration and Adaptation." Ph.D. diss., Emory University, 1991.

Rosenberger, Homer T. *The Pennsylvania Germans, 1891–1965 (Frequently Known as the "Pennsylvania Dutch"): Seventy-fifth Anniversary Volume of the Pennsylvania German Society.* Lancaster, Pa.: Pennsylvania German Society, 1966.

Roth, Randolph A. *The Democratic Dilemma: Religion, Reform, and the Social Order in the Connecticut River Valley of Vermont, 1791–1850.* New York: Cambridge University Press, 1987.

Rothermund, Dietmar. *The Layman's Progress: Religion and Political Experience in Colonial Pennsylvania, 1740–1770.* Philadelphia: University of Pennsylvania Press, 1961.

———. "Political Factions and the Great Awakening." *Pennsylvania History* 26 (October 1959): 317–31.

Rouse, Parke, Jr. *The Great Wagon Road from Philadelphia to the South.* New York: McGraw-Hill, 1973.

Rumple, Jethro. *History of Rowan County, North Carolina, containing Sketches of Prominent Families....* Salisbury, N.C.: J. J. Bruner, 1881; reprint, n.p.: Elizabeth Steele Chap., D.A.R., 1916.

Sabean, David Warren. *Power in the Blood: Popular Culture and Village Discourse in Early Modern Germany.* New York: Cambridge University Press, 1984.

Sachse, Julius Friedrich. *The Wayside Inns on the Lancaster Roadside Between Philadelphia and Lancaster.* Lancaster, Pa.: Pennsylvania German Society, 1914.

Salamon, Sonya. *Prairie Patrimony: Family, Farming, and Community in the Midwest.* Chapel Hill: The University of North Carolina Press, 1992.

Sánchez, George J. *Becoming Mexican American: Ethnicity, Culture, and Identity in Chicano Los Angeles, 1900–1945.* New York: Oxford University Press, 1993.

Sapio, Victor A. *Pennsylvania and the War of 1812.* Lexington: The University Press of Kentucky, 1970.

Sarna, Jonathan D. "From Immigrants to Ethnics: Toward a New Theory of 'Ethnicization.'" *Ethnicity* 5 (December 1978): 370–78.

Schaeffer, Charles E. "The Helfenstein Family." *Bulletin: Theological Seminary of the Evangelical and Reformed Church* 26 (July 1955): 12–37.

Schaff, David S. *The Life of Philip Schaff, in part Autobiographical.* New York: Charles Scribner's Sons, 1897.

Schalk, Carl F. *God's Song in a New Land: Lutheran Hymnals in America.* St. Louis: Concordia Publishing, 1995.

Schneider, Carl E. *The German Church on the American Frontier: A Study in the Rise of Religion Among the Germans of the West, based on the History of the Evangelischer Kirchenverein des Westens, 1840–1866.* St. Louis: Eden Publishing House, 1939.

Schwartz, Sally. *"A Mixed Multitude": The Struggle for Toleration in Colonial Pennsylvania.* New York: New York University Press, 1987.

Sellers, Charles C. *Lorenzo Dow: The Bearer of the Word.* New York: Milton, Balch, 1928.

———. *Theophilus the Battle-axe: A History of the Lives and Adventures of Theophilus Ransom Gates and the Battle-axes.* Philadelphia: Patterson and White, 1930.

Sellers, Charles G. *The Market Revolution: Jacksonian America, 1815–1846.* New York: Oxford University Press, 1991.

Shalhope, Robert E. "Republicanism in Early America." *William and Mary Quarterly*, 3d ser., 39 (April 1982): 334–56.

Shaughnessy, Gerald. *Has the Immigrant Kept the Faith? A Study of Immigration and Catholic Growth in the United States, 1790–1920*. New York: Macmillan, 1925.

Sheatsley, Clarence V. *History of the Evangelical Lutheran Joint Synod of Ohio and Other States, from the Earliest Beginnings to 1919*. Columbus, Ohio: Lutheran Book Concern, 1919.

Shoemaker, Alfred L. *Christmas in Pennsylvania: A Folk-Cultural Study*. Kutztown, Pa.: Pennsylvania Folklife Society, 1959.

———. "Whit-Monday: Dutch Fourth of July." *The Pennsylvania Dutchman* 5 (May 1953): 5, 12.

Smith, Timothy L. "Religious Denominations as Ethnic Communities: A Regional Case Study." *Church History* 35 (June 1966): 207–26.

Sollors, Werner, ed. *The Invention of Ethnicity*. New York: Oxford University Press, 1989.

Sommer, Elisabeth W. *Serving Two Masters: Moravian Brethren in Germany and North Carolina, 1727–1801*. Lexington: The University Press of Kentucky, 2000.

Spaeth, Adolph. *Charles Porterfield Krauth, D.D., LL.D. . . .* Vol. 1, New York: Christian Literature, 1898; vol. 2, Philadelphia: General Council Publishing House, 1909.

Splitter, Wolfgang M. "The Germans in Pennsylvania Politics, 1758–1790: A Quantitative Analysis." *Pennsylvania Magazine of History and Biography* 122 (January–April 1998): 41–76.

———. *Pastors, People, Politics: German Lutherans in Pennsylvania, 1740–1790*. Trier: Wissenschaftlicher Verlag Trier, 1998.

Spotts, Charles D. "The People of Bowmansville." *Community Historians Annual* 9 (July 1970): 34–37.

Stine, Clyde S. "The Pennsylvania Germans and the School." In *The Pennsylvania Germans*, edited by Ralph Wood, 103–27. Princeton: Princeton University Press, 1942.

Stoeffler, F. Ernest. *German Pietism During the Eighteenth Century*. Leiden: E. J. Brill, 1973.

———, ed. *Continental Pietism and Early American Christianity*. Grand Rapids, Mich.: William B. Eerdmans, 1976.

Stout, Harry S. *The New England Soul: Preaching and Religious Culture in Colonial New England*. New York: Oxford University Press, 1986.

Stump, Adam, and Henry Anstadt, eds. *History of the Evangelical Lutheran Synod of West Pennsylvania . . . 1825–1925*. Chambersburg, Pa.: J. R. Kerr, 1925.

Swank, Scott T., et al. *Arts of the Pennsylvania Germans*. [New York]: Norton, 1983.

Taylor, Alan. "From Fathers to Friends of the People: Political Personas in the Early Republic." *Journal of the Early Republic* 11 (Winter 1991): 465–91.

———. *Liberty Men and Great Proprietors: The Revolutionary Settlement on the Maine Frontier, 1760–1820*. Chapel Hill: The University of North Carolina Press, 1991.

Thernstrom, Stephan, ed. *Harvard Encyclopedia of American Ethnic Groups*. Cambridge: Harvard University Press, 1980.

Thompson, Henry A. *Our Bishops: A Sketch of the Origins and Growth of the Church of the United Brethren in Christ as Shown in the Lives of Its Distinguished Leaders.* Dayton, Ohio: United Brethren Publishing House, 1904.

Tinkcom, Harry M. *The Republicans and Federalists in Pennsylvania, 1790–1801: A Study in National Stimulus and Local Response.* Harrisburg, Pa.: Pennsylvania Historical and Museum Commission, 1950.

Trommler, Frank, and Joseph McVeigh, eds. *America and the Germans: An Assessment of a 300-Year History.* 2 vols. Philadelphia: University of Pennsylvania Press, 1985.

Tully, Alan W. "Englishmen and Germans: National-Group Contact in Colonial Pennsylvania, 1700–1755." *Pennsylvania History* 45 (July 1978): 237–56.

Van Horne, David. *A History of the Reformed Church in Philadelphia.* Philadelphia: Reformed Church Publication Board, 1876.

Vaughn, William P. *The Antimasonic Party in the United States, 1826–1843.* Lexington: The University Press of Kentucky, 1983.

Vincent, John M. *Costume and Conduct in the Laws of Basel, Bern, and Zurich, 1370–1800.* Baltimore: The Johns Hopkins University Press, 1935.

Waldstreicher, David. *In the Midst of Perpetual Fetes: The Making of American Nationalism, 1776–1820.* Chapel Hill: The University of North Carolina Press, 1997.

Walker, Mack. *German Home Towns: Community, Estates, and General Estate, 1648–1871.* Ithaca: Cornell University Press, 1971.

Wallace, Paul A. W. *The Muhlenbergs of Pennsylvania.* Philadelphia: University of Pennsylvania Press, 1950.

Ward, W. Reginald. *The Protestant Evangelical Awakening.* Cambridge: Cambridge University Press, 1992.

Watts, Franklin P. "The Free Synod Movement of the German Reformed Church, 1822–1837." S.T.D. diss., Temple University, 1954.

Watts, Steven. *The Republic Reborn: War and the Making of Liberal America, 1790–1820.* Baltimore: The Johns Hopkins University Press, 1987.

Weaver, Ethan A. *"The American Eagle:* The First English Newspaper Printed in Northampton County, Pennsylvania." *Pennsylvania Magazine of History and Biography* 23 (January 1899): 69–76.

Weaver, William Woys. *Sauerkraut Yankees: Pennsylvania-German Foods and Folkways.* Philadelphia: University of Pennsylvania Press, 1983.

Weber, Samuel E. *The Charity School Movement in Colonial Pennsylvania.* Philadelphia: William V. Campbell, 1905. Reprint, New York: Arno, 1969.

Weiser, Clement Z. "The External History of the Theological Seminary of the Reformed Church in the United States, Lancaster, Pa." *Mercersburg Review* 23 (January 1876): 5–58.

Weng, Armin G. "The Language Problem in the Lutheran Church in Pennsylvania, 1742–1820." *Church History* 5 (December 1936): 359–75.

Wentz, Abdel Ross. *A Basic History of Lutheranism in America.* Rev. ed. Philadelphia: Fortress Press, 1964.

———. *History of the Gettysburg Theological Seminary ... 1826–1926.* Philadelphia: United Lutheran Publication House, [1926].

———. *Pioneer of Christian Unity: Samuel Simon Schmucker.* Philadelphia: Fortress Press, 1967.

———. "Relations Between the Lutheran and Reformed Churches in the Eighteenth and Nineteenth Centuries." *Lutheran Church Quarterly* 6 (July 1933): 301–27.

Wentz, Richard E. *John Williamson Nevin, American Theologian.* New York: Oxford University Press, 1997.

West, John G., Jr. *The Politics of Revolution and Reason: Religion and Civic Life in the New Nation.* Lawrence: University Press of Kansas, 1996.

Wickersham, James P. *A History of Education in Pennsylvania . . . to the Present Day.* Lancaster, Pa.: Inquirer Printing, 1886.

Wiebe, Robert H. *The Opening of American Society: From the Adoption of the Constitution to the Eve of Disunion.* New York: Alfred A. Knopf, 1984.

Wigger, John H. "Taking Heaven by Storm: Enthusiasm and Early American Methodism, 1770–1820." *Journal of the Early Republic* 14 (Summer 1994): 167–94.

———. *Taking Heaven by Storm: Methodism and the Rise of Popular Christianity in America.* New York: Oxford University Press, 1998.

Winpenny, Thomas R. *Bending Is Not Breaking: Adaptation and Persistence Among Nineteenth-Century Lancaster Artisans.* Lanham, Md.: University Press of America, 1990.

Wokeck, Marianne. *Trade in Strangers: The Beginnings of Mass Migration to North America.* University Park: The Pennsylvania State University Press, 1999.

Wolf, Edmund J. *The Lutherans in America: A Story of Struggle, Progress, Influence, and Marvelous Growth.* New York: J. A. Hill, 1890.

Wolf, Stephanie Grauman. "Hyphenated America: The Creation of an Eighteenth-Century German-American Culture." In *America and the Germans: An Assessment of a 300-Year History,* edited by Frank Trommler and Joseph McVeigh, 1:66–84. Philadelphia: University of Pennsylvania Press, 1985.

Wood, Gordon S. *The Creation of the American Republic, 1776–1787.* Chapel Hill: The University of North Carolina Press, 1969.

———. *The Radicalism of the American Revolution.* New York: Alfred A. Knopf, 1992.

Wood, Ralph, ed. *The Pennsylvania Germans.* Princeton: Princeton University Press, 1942.

Wust, Klaus G. *The Virginia Germans.* Charlottesville: The University Press of Virginia, 1969.

———. *Zion in Baltimore, 1755–1955: The Bicentennial History of the Earliest German-American Church in Baltimore, Maryland.* Baltimore: Zion Church, 1955.

Wyatt-Brown, Bertram. "Prelude to Abolitionism: Sabbatarian Politics and the Rise of the Second Party System." *Journal of American History* 58 (September 1971): 316–41.

Yoder, Don. "The Bench Versus the Catechism: Revivalism and Pennsylvania's Lutheran and Reformed Churches." *Pennsylvania Folklife* 10 (Fall 1959): 14–23.

———. "The 'Dutchman' and the 'Deitschlenner': The New World Confronts the Old." *Yearbook of German-American Studies* 23 (1988): 1–17.

———. "*Der Fröhliche Botschafter:* An Early American Universalist Magazine." *The American-German Review* 10 (June 1944): 13–16.

————. Introduction to *Christmas in Pennsylvania: A Folk-Cultural Study*, edited by Alfred L. Shoemaker, 1–18. Kutztown, Pa.: Pennsylvania Folklife Society, 1959.

————. "Lutheran-Reformed Union Proposals, 1800–1850: An American Experiment in Ecumenics." *Bulletin: Theological Seminary of the Evangelical and Reformed Church* 17 (January 1946): 39–77.

————. "The Palatine Connection: The Pennsylvania German Culture and Its European Roots." In *Germans in America: Retrospect and Prospect*, edited by Randall M. Miller, 92–109. Philadelphia: German Society of Pennsylvania, 1984.

————. "Palatine, Hessian, Dutchman: Three Images of the German in America." In *Ebbes fer Alle—Ebber Ebbes fer Dich: Something for Everyone—Something for You*, edited by Albert F. Buffington, 107–29. Breinigsville, Pa.: Pennsylvania German Society, 1980.

————. "Pennsylvania Germans." In *Harvard Encyclopedia of American Ethnic Groups*, edited by Stephan Thernstrom, 770–72. Cambridge: Harvard University Press, 1980.

————. "The Pennsylvania Germans and the American Revolution." *Pennsylvania Folklife* 25 (Spring 1976): 2–17.

————. *Pennsylvania Spirituals*. Lancaster, Pa.: Pennsylvania Folklife Society, 1961.

————. "The Reformed Church and Pennsylvania German Identity." *Yearbook of German-American Studies* 18 (1983): 63–82.

Young, Alfred F. *The Shoemaker and the Tea Party: Memory and the American Revolution*. Boston: Beacon Press, 1999.

Young, Henry J. "The Treatment of the Loyalists in Pennsylvania." Ph.D. diss., The Johns Hopkins University, 1955.

Yrigoyen, Charles, Jr. "The Second Great Awakening and Finney's Revival in Reading." *Historical Review of Berks County* 38 (Spring 1973): 65–73.

Zelinsky, Wilbur. *Nation into State: The Shifting Symbolic Foundations of American Nationalism*. Chapel Hill: The University of North Carolina Press, 1988.

Zuckerman, Michael, ed. *Friends and Neighbors: Group Life in America's First Pluralist Society*. Philadelphia: Temple University Press, 1982.

Zuckert, Michael P. *Natural Rights and the New Republicanism*. Princeton: Princeton University Press, 1994.

INDEX

democratic republicanism and individual, 24, 26, 160 n. 35
ethnicity and, 68
Free Synod defenders and, 82–84
Free Synod opponents and, 84–86
Pennsylvania German conception of, 17, 31–32, 32, 43, 44, 92, 100, 103, 131
Roman Catholics perceived as threat to Protestant, 111–12
Liberty Men, 24
Livingston, John H., 70–71, 72, 172 n. 10, 174 n. 27
localism
democratic, 162 n. 65
Gock on, 107
Pennsylvania German conception of liberty and, 92, 100, 103
in Pennsylvania German religiosity, 61
Pietism and, 32
Republican party and, 39–40
versus social reform, 103–5
versus Whiggish vision, 139
Lochman, Johann Georg, 112–13
Loetscher, Lefferts A., 179 n. 8
Long Swamp German Reformed Church, 167 n. 40
Loysville Lutheran congregation, 58, 60
Luther, Martin, 60, 123, 170 n 61, 179 n. 10, 191 n. 81
Lutheran Church, 63. *See also* General Synod, Lutheran
Americanization process and, 125–27, 141, 188 n. 46
catechisms in, 60, 170 n. 61
choosing ministers in, 33, 172 n. 6
confessional consciousness and, 111
congregations in Pennsylvania counties, 18
custom and tradition versus post-Revolutionary War political order, 35
denominational union with Reformed, 121–26, 191 n. 86
differences from Reformed, 114, 158 n. 22
ecumenism and, 114–15, 119–20, 186 n. 23
ethnic ecumenism and, 120–26
eucharistic theology in, 187 n. 31
evangelical techniques in, 55–56
German Reformed Church and, 71, 113, 120–26

hymnals of, 113–14, 187 n. 28
laity in, 33, 158 n. 21
membership numbers in, 14, 16, 55, 145 n. 4, 151 n. 21, 188 n. 44, 192 n. 95
Ministerium of (*see* Lutheran Ministerium)
"Old Lutherans," 131
opposition to denominational union with Reformed, 125–26
organization of, 191 n. 75
peasant republican ideals in, 32
Pietism and (*see* Pietism)
publications of (*see* publications, Lutheran Church)
Reformation Festival and, 110–15, 184–85 n. 7
reorganization of, 115–16
revivalism and, 52–53, 111
role in America, 118
Roman Catholics and, 118, 187 n. 33
schism in, 126
seminary of, 117, 188 nn. 40, 41, 45
statistics keeping in, 168 n. 43
Sunday schools programs and, 183 n. 46
synods of, 115–17, 125, 126
as theological "outsider," 16, 17
The Lutheran Magazine, 100–101, 182 n. 33
Lutheran Ministerium, 111. *See also* Lutheran Church
Americanization and, 188 n. 46
Brauns and, 190 n. 68
ecumenism and, 124
Evangelical Alliance and, 190 n. 65
Free Synod and, 193 n. 10
German Reformed Church and, 113, 121
membership of, 188 n. 44
organization of, 191 n. 75
on Reformation Festival, 111
reorganization of, 115–16
response to revivalism, 52
schism at 1842 synodic meeting, 126
support of Francke Foundation, 110
Lutheran Observer, 56, 62, 118, 169 n. 48, 180 n. 12
Lutheran Seminary, 117, 188 nn. 40, 41, 45
Lutheran Synod of Pennsylvania, 101–2

Magazine of the German Reformed Church, 56
magazines. *See entries under* "publications"
Mahnenschmidt, John Peter, 36, 160 n. 37